Design a Z80 Computer
Design and build a fully functional Z80 Computer System

A practical approach to designing and building a working Z80 Computer
system from theory to a working prototype.

Edition 1

J. S. Walker

Copyright © 2023 J. S. Walker

First published in the United Kingdom in 2023 by

Oldfangled Publishing

ISBN 978-0-9957072-2-1

Contents

Designing a Z80 Computer

In Loving Memory of

IZZY

ꠉꠝꠤ

Chapter 1   - Introduction

At the beginning of the 1970's there were very few small scale computers available and none which were available at a reasonable cost to the general public. Only individuals with extremely deep pockets or large corporations could get their hands on a computer system for their own use and even then they were usually tied to very specific operational limitations.
However things were about to change because by the end of that decade computer systems started to become available which were built around relatively low cost single chip integrated circuits.
The era of commercially available microprocessor computer chips had arrived and this spawned a rapid growth in the availability of small computer systems which served to make such machines available to individuals. Initially they were still very expensive but as more companies began to embrace this technology and designed their own versions the competition to make these computers cheaper and available to a wider market accelerated very rapidly.
Many companies competed in the race to create their own versions of small scale computer systems in the hope of cornering the market and making a name for themselves along with the huge profits which they hoped would go with it.
The technology behind this growth was based very heavily on the introduction of the single chip microprocessor integrated circuit and it was not long before several manufacturers had designed their own version although some were more successful than others.
In fact a number of the early devices never made it much past the prototype phase before they were considered obsolete.

Most of the remaining devices had a fairly short production life and did not find their way into very many products and those that did were soon replaced with newer versions or made totally obsolete by the introduction of alternative types.

Each early type of processor was very different and the system designers could not easily switch from one type of device to another. They all had their own instruction sets and were for the most part totally incompatible with each other as were the computers that they were used in. This was because the industry was in its infancy and so no real standards had been established which the manufacturers could readily use to target their ideas.

In some ways I believe it was very fortunate that no such standards existed in the early days of microprocessor development as this lack of formality paved the way for inventive thinking which may have otherwise been hampered by commercial pressures.

At that point in history some processor system designs still used discrete components and the direction for integrated computer chip development was still not clear.

The amount of time and effort which went into developing many of these discrete designs is absolutely staggering as is the variety of approaches taken by the designers.

I have worked on repairing many of these discrete component designs over the years and I am frequently stunned by the level of inventiveness and sheer genius which was exhibited by the designers of the time.

One thing that was consistent across the designs of the time was their inconsistency and the result was each system requiring its own software platform which could not be simply transferred from one type of machine to another.

This could even apply if the machines in question were based on the same type of microprocessor.

These days we take for granted the ease with which a program designed for one computer can be ported onto another machine with very little effort.

For anyone running a company at the time and wanting to invest in a computer system it was a very difficult decision to determine the best direction to jump. Selecting the wrong system could well lead to the waste of a significant investment and even possibly the failure of the company.

Once again things were about to change and while I am not certain that the changes were all for the best what is clear is that these changes were inevitable and there was no going back.

Small scale computer systems had begun to appear and as with all new technology they were seen as commercial imperatives which meant that they were here to stay even if some companies had to invent a purpose for them.

The problem facing any fledgling microprocessor development company was in determining exactly what functionality their device should provide in order for it to compete in the market.

It is easy these days to say what features a computer processor should have as a minimum but back then it was down to the inventive minds of development engineers to come up with something new. What may seem obvious today with the benefit of hindsight has taken many attempts resulting in equal numbers of triumphs and failures, or possibly more failures than triumphs. These were the days long before the internet existed so you could not simply search for help or ideas and as a result there was much more limited access to wider thinking or marketing demands.

Once again this may well have been a good thing as it helped to prevent the tendency for new devices to simply copy existing ones.

An important limitation whenever considering a new large scale integrated circuit design and development was the enormous costs associated with the fabrication and manufacturing process.

The tools available for the design and visualisation of such devices were also much more limited than they are today.

The manufacturing technology for integrated circuits was also much more restrictive than it is today which added further limitations to the design of new devices.

In modern integrated circuit design it is possible to not only design a new device entirely in a visual computer development system but they can also be fully tested and simulated before any silicone is ever sliced. In fact modern large scale integrated circuits are so complex and contain such a staggering number of elements that it would be impossible for humans alone to design them.

With these commercial pressures and development restrictions in mind it is all the more remarkable that a new computer processor was developed which would find its way into many thousands, if not millions, of devices and would remain in production for almost 50 years and counting (at the time of writing).

Amazingly this particular device is still used for new designs, including the one I will be describing in this book.

This is all the more astounding when you consider that there are currently thousands of very much cheaper and more powerful processors and microcontrollers available.

It is hard to say exactly why this processor lives on and has been so popular for so long but it is most likely because it is a relatively simple device to program and yet has some features which make it extremely flexible in a very wide variety of applications.

This device has found its way into almost every conceivable type of application from full commercial computer systems to embedded process controllers.

It has gone through a number of significant development steps since its introduction although it has still retained much of its fundamental character to the extent than anyone familiar with the earliest version would still recognise the current devices.

I myself have designed over 20 different systems using this device although I must confess that until I started the project outlined in this book I had not considered it for a new design for quite some time although this project did rekindle my appreciation of it.

As this project progressed I was once again struck by the power and versatility of this processor along with the ease with which a system could be designed around it.

It is also fair to say that the instruction set supported by this device further adds to its utility and simplicity of use which is all the more surprising when you consider the time in which it was created.

These days it is so easy to jump into designing embedded computer systems because there are so many development starter kits which can be used to bypass a lot of the initial learning that was required back in the day if you wanted to implement a microprocessor design.

I feel that this is unfortunate as the sense of satisfaction obtained in learning the basics of computer operation using nothing more than data sheets and imagination cannot be replaced.

In my case I did not start my career with the device I am referring to although in many ways I think that if I had done so it may have made my early life so much easier.

When I began working with microprocessors the internet was not available and most data sheets had to be purchased from the manufacturer and often the cost was not insignificant.

There were also very few books on the subject which could provide reference material or guidance and so almost all aspects of the circuit design needed to be gleaned directly from the data sheets.

As with the microprocessors themselves there was no real standard for how the data sheets were written and a typical datasheet for a microprocessor could easily run into more than a thousand pages.

Unlike more recent data sheets they were very detailed with information such as internal operation and timing diagrams.

I can remember spending several weeks reading through these data sheets in order to get an understanding of how to design a circuit around them.

Naturally this also made comparing one processor against another very difficult because the only information available may have been the data sheets themselves. This made initial development very time consuming although I have to say that it was also an immense amount of fun.

So which device am I referring to?

This processor is of course the

Zilog Z80

Figure 1-1 shows a close up view of the inner workings of this device.

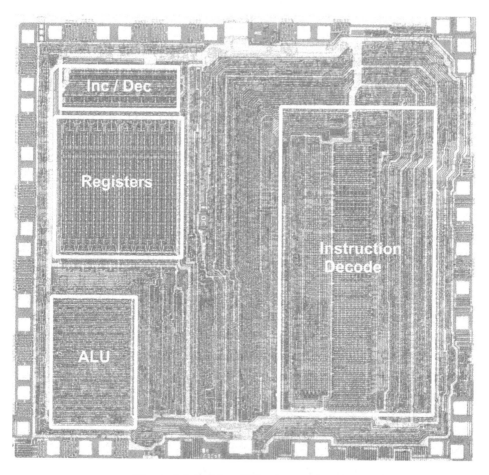

Figure 1-1 Inside a Z80 microprocessor

While there have been a number of different versions of the Z80 with a few different identification codes the basic device has remained almost unchanged in terms of its features and capabilities since it was first released.

In this book I be will describing how to design and build a simple computer based on the Z80 processor but unlike many small Z80 based computers available today I will be trying as much as possible to design a system which would have been familiar to developers who were the first to get their hands on the new Z80 microprocessor back when it was first released.

To that end I will be avoiding the use of the large scale integration support devices that became so popular and will stick to discrete logic designs for the core design.

Origin of the Z80

In general terms the first single chip processor was developed by Intel and was called the 4004, probably because it had a 4 bit address bus and a 4 bit data bus.

This may sound like a very limited device and by modern standards it was but cramming an entire microprocessor system into a single chip was a technical marvel at the time but this was just a sign of things to come.

The 4004 was release around 1969 and was quickly followed by the 4040 which was an improved version of the 4004 although it still retained the 4 bit address and data busses.

Following on from the excitement in the engineering world along with a good commercial response to the emergence of these devices they were incorporated into early microprocessor controlled products by a number of manufacturers.

Some of these would lead on to highly successful commercial successes and others would fall by the wayside.

Encouraged by their success Intel then went on to produce the 8008 which was the first 8 bit single chip processor. It is important to remember that up to that time there had been quite a number of programmable processor based machines but they had all been based on discrete component circuitry or multiple processor chip sets which normally occupied several large circuit boards and consumed a lot of power making them unsuitable for many designs.

The number of bits used for data in these systems was also not always the same which may sound very odd these days.

Intel was able to condense a great deal of electronic circuitry into a very small package and yet still provide a reasonable set of instructions for developers to make use of.

The 4004, 4040 and 8008 were no where near as powerful as most of the discrete designs available at the time but they did pave the way for incorporating a microprocessor into designs where previously the cost, size and complexity would have made this impractical or physically impossible.

Not long after the 8008 was released Intel produced the 8080 which had a different architecture to be the 8008 and was to be the starting point for the range of microprocessor chips that are still in use today and are being constantly developed for modern PC's.

The 8080 was release in 1974 and it was very quickly apparent that this device was going to become a useful and popular processor. Many of you will no doubt be familiar with this processor as it was used in machines such as the Altair 8800.

At this point the origins of the 4004 re-emerged and some of the engineers responsible for its development joined forces to create a company which they called Zilog.

As they had also been instrumental in the design of the processors which followed on from the 4004 they were very well aware of how to design a working processor and also how to build on the success of the Intel devices.

To that end they developed a new processor based on the 8080's instruction set and it would in fact reliably process all the 8080 instructions but they incorporated many new capabilities which pushed the new processor way ahead of its rivals.

The new processor added over 100 new instructions and many of these were to support the additional hardware features of this new processor such as its I/O mechanism and interrupt vectoring along with powerful memory access pointers.

Despite its more advanced capabilities the new processor was actually easier to interface to external support electronics and so made designing computer systems around it much easier.

This new processor was of course the Z80 and despite the rapid development of the 80xxx range of processors the Z80 remained largely unchanged and yet, almost mystically, it still continues to be in widespread use many decades later.

The Z80 has been used in countless designs and its simplicity coupled with good performance makes it a popular choice for both commercial systems and hobbyists.

Released in July 1976 the original Z80 could run at a maximum clock speed of 2.5MHz but later versions could run up to 10MHz and compatible new versions can run at up to 20MHz. These later processors still retain compatibility with the first versions making the Z80 a true long lived entity.

In the next chapter we will look more closely at the Z80 architecture and the instruction cycle that it uses.

The computer design I will be presenting in this book is not the most efficient or powerful way to use a Z80 but I am hoping to keep the design as clear as possible and accessible to anyone interested in building their own version or anyone just interested in this subject.

All the components I will be using are readily available (at the time of writing) and so you can easily use the design shown as a starting point for your own version. This computer can also be used as a good platform on which to develop simple or complex Z80 code.

As with all designs there will be an almost unlimited number of ways to improve and add to the design but the circuits shown should be a good starting point.

Figure 1-2 shows the first prototype computer running an early boot and monitor ROM the listing of which is shown later in appendix E.

Figure 1-2 Early Prototype

The board show in Figure 1-2 is version 3 of the prototype boards although this project required the design and building of many other boards and assemblies along the way.

I will detail each of these are we progress through the design but if you wish to build your own system then you can of course simply build the final version without the need to build all the prototypes.

Each step in the development of this machine was carefully considered with the hope that the end result would not only be a useful computer but that the process would also be of interest.

It is very easy for a project like this one to go off course and end up never being completed but with any luck this book will help anyone who wishes to develop their own machine.

This computer is a multi memory bank machine which is fully capable of running complex software applications including several of the well known operating systems.

In a follow up book I will also be including a monitor program to allow programming and a boot loader / operating system to allow booting of the computer from a remote source.

I do however present a basic monitor program in this book.

Developing this computer was a huge amount of fun and I would encourage anyone interested in vintage computers to have a go at designing their own. While a project such as this one is not for the feint hearted there are few things as exciting as seeing a discrete device computer that you have designed and built booting up and running your software.

It is probably safe to say that a project like this is never finished as there are always things you can add to it or improve and there are of course also unlimited options as far as software development.

The computer we will develop in this book will be fully capable of running complex software applications so the sky is the limit.

In chapter 3 we will discuss the features which I will be including along with some which although I will not be incorporating just yet it would be easy to add them.

ℰ ഏ ℭ

Chapter 2 – Why Use A Z80

When I was starting to plan this project I began by thinking about which of the many available processors I was going to base it on.
As I have said in the previous chapter there were a number of different processors to choose from and I could have selected any one of them. In all honesty it was really a foregone conclusion that I would select the Z80 although I did briefly give consideration to both the 8080 and the 6502.
I selected the Z80 not just because it is an iconic processor which most people would have heard of but it also has some features which make it a very attractive proposition for a project such as this. It seems to be apparent that a similar conclusion was reached by numerous system developers over the decades since the Z80 first became available judging by how often it has featured in computers and embedded control systems.
In this chapter we will take a look at just a few of these features and I will explain why the Z80 was an easy choice for our project.

I should probably mention at this point that the design I will be presenting is by no means the simplest approach that could be taken if you wish to create a Z80 based computer system. However I wanted to design a system that is more typical in its general configuration to a vintage computer system. I therefore decided not to follow the modern trend of trying to reduce the complexity and so I would avoid using devices which are more readily available today than they were back when the Z80 was in its hay day.

For example I will use discrete logic gates for the vast majority of the design rather than dropping in large scale integrated circuits which are so common today despite the unavoidable fact that this would greatly simplify the design process.

Most modern computer designs use static ram (SRAM) memory devices rather than the dynamic ram chips (DRAM) which were more typical of the time we are aiming for with this project.

Back in the 1970's and 80's the cost of SRAM memory devices was very high and their capacity was relatively small so it was mostly only used in small capacities for things such as video ram.

Bulk system ram was much more commonly comprised of DRAM devices for the simple reason that it was far less expensive and generally available in higher capacities. This made it ideal for use in lower cost computer systems although it does have a significant drawback. It is much more complex to implement a memory system using DRAM than it is to use SRAM and this complexity increases rapidly when using discrete component circuit designs such as the one we will be creating.

Memory Refresh

When data is written into a static RAM device that data will be retained unless it is intentionally altered for as long as power is applied to the system without the need to carry out any further actions, hence the term 'static'. This means that all any processor needs to do to use SRAM is to decode the memory address and determine when to assert read and write signals using some simple control logic. In fact the Z80 processor can be connected directly to a static RAM memory device and it can then immediately make use of it because the processor has memory control output pins which are capable of performing the simple actions required by the SRAM.

Unfortunately things are not as simple as this when implementing dynamic memory and for a system to make use of DRAM things get much more complicated. This is because of the fact that DRAM is very forgetful which is a bit of an unfortunate characteristic for a memory device.

If data is written into a DRAM memory chip then just a few milliseconds later the data will be lost unless something is done to prevent it.

That something is referred to as a memory refresh and in its most basic form it is implemented by simply reading the memory device at regular intervals. Each time the memory is refreshed the stored data is re written and the cycle starts again. The reason for this is that the DRAM actually consists of an array of tiny capacitors which are what are used to store the actual data bits.

When data is written into the memory device the capacitors are charged to represent a '1' or discharged to represent a '0'. These tiny capacitors will very rapidly discharge if nothing is done to prevent it so the DRAM chip has a special mechanism whereby a refresh cycle will recharge any capacitors that contain a '1' and leave any discharged capacitors in their discharged state. The interval that this refresh cycle must be repeated is called the refresh interval and it is typically just a few thousandths of a second (mS). The memory cannot be read or written during these refresh cycles unless the refresh is actually being performed as part of such a cycle and so this creates the need for much more complicated memory control logic.

The refresh cycles must also continue even if the computer is not currently trying to access the memory devices or the result will be very rapid data loss.

Fortunately the DRAM manufactures took pity on the system developers and designed these memory devices in such a way that refresh cycles could operate on more than a single memory cell during each pass.

Most dynamic memory devices are organised internally in a way that simplifies the refresh requirements by configuring the memory storage cells in an array of rows and columns. Typically these arrays are symmetrical where there are the same numbers of rows as there are columns although this is not always the case.

In general the refresh operation refreshes an entire memory row in each chip during a single refresh cycle and this makes the refresh logic less complicated and in addition it reduces the number of refresh cycles which are needed.

For example a 16k DRAM would need 16,384 refresh cycles every few mS if each cell had to be refreshed individually but by using entire row refresh techniques this is reduced to just 128 cycles.

However the memory control logic is still much more complex than it would be for a static ram design because it needs to not only produce a refresh cycle for each internal memory chip row every few mS but it must also handle the reading and writing operations while ensuring that these operation do not interfere with each other. It must continue to refresh the memory as long as the system is powered up even if the memory is not currently being accessed.

An additional cost reducing feature was to manufacture these memory devices in smaller packages with lower pin counts and so DRAM chips generally use multiplexed address inputs where the supplied memory address is presented to the memory chip in two steps rather than as a single binary value.

The need to keep track of which memory row needs to be refreshed next along with the need to separate the refresh and read / write cycles while supplying a two step memory address can easily result in very complicated logic circuits.

This is where the first Z80 specific feature entices us towards using this processor instead of one of its competitors although this can also be a bit of a false temptation.

The Z80 was the only device which had inbuilt DRAM control functions which could be used to simplify the circuit design and also improve system performance.

I will describe this function in more detail in the chapter in which we design the memory control circuits but in brief the Z80 contains a DRAM address counter which keeps track of the next memory row address which needs to be refreshed. This is a very useful feature which was intended to reduce system complexity and component count although it does have a limitation which we will have to deal with.

It also has a refresh control output pin which is controlled by the Z80 to allow us to refresh the DRAM during a part of the instruction cycle that would otherwise result in idle bus time. This again simplifies circuit complexity while also increasing memory bandwidth by effectively producing 'hidden' DRAM refresh cycles.

This feature alone would have made the Z80 a very attractive proposition for a developer back in the day. It is also why I chose to make life more difficult for myself by selecting DRAM instead of SRAM despite the latter being much cheaper these days.

It is almost certain that SRAM would have been selected by the system designers in preference to DRAM if they had an option but I wanted to design a system which showcased some of the more important Z80 features.

The next very useful feature of the Z80 is the very powerful and versatile In / Out mechanism and supporting instructions.

The 'IN' instruction allows data to be read from one of up to 256 ports although they can be mapped to anywhere in the 64k address range. The 'OUT' instruction allows writing data to the same number of ports. This capability is built seamlessly into the processor and a dedicated pin is provided to allow control of the port addressing. While this may initially seem a fairly trivial feature it is certainly one of the major contributions to the ease with which a Z80 can be used to control systems which need large amounts of additional hardware.

A related topic is the large array of support IC's which were developed to allow very easy system expansion.

Devices such as peripheral controllers and adaptors can be interfaced directly to the Z80 with an absolute minimum of control circuitry.

As with the memory selection I have decided not to use these types of devices because I wanted to make the design as clear and open as possible without the need to explain the inner workings of complex large scale integration support devices.

These devices certainly expanded the possibilities in system design but they are not really needed when discussing the fundamental design of a Z80 based computer.

If you look back at the timeline for computer and embedded system development you will see that these large scale devices were adopted by developers as soon as they became available but even so we will try to avoid using them.

There are other hardware features included in the design of the Z80 which we will come back to in later chapters but the main point I am trying to get across is that the Z80 was designed from the outset with features which greatly simplified the design of systems and at the same time reduced component count and hence system cost.

Intelligent Instruction Set

If you have spent any time writing code for the Z80 then you probably already appreciate how easy it is compared to other processors of the time. Not only does it have a tightly uniform approach to the instruction formats but it also contains some surprisingly powerful instructions which can save a great deal of code space and therefore allows the use of smaller ROM's but some of these instructions also have the added advantage in that they provide a big increase in both speed and performance.

The Z80 designers also fully understood that trying to push a new processor into a rapidly developing market which was already beginning to establish favourites could be difficult.

Engineers and developers of the time may well have spent a great deal of time and effort learning how to make the most of the instruction set which was available in the alternate mainstream processor, the 8080.

In order to minimise or offset the possibility of reluctance to learn a totally new instruction set and avoid having to throw away all code developed prior to the Z80 becoming available the designers allowed the Z80 to support the full 8080 instruction set at the bit level. This would allow the Z80 to execute code written for the 8080 without modification despite the new processor having a totally different internal structure.

It should be noted here that because the Z80 contains many additional instructions compared to the 8080 then the reverse is not true and so trying to run Z80 code on an 8080 will probably not end at all well.

Although the Z80 could execute the native 8080 instructions the instruction set was greatly expanded to include well over 100 new instructions. Many of the new instructions were required to give access to the new hardware features but some were included to allow code written for the Z80 to be compact and powerful.

I do not intend to describe each of the Z80 instructions as there are many books and on line resources which will provide this information.

However I do wish to give a few examples in this chapter of the type of Z80 instructions which I think demonstrate the amount of thought which went into the design of this device.

That is not to say that similar instructions were not available in other processors but the Z80 was certainly ahead of its time in this respect.

If you are not familiar with the Z80 then I strongly recommend picking up a book on how to program it.

We will now look at a few Z80 instructions and hopefully you will see how well thought out they are.

LDIR Instruction

This instruction is simple to use and yet very powerful as it only requires that we load one register with a source memory address and another with a destination address and a third register with a byte count.

The LDIR instruction can then be invoked and this single instruction is able to move a large block of data from the source memory address to the destination address without the Z80 needing to read any further instructions.

In most other processors this action would require an entire code function but in the Z80 it only requires a few bytes of code space. This instruction is also not limited to single byte address pointers but can access any address within the entire 64k memory space.

This instruction is very useful for general purpose data handling and it is also very useful in systems such as the one I am presenting here where direct memory address hardware (DMA) will not be implemented.

A second example is the RRA instruction

RRA Instruction

This instruction may seem a little odd when you first encounter it but once the possible uses for it are appreciated then it can be surprisingly useful.

When executed it causes 12 bits of data to be rotated by 4 bits but in a very interesting way and in my opinion it is an instruction that really goes to demonstrate the amount of though which went into the design of the Z80.

When invoked the instruction moves the lower 4 bits of the address pointed to by the HL register into the upper 4 bits of the same address.

The upper 4 bits of this memory address are rotated into the lower 4 bits of the A register while the upper 4 bits of the A register remain unchanged.

The original lower 4 bits of the A register are rotated into the memory location pointed to be the HL register.

In short the 12 bits comprising the 8 bits at the memory address and the lower 4 bits of the A register are rotated 4 bits while leaving the upper 4 bits of the A register unchanged.

While this may not sound as if it has many practical uses it actually has some very good applications and specifically operations such as packing BCD or HEX numbers is made very simple and efficient using this instruction.

As with so many of the Z80 instructions this type of construct can greatly reduce the overall size of code while at the same time increasing system performance.

You could of course achieve the same thing with other code but the ability to perform what is a relatively complex task in a single instruction greatly adds to the power of the Z80.

CALL Instruction

Although all processors have at least one call instruction which allows the executing code to branch to subroutines and then resume where it left off once the subroutine has finished. The Z80 in particular has some very useful CALL instruction variations.

One variant of the CALL instruction which is very interesting is the conditional call which allows calls to be made based on the state of the flags register.

This can be very useful in many applications such as call look up functions which are frequently required in order to determine which subroutine to call.

For example if the program needs to use the value stored in a register as a subroutine selection code then this is very simple using the Z80. With a single instruction the processor can examine the state of particular flags and decide if a call should be performed.

The following code snippet shows how this can be achieved.

```
CP      'O'
CALL    Z, SUBROUTINE_ONE
CP      'T'
CALL    Z, SUBROUTINE_TWO
```

This code will call subroutine 'SUBROUTINE_ONE' if the value in register 'A' is the character 'O' and it will call subroutine 'SUBROUTINE_TWO' if the value in register 'A' is the character 'T'.

This can of course be extended to include as many subroutines as required.

LD Instruction

The last instruction I will mention is the load instruction (LD) of which the Z80 has many variations.

This instruction allows direct or indirect memory addressing and the versatility of this instruction allows the creation of very simple constructs for handling both register data and memory data.

If you intend to build your own version of this computer then one aspect of development that I highly recommend is using the resulting hardware to fully investigate the Z80 instruction set.

This in itself is a fascinating process and will serve you well if you wish to develop your own operating system or applications.

The Z80 has been made available in a number of different packages but it continues to be available in the original ubiquitous 40 pin 0.1" pitch DIL package. This package is very familiar and easy to handle without the need to resort to special tools or handling.

This adds yet another facet to its popularity amongst hobbyists because it is robust and can be simply plugged into a cheap breadboard by anyone who wants to have a play with it.

In an era where modern microprocessors are being manufactured in ever smaller packages with ever decreasing pin pitches and surface mount package designs the Z80 remains accessible to all.

It is this combination of brilliant processor hardware design along with a well thought out and consistent instruction set which makes the Z80 a truly remarkable processor and it also makes it a lot of fun to work with.

There are yet more reasons why I selected it for this project but I will come back to those later in this book.

I would also like to point out that my aim in writing this book is not to railroad anyone into designing and building a computer by implying that the Z80 is the only possible choice.

Indeed I hope that many readers will want to design systems using other types of processors.

Most of the circuits I will be presenting in this book could easily be adapted for use with other types of microprocessor.

Z80 Technology

From a technology perspective the Z80 contains around 8500 transistors and while this is a minute amount compared to modern processors there can be little doubt that this processor has been used as the heart for thousands of systems and continues to be a firm favourite with many professionals and hobbyists alike.

The Z80 is not particularly well suited to maths intensive applications where rapid processing of large floating point numbers will be required although like all microprocessors it can certainly be programmed for this purpose.

It is however in its element when it is called on to control large amounts of hardware because the versatile instruction set and simple interface can easily be called on to form the basis of surprisingly complex and powerful systems.

There is of course no getting away from the fact that the Z80 is only an 8 bit device but for many applications this really is not a limitation.

I hope that by the end of this book you are able to add your own reasons for liking this processor but at the very least it will be an interesting journey.

In the next chapter we will look at the Z80 architecture and put together an overall design plan for the computer which we will be developing throughout the remainder of this book.

ᘓ ᦓᐰᦕ

Chapter 3 – The Z80 Architecture

Before we can start to outline the design of our new computer we should take a moment to look at the Z80 a bit more closely so we can then decide how to make best use of it for our new system. I am using the word 'best' here although there are of course many other ways to design a computer system based on the Z80.
In this case I am attempting to make use of the Z80 in a way that is best for my particular application but you may wish to design your system differently if your requirements are not the same.
This project is not intended as a guide on how to develop within a commercial environment so I will not be presenting a typical development cycle approach to our project but it will still be of benefit to take a look into the Z80 before we begin.

Z80 Architecture

Figure 3-1 shows the simplified internal architecture of the Z80 and this is a very good place to start our project investigation.
If you are unfamiliar with the Z80 processor then it is well worth spending some time reading through the Zilog Z80 Handbook as this contains a lot of very useful technical information which will make the explanations in this book much clearer.
Should you wish to base your design around a different type of processor then hopefully most of the circuits and explanations in this book will still make sense although I am targeting the Z80.

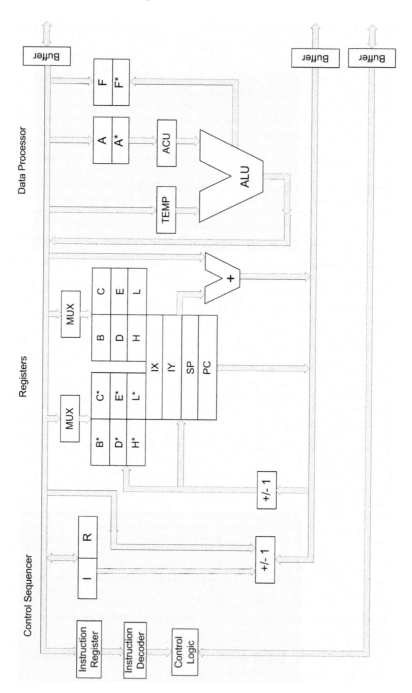

Figure 3-1 Simplified Z80 Architecture

For anyone that really wants to understand how a processor works then my book 'Computer Time Travel' describes how to build a micro processor from discrete transistors and in it I go into a lot of detail on the inner workings of these fascinating devices.

While you really do not need to know the details of how a microprocessor works a basic understanding of the principles involved would certainly help to clarify many of my design decisions as we progress.

The Z80 has been around for so long and it has been used in so many machines that it is almost impossible to come up with unique designs but my intention in this book is to design a computer system which is in keeping with the way they may have been designed back when the Z80 was still becoming established as a commercial contender in the single chip processor market.

A quick review of the major features available in the Z80 will help to get the project started.

Referring to Figure 3-1 we can see that the Z80 is a deceptively simple processor although it has been very cleverly thought out and so this apparent simplicity belies its real power.

Starting at the top left corner of the image we have the Instruction register and this is of course used to store the last instruction which was retrieved from memory at the beginning of the current instruction cycle.

Instruction cycles are divided into clock phases and can vary in length depending on which particular instruction is currently being processed. We do not need to concern ourselves with this until much later in our design.

The instruction stored in this register is decoded by the instruction decoder and this decoded information is used by the processor to determine which operations are required to complete the current instruction cycle.

Once it is decoded the required instruction sequence is taken care of by the Control Logic which will make use of the various processor circuits in order to complete the particular instruction operations.

To allow the Z80 to carry out the operations needed to support its instruction set it contains a collection of carefully designed building blocks each of which is used to perform the specific steps in a complete instruction cycle.

To the right of the Instruction register there are two special purpose registers which are used to control specific system interactions.

The 'I' register is used to store any interrupt information which is currently being processed and next to it is the 'R' register which is used to maintain a refresh address count. We will be making use of both of these registers so I will come back to them in later chapters.

In the centre of the diagram we see a large group of registers and these are the main user software accessible registers which the Z80 uses to store the data which it is currently processing.

You will notice that there are two identical sets of 8 registers if we include the 'A' and 'F' registers and this is a very interesting feature of the Z80.

The contents of these two sets of registers can be exchanged under software control and this can be a very useful feature for complex software applications and is especially useful in multitasking code.

Above these two sets of registers are two multiplexers which allow either set of registers to be connected to the internal bus. It seems more likely that the data exchange instruction works by simply swapping the multiplexer control rather than actually moving the data between the registers but I have been unable to determine if this is the case.

Each pair of registers in the centre groups of 6 registers can either be treated as two individual eight bit registers or as single sixteen bit registers. They can also be treated as single sixteen bit registers but each eight bits can be accessed separately.

This makes manipulation of data very simple and can save a lot of additional code.

For example the 'H' and 'L' registers can be treated as two independent registers or referred to as 'HL' and used as a single sixteen bit register. Again this provides a great deal of flexibility for the software developers.

Some of these registers also have special functions such as 16 bit memory pointers or 8 bit counters giving the Z80 some very useful hardware capabilities.

Below the two sets of 6 registers are 4 special purpose registers which are called IX, IY, SP and PC.

The first two are special purpose 16 bit pointers which allow direct access to any memory location within the Z80 address space.

The 'SP' register is the stack pointer register and is used by the Z80 to keep track of the current 'Top of Stack' address.

As with most processors the Z80 stack 'grows' downwards in memory as values are pushed onto it.

The 'PC' register is the Program Counter and it is a 16 bit pointer which points to the next instruction which will be fetched at the beginning of the next instruction cycle unless it is changed by the currently executing instruction, For example by a jump.

To the immediate right of these four special purpose registers is a pointer modifier which allows the pointers to be loaded or automatically incremented or decremented by the currently executing instruction. Once again this sort of feature gives software developers a great deal of power and can really help to reduce the amount of code required to perform certain tasks.

At the right side of the diagram is the data processing unit and this is where the Z80 does most of its mathematical data processing. It contains an Arithmetic Logic Unit which is used to perform the actual mathematical tasks such as addition, subtraction, multiplication etc.

It includes a temporary register along with an accumulator and these two registers are used during the execution of an instruction where data values need to be manipulated but they are not directly available to the software programmer.

At the top right of this block are two special registers which are used to store status information generated by the execution of instructions. There is also a set of duplicate status registers.

Each of the externally available busses has a buffer to provide a consistent input and output signal level and also to help protect the Z80 from damage due to external misuse although they do not make the Z80 indestructible.

As you can see the Z80 is a relatively simple device compared to modern processors but its mix of clever features and a powerful instruction set combined with this simplicity make the Z80 one of the most successful micro processors ever conceived.

Although we will be focussing this project on a discrete logic circuit design I feel that no discussion about the Z80 would be complete without at least mentioning the wide selection of large scale support devices which emerged throughout the early life of this processor.

Z80 Support Devices

DMA controller (Z8410)
PIO Parallel I/O Controller (Z8420)
CTC Timer / Counter Controller (Z8430)
SIO Serial I/O Controller (Z8440)
DART Dual Asynchronous Receiver / Transmitter (Z8470)
SCC Serial Communications Controller (Z8530)

This is by no means an exhaustive list of the devices which can be very easily interfaced to the Z80 processor but it should serve to show just how much was available for the Z80 and the level of support which was available for it.

There are of course many other non Z80 specific devices which can be connected to the Z80 ports such as display controllers and floppy drive controllers.

The final version of the computer I will be presenting in this book will include a number of In/Out ports which if required can be used to interface to additional control circuits. Once again this will depend entirely on the type of hardware devices you wish to attach to your machine.

As I stated earlier we will hopefully be able to avoid resorting to the use of any of these devices in this project but you may want to incorporate one or more of them into your own design if you believe it would improve the purpose and functionality of your computer. There is no doubt that they can make the design process much less complicated but where is the fun in that?

The Z80 provides a good balance of simplicity and processing power which we will make good use of as we develop our computer system.

In the next chapter I will start looking at the specifics of the computer we will be designing and we can then start the project.

ℰ ℐ ℱ

Chapter 4   – Introducing the JMZ

All new computers need a name and the computer we will be developing in this book is no exception. It was an easy decision as I name all my projects after my website and as this machine will be using a Z80 processor I simply added the Z to give…

JMZ

This computer will therefore be designated as JMZ from now on.
Of course it does not exist yet and these are currently just 3 letters so we had better get on with the design.

To keep this project moving and avoid the usual tedious process of white paper design which is normally an early step in any development project we will skip that step and move directly to the hands on design of our new computer.
We do however need to decide what particular features and capabilities the machine is to have and from there we can put together a general design outline for our machine. There is no need to fully design each circuit in order to figure this step out as we can design the specific circuits later so we will start by developing a block diagram of the JMZ. In later chapters we will turn each element in this diagram into functional electronic circuits and test each one as we go.
Figure 4-1 shows the simplified block diagram of the JMZ.

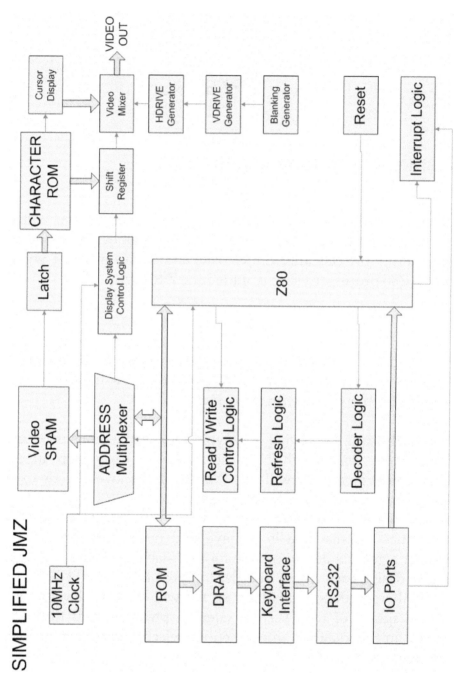

Figure 4-1 JMZ Simplified Block Diagram

This diagram only shows the major elements of the design and none of the detail. In this chapter I will give a brief explanation of each block within this diagram and try to explain the thinking behind my decisions.

It is probably fair to say that almost all of the functionality which I will be designing into the JMZ could be achieved much more easily and using far fewer devices if the large scale integration support chips were used. However what I am attempting to demonstrate is how to go about the development of each section of a fully functional Z80 based computer and I feel that the best way to do this is to unveil the inner workings of such devices. While we will be using discrete logic gates for the majority of the circuits in this system you should bear in mind that the large scale devices simply serve to encapsulate the same circuitry into single devices.

It is also useful for anyone wanting to fully understand how to implement such systems to have a detailed knowledge of the inner workings of such devices and the best way to achieve this is to build your own versions from scratch.

It is probably only fair to warn you at this stage that discrete designs such as the one I will be presenting in this book tend to grow very rapidly and so the final build will be a fairly significant undertaking for anyone wanting to build their own version.

I fully expect the final design to require at least 100 logic devices and possibly many more depending on how many peripheral circuits I decide to add.

Each circuit will be designed and built initially on breadboards and I will explain each part of the design in detail along with the reasoning behind them.

This book is not a simple description of a computer I have already designed and while I have designed quite a few over the years the JMZ will be different due to my avoidance of the support devices.

I therefore recommend that you read to the end of the book before commencing any build of your own as certain aspects of the design may very well change as the design takes shape.

You may of course want to follow the same steps in the project which I will be taking but just bear in mind that some of the circuits I show may not make it into the final design.

During development I will be making use of equipment such as oscilloscopes, Logic analysers, in circuit emulators and EPROM programmers and while these are invaluable tools for developing a system such as the JMZ you do not really need them in order to build the final version of this system as I will be fully testing all the modules as we proceed. These tools would however be useful for investigating the operation of your build and as a minimum I would recommend a good oscilloscope and a basic EPROM programmer.

You will need the programmer to create your own system or characters ROM's although I hope to include a monitor program which will allow the entry of simple programs through the computer keyboard.

As I mentioned earlier the Z80 is a surprisingly easy processor to write code for but it is no trivial task to create a boot ROM for a multi-bank computer system. It requires a great deal of care and attention to detail to ensure that the correct bits of code end up in the correct parts of the memory system.

It is also true that the sense of accomplishment when a system you have built and written the operating system for boots for the first time is immense. Indeed this is something that I never get bored with and if nothing else the computer system I will be creating throughout this book could be used as the basis for virtually unlimited experimentation or educational purposes.

Unfortunately it is a fact of life that anything worthwhile can take considerable effort to achieve and this sort of design is no exception to that so unless you are already very familiar with developing systems of this type then you should be prepared for a bumpy ride.

So let us now take a very brief look at the various blocks which will be included in the JMZ computer.

Z80 Processor

This is of course the Z80 processor itself and it will be the only large scale integration device I will be using in the basic design of the system. Large scale devices may be added to later versions of the JMZ.

10 MHz Clock

This is the main clock generator for the system and it will be a simple circuit along with a few dividers in order to generate the various clocks which will be needed by the computer circuits.

Reset

The Z80 requires a fairly specific reset signal applied to its reset pin following initial power up and this circuit will ensure proper initialisation of the Z80 processor. It will also allow manual resetting of the computer by pressing a reset button.

ROM

The ROM will contain a boot loader and monitor program along with any system specific functions.

DRAM

The system main RAM will consist of 64k of banked dynamic RAM.

Keyboard Interface

I have decided to use a PS2 keyboard for the system rather than design a custom keyboard which would not really add much to the design and make it difficult for anyone wanting to build their own version of the JMZ. The keyboard interface circuit will allow easy connection of a PS2 keyboard and be hooked into the system hardware interrupt circuit.

It will of course be possible to include a key lookup table should this be required.

RS232

The JMZ will have a bi directional RS232 interface circuit which will allow serial communications between the JMZ and a host machine or device. Several different BAUD rates will be available and the circuit will allow either polled or interrupt driven protocols to be created.

IO Ports

A number of parallel input and output ports will be included along with port status information to allow efficient connection of most types of hardware device.

Address Multiplexer

The JMZ will use a multi banked memory mapped architecture and it will also allow both reading and writing of all RAM areas including the video RAM. To facilitate these features the system will require a bi directional data and address multiplexer.

Read Write Control Logic

To enable the memory banks and ports to be properly accessed the system will need a well designed read / write decoder circuit.

Refresh Logic

The main bulk RAM will be constructed using dynamic RAM memory and so the JMZ will need to implement some form of DRAM refresh control circuitry and access control logic.

Decoder Logic

Because we will be designing a banked memory mapped system along with mapped input / output ports plus memory mapped video RAM we will need to design a memory decoder circuit.

This circuit will be responsible for allowing the Z80 to access the desired hardware based on the address and type of instruction.

Video SRAM
The video display data will be stored in static RAM which will be both readable and writable.

Character ROM
This ROM will contain the system character map to allow efficient generation of our character set on the display.

Video Latch
A data latch will be required between the video RAM and the character ROM to allow zero wait states for the video system.

Cursor Display
This circuit will be responsible for presenting a cursor on the video display in order to indicate where the next typed character will be entered. It will also allow inverse character display at any location.

Video Shift Register
The video shift resister is responsible for translating the parallel video byte data into a serial data stream which can be sent to the display. The timing of the signals controlling this shift register will be very important to ensure a clear and stable display output.

Video Mixer
This circuit will accept incoming cursor data and character data and blanking data and mix them together to determine the current pixel intensity. It will also allow external video data to be mixed into the video data stream which could allow a graphics mode to be added.

Display System Control Logic
Each part of the video display sub system requires careful timing control to ensure a stable display and this circuit is used to allow the various parts of the system to work properly together.

HDrive Generator

This circuit generates the required monitor horizontal drive signal.

VDrive Generator

This circuit generates the required monitor vertical drive signal and also resets the video generation counters.

Blanking Generator

This circuit ensures that areas outside the intended display area on the screen remain blank and it also generates the inter character blanking signals in order to suppress screen artefacts.

Interrupt Logic

The JMZ will use the Z80 mode 2 hardware interrupt system and this circuit will allow devices to generate interrupts if required.

I will explain each of these circuits in detail as we progress through the project and although this block diagram is a very simplified version of the JMZ it does contain all the main elements required to get our system working.

In the next chapter we will begin designing the actual circuits beginning with the video output system.

ℒ ℋ ℰ

Chapter 5 – Video Output System

It may seem odd to begin developing our Z80 system by designing the video output system. After all the video output is a long way down the chain as far as system operation is concerned and so it may seem that it would be better to begin our project with something more directly related to the Z80 processor itself rather than one of the computer sub systems.

However the reason that I decided to develop the video output electronics so early is because in many ways it is one of the most complex parts of the system to get working reliably. If I go down the route of designing a lot of the Z80 system first then it would be very easy to end up with an over complicated or unreliable video output sub system because it would need to fit into whatever I had already developed. By developing the video system first I am free to design it in the way that makes most sense for this project and then the Z80 system can be easily designed to accommodate the requirements of the video system.

I should point out at this stage that this computer will only have character mode output and character mode graphics. The aim of this project is to describe the design and construction of a Z80 system rather than how to add peripheral devices to it. However once the computer is up and running it would be very easy and a lot of fun to begin adding more advanced features such as full graphics or even colour display but that will be for a later project.

As we progress through this chapter it will hopefully become apparent why I am taking this approach and how complex even a simple design can become.

Most simple Z80 single board computers currently output data through an RS232 port and while that is fine for a basic system my intention is to demonstrate how much more difficult computer development was before modern large scale integrated circuits appeared. They encapsulated much of the complexity in creating such systems and in my opinion they made it much easier to design low cost computers.

By bringing down the cost of small computers they could be made available to far more people. This is of course a very good thing but in some ways it removed a lot of the transparency to the inner workings of them. As small computers continued to develop this trend continued and we are now at the point where it is possible to buy a small embedded computer development system for a very low cost and download some code to run on it. In just a few minutes a fully functional mini computer system can be up and running but I wonder how many of the users really appreciate what has gone into the creation of such devices.

Beginning with this chapter I hope to demonstrate just what is involved in designing a computer from scratch using basic circuits and the same techniques which were employed back when the Z80 was young. Much of the material in this book and in this project may seem unrelated to modern embedded computer systems but the modern devices have their roots firmly embedded in the techniques and methods we will be investigating. The modern devices still use many of the complex electronic methods which we will design in our Z80 computer.

The real difference is that to design a system like this we will need to understand the inner workings of such systems and this is much easier when these workings arc fully exposed.

Starting Development

So it is time to begin our design and as I said we sill start by designing and building the video output sub system.

Step one in any development project is to figure out what we are aiming to achieve (Actually it is getting funding but lets assume that has been taken care of).

Our video sub system will need to be able to take data values from our computer video memory and use these values to display data on our display in a readable form.

In keeping with the vintage theme of this project I decided to use a Cathode Ray Tube display (CRT) which was typical of the type of display used during the period we are considering.

For test purposes I selected a 12 inch black and white CRT from a dumb terminal as this is a reasonable size to experiment with and it is also a very basic device although it does have some very particular drive requirements.

The monitor does not have any in built display ability as its driver board does nothing more than produce the high voltage required by the CRT and also generates the deflection currents required to move the electron beam across the face of the tube.

In fact it cannot even do that unless we feed it with suitable drive signals so I will begin by describing how we will make use of the CRT display to create a character based computer output system.

Designing a video system such as this is surprisingly complex as quite a few elements within the drive circuits need to work in harmony to produce a clean and readable display.

We will also need to include methods for writing data into the video system and reading data out of it as well as generating a cursor along with accurately timed drive signals for our monitor.

CRT displays can in general generate display output using one of two basic methods.

The first method is called 'Vector' display and in these systems the electron beam in the CRT is used to directly 'draw' an image on the face of the screen. That is it simply moves the electron beam in the same way that you would if you were using a pencil to draw an image. For example if a circle is needed then the electron beam is moved in a circle and the phosphor on the face of the tube glows where the electron beam strikes it and a circle is produced.

The image is redrawn repeatedly very quickly at short intervals and the human eye is fooled into thinking that a continuous image is being presented.

This method is useful for simple displays but has limitations which make it unsuitable for the type of information we wish to output.

Vector display is fairly slow and this limitation becomes increasingly apparent as the number of required display elements increases.

We wish to display quite a few characters on screen simultaneously which means that we must use a different technique.

Raster Scan Display

We will use the second common type of CRT drive method which is the 'Raster Scan Display'.

While designing this sort of display system adds complexity it rewards us by allowing us to display as many elements on the screen as we wish all at the same time without any slowing down of the video output. The only limitation in the number of items we can display on the screen is due to the size of the individual screen picture elements or 'pixels' and this is only limited by how fast we can turn the CRT electron beam on and off.

For the type of CRT we are going to be using this limiting time is approximately 80nS and at the speed we will be scanning the tube this results in a horizontal pixel count of around 800 and a vertical pixel count of around 300.

In other words we can construct any image on the screen which can be represented using around 250,000 individual pixels.

For practical reasons we will be using a little less than this but our display will still be made up from over 200,000 pixels.

So how are we going to go about designing a circuit which can read values from a computer memory and accurately translate them into rows of characters on a CRT screen?

Let us begin by looking at the basic scanning geometry of our monitor system.

Figure 5-1 shows how the electron beam in our monitor will be scanned across the face of the tube.

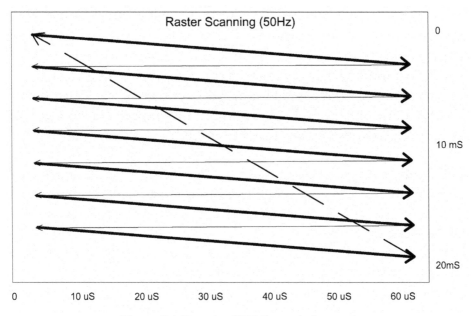

Figure 5-1 How the CRT Raster is Scanned

As we can see in Figure 5-1 the electron beam starts at the top left corner of the display and it then moves at a fairly steady speed horizontally across the face of the display.

When the beam gets close to the right hand edge of the display it is rapidly moved back to the left of the screen and it again begins moving at a fixed speed back across to the right.

While it is scanning left to right and back it is also moving down the tube face as a steady but much slower rate and as you can see in Figure 5-1 the combined movements produce a zig zag pattern which progresses down the display.

Once the beam reaches the bottom right corner of the display area the beam rapidly moves back to the top left of the display and the next scan begins. We refer to this as raster scanning.

I have exaggerated the amount it moves down on each horizontal pass in order to make the motion clear. In practice there are approximately 250 horizontal lines in each full screen of scan lines.

I said that the lines are horizontal but as you can see in Figure 5-1 they actually slope down towards the right of the display. The rapid return lines also slope down and to the left but as the return (known as retrace) is much faster than the scan to the right the downward movement during the retrace periods is much less.

This results in a raster which is tilted down towards the right but the scan coils on the CRT are normally rotated slightly in order to make the scan lines appear to be horizontal.

As I mentioned earlier the monitor drive electronics cannot produce this motion on their own so we need to provide what are known as sync or drive pulses in order to get the monitor to produce the required raster pattern.

To be precise the horizontal signal is actually a drive signal and the vertical signal is a synchronisation, or sync, signal.

The reason for this is due to the fact that the monitor drive board requires an external drive signal applied to its HDRIVE input to cause the electron beam to move.

This is also needed in order to generate the very high voltage required by the CRT which is around the region of 9000-12000 volts (so be careful if you start experimenting).

In contrast the monitor drive board has an in built vertical scan oscillator which runs whenever power is applied and so the pulse applied to VDRIVE input is only required to force this oscillator to run at the correct speed.

While the monitor is capable of working over a range of scan speeds this range is very small and unless the applied pulses are within the small acceptance range the monitor will not work correctly and could even be damaged.

Our circuits will be responsible for accurately generating the required drive signals and ensuring that they are properly synchronised with the video output signals which it will also need to produce.

Before we begin designing the drive electronics for the video display system it is worth looking more closely at exactly how the CRT monitor actually produces an image. As I have shown in Figure 5-1 the monitor creates an image by progressively scanning an electron beam across a phosphor coated surface and the phosphor glows where the electron beam hits it. The beam moves fairly rapidly and at any moment in time it is only creating a very small dot on the screen. While the phosphor does have some persistence which causes it to continue glowing for a short time after the beam moves on it is actually your eye and brain that is largely responsible for generating the final image.

Our primary concern in our design task is the basics of how the electron beam moves and how we can control it because it may not be as obvious as it first sounds.

There are 3 signals we need to generate in order to correctly drive the monitor and the way these work together and the way they interact is fairly important to the success of our design.

We already know that the electron beam starts at the top left corner of the screen and follows a zig zag path down the face of the display tube and ends at the bottom right corner.

However everything is not as simple as it first sounds.

To begin with we need to determine how many times the beam moves across the screen during each full display cycle. We will refer to a full screen update from top left to bottom right and back as a 'Frame' and so the number of these cycles each second is our frame rate.

This is where things start to get a bit complicated because we can decide how many characters we will display across the screen and also how many rows of characters we will produce. There are of course limits imposed on us due to the way the monitor works but there is some scope for us to set the display parameters.

The first thing to come to terms with is the fact that while we can set the number of passes the electron beam makes across the screen each second we cannot actually alter the speed at which it travels.

This may sound like a contradiction and to a certain extent it is but I will elaborate on this to hopefully make it clearer.

The drive board inside the monitor is very simple and one of the three signals it needs is a horizontal drive. This signal is used to tell the drive board to start moving the electron beam across the screen. Once it receives a trigger pulse the beam begins sweeping across the screen from left to right but it always takes the same amount of time to complete a full sweep and this is set by the drive electronics inside the monitor.

While we cannot make the electron beam go any faster, what we can do is make it complete more sweeps each second. I appreciate that this sounds like double talk but bear with me and I will try to explain.

Once the electron beam is moving across the screen it will continue to move to the right until we send the next horizontal drive signal and at that time the beam rapidly moves back to the left and it then begins the next sweep.

By shortening the time between these signals we can cause the electron beam to complete more sweeps each second and we will refer to this repetition speed as the horizontal frequency. Although we can vary the horizontal frequency the range which most monitors will accept is fairly limited and if you try to go outside the allowable limits the monitor will not work correctly, if at all and it may even be damaged due to inappropriate drive currents being generated.

The monitor I am using can be made to work at horizontal frequencies from around 15 KHz to a little over 20 KHz so we must bear this in mind as we design our video drive system.

You may have realised that if we force the electron beam to end its current sweep and start the next before it has got all the way to the right hand side of the screen then the image will not extend the full width of the display.

Although I said we cannot alter the speed at which the electron beam travels this is not strictly accurate because we can adjust the width of the displayed image.

If we increase the width of the image then the electron beam will travel faster during each sweep and so even if we increase the horizontal frequency by speeding up the horizontal drive signal we can adjust the image to span the screen by adjusting the display width. This does cause the beam to move faster but you must remember that the time taken for the beam to move back from right to left is fixed and so we cannot make random changes to the scan frequency as this would cause unstable display output.

So to set the number of horizontal raster lines we simply select a suitable horizontal drive signal frequency and then we can adjust the display width control to produce a full width scan.

The next item to consider is the vertical drive signal frequency and the second drive signal we need to generate and send to the monitor is the vertical synchronisation pulse.

This works differently to the horizontal drive signal because the monitor has a built in vertical drive oscillator which runs all the time even in the absence of synchronisation pulses.

This is unlike the horizontal drive which does nothing unless drive pulses are applied.

In general terms we adjust the vertical drive oscillator to run close to the required speed and then the pulses we provide are just used to fine tune this speed to exactly match our system.

As with the horizontal drive there are limits and for this monitor the vertical drive is limited from around 46 Hz to 61Hz and if we try to go beyond these limits the monitor will complain.

The third input to the monitor is the video signal and this allows us to turn the electron beam on or off. The electron beam continues to scan when it is not illuminating the phosphor but nothing appears on the screen. By turning the beam on and off at the correct times during each display scan frame we can build up an image and the trick is to coordinate all three input signals to generate the required display.

There are a few additional complications we will need to deal with but let us start by figuring out what frequencies we will need to use for the drive signals.

Now that we know what each monitor input signal does we can begin calculating the required drive signal parameters.

Columns and Rows

The characters we will display on the screen will be organised in rows and columns so the first decision we have to make is how many rows and how many columns do we want.

This is also not a simple decision as we need to take a number of things into consideration in order to get the best from our design.

I should point out that when I say 'Get the Best' this is of course a matter of personal choice and will depend on what you want from your own design.

For my computer I want a display that gives me a good balance of line text length and the number of lines I can display on the screen.

As we intend to use a 2k byte RAM to store the video text data we actually have 2048 bytes and so a maximum of 2048 characters for each full screen of data.

Many displays use 80 columns of characters and if we select this we will be able to store a maximum of 25 rows of characters.

However for my use I do not think that 80 characters is the best choice because this would result in the vast majority of text lines only occupying the left quarter of the screen.

That is because most text lines I enter are less than 20 characters in length and so most of the video display area would be blank and the text would be cramped towards the left side of the display.

I did initially design a circuit to give me 80 columns by 25 rows but I was not happy with it for the reasons given above.

I therefore used a word processor to try different formats starting with an 80 x 25 character layout and I began decreasing the length of each line and increasing the number of rows.

I found that something around 65 characters on each line gave me the best compromise and would result in a good balance of line length combined with the number of rows.

At the same time I was also considering another seemingly unrelated design decision which I could resolve as part of this process.

Non Volatile Storage

Most computers will benefit from some form of non volatile storage which they can use to store things such as system configuration settings. In modern microcontroller based systems this is very simple to implement as most devices include some EEPROM memory but I do not want to resort to this approach as it goes against the vintage goal of our design.

One method used for storing non volatile data in the early days of the Z80 was the use of battery backed SRAM.

Many SRAM devices were designed to support a standby mode in which they could be put into a very low power state without losing their stored data. The SRAM I have selected for this design is such a device and so we can use one of these to store our non volatile system data by including a battery backup circuit.

It is most likely that we will only ever need a few bytes of non volatile RAM and so adding another SRAM device along with the required decoding to address it seemed a bit excessive so I have decided to use a small portion of the video SRAM for this purpose. All we will need to do to implement the non volatile storage is to add a small backup battery and a few power steering diodes and also avoid using the same bytes for video display data.

So taking this into consideration when determining the text layout of the video display I ended up with a final decision of 64 characters by 30 rows. This leaves 128 bytes of the SRAM which we can use for the non volatile storage and as we already have memory address decoding in place to access the video SRAM we have everything we require to implement this feature.

Video Memory Array Addressing

When I designed the first version of the video display circuit I spent some considerable time designing a circuit which resolved the 7 bits from the Column counter and the 5 bits from the Row counter into a single 11 bit memory address.

This is not as simple as it may sound and required the addition of two 5 bit adders and 2 multiplexers along with some relatively complex logic to make it all work. There is actually a point worth making here which is not to confine your design process because of any time you may have spent on part of the design. Do not be afraid to throw away something which no longer meets the design needs and move on to an alternative option.

That is exactly what I did in this case by removing the hard won address resolution circuitry and replaced it with a much simpler alternative. This was a bit of a shame because the circuit was interesting and had taken considerable time and effort but it was simply part of a design process so was not really time wasted.

The reason I could simplify the video addressing circuit design is because I initially ended up with a determination that 65 columns by 31 rows would work very well for this design but by removing one column I could get 64 by 32 rows and this fits perfectly into 6 bits of column address and 5 bits of row address. This completely removes the need to resolve an address from the two counters as each can be used directly.

It was apparent that implementing 32 rows would require a fairly compressed vertical adjustment to the monitor which would in turn give a fairly 'squashed' appearance to the text but by reducing the row count by just two to 30 it not only resulted in very good display proportions but it also freed up 128 bytes of the video SRAM which we can now use for non volatile storage.

So we now have our desired target text layout of 64 columns by 30 rows so how do we go about designing a circuit to provide this format of display output?

I said that we will be using a 2048 byte RAM device for storing the video information but we now need to determine exactly how the video information will be stored within this memory space.

Each RAM byte can only store 8 bits of information and this is of course not enough to store sufficient data to display an entire character on the screen.

Each character will be displayed using a small grid of dots on the screen and in our design every character will actually need 64 of these dots to form the required character image. That means that if we simply store the video image as a series of dots then our 2k of video RAM would only be able to store a maximum of 256 characters.

That would limit us to displaying an absolute maximum of 4 rows of characters at any one time (2048 / 8 = 256).

Clearly we need to find a more efficient way to store our video data if we want to be able to simultaneously display the required 1920 characters on the screen.

Fortunately there is a very good way to store the required video information in such a way that we can display a full screen of information using just 2k of RAM and still have bytes to spare.

This is a widely used technique which is found in almost all vintage computers and is normally referred to as a bitmapped display.

Character Bitmaps

We know how the monitor scans its electron beam across the face of the CRT so we just need to arrange to send it some accurately timed video information in order to produce an image.

A third input to the monitor is the VIDEO, or brightness signal and it is used to determine which parts (or pixels) on the display are illuminated (on) or dark (off).

The monitor can actually produce a grey scale image with individual pixels ranging from black up to full white or anything in between but for our purposes we will be turning them either fully on or fully off, we just need to determine when this has to happen for each pixel we wish to display.

The display raster scan runs continually and at relatively high speed. In our application each horizontal line will take approximately 54uS for the beam to travel from the left of the screen to the right and around 20mS to travel from the top to the bottom of the screen.

This means that a full screen raster scan takes approximately 20mS or in other words it repeats 50 times each second which is fast enough to make it appear as if the display is static with minimal flicker.

It may already be apparent that we will need to design a circuit which can output a lot of pixel information at fairly high speed in order to keep up with the raster scanning. Naturally we cannot use the Z80 to send the pixel information one pixel at a time because it is no where near fast enough to do that and also we really want the processor to concentrate on running our programs and not doing its housework.

The method we will employ to help us is know as 'bitmap' image production and as it sounds it consists of generating an image using collections of bits arranged in specific patterns.

As we only need to store the required bit map number and only one copy of each bitmap this is a very efficient way of storing video display data.

If we think about the information we want to display then it will be easier to describe this method.

Figure 5-2 shows an example for the top left corner of our display where two words are required at the beginning of the first two lines.

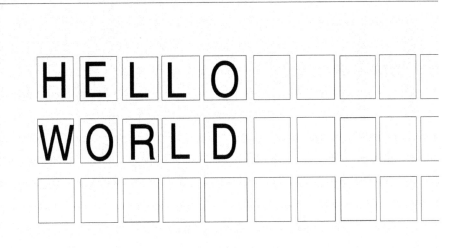

Figure 5-2 Example Display Text

In order to display text like this we will need to work with the display raster scan in such a way that we can form individual letters or characters as the raster progresses.

We will do this by sending a serial stream of video data to the monitor VIDEO input as the raster is scanned across the screen.

Because the raster scans the entire width of the screen in each raster line we cannot complete each character entirely before moving on to the next. Instead we must form rows of partial characters from their bitmap patterns before moving on to the next row of characters.

In the example shown in Figure 5-2 we would need to form all the characters in the line which starts 'HELLO' before we move on the line which starts 'WORLD'.

This is most easily described if we examine one of these bitmaps and the bitmap for an uppercase 'H' is shown in Figure 5-3.

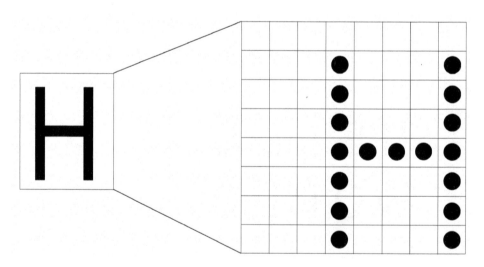

Figure 5-3 Bitmap for an Uppercase H

As you can see the bitmap is actually a series of short rows of dots which are arranged in such a way that they display characters.

Different computer systems use different bitmaps for the characters but they generally all work in very similar ways.

In our system I have decided to use bitmaps formed from an 8 by 8 grid of dots as shown in Figure 5-3.

Before we can use such a bitmap in a computer display system we must convert it into a form that can be used in an electronic circuit.

In other words we must convert this bitmap into a series of numbers which we can store in our computer.

This will be much easier to understand if you are familiar with the binary number system (and also the Hexadecimal number system).

If we decide that each blank square in the bitmap grid is a '0' and that each dot is a '1' then we can represent each line in the bitmap as an 8 bit binary or hexadecimal number.

Figure 5-4 shows how this would look for the uppercase 'H' character. Alongside the bitmap grid is the hexadecimal equivalent of the 8 bit binary number for each bitmap grid row.

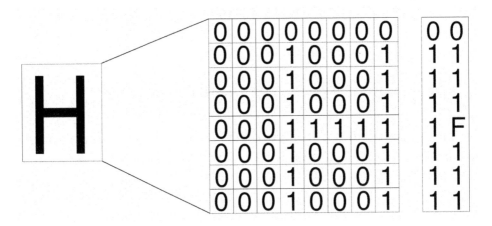

Figure 5-4 Converting the bitmaps to numbers

In this way we can describe each bitmap character using a series of 8 numbers and we can of course also create graphics characters in the same way or indeed any pattern which will fit into the grid.

Each number is a very conveniently 8 bits in length or to put it another way each number is one byte which exactly matches the byte storage size used by our selected SRAM.

This means that we can fit a character bitmap number into each memory location and so we now have a very simple way to store the video data we wish to represent on the screen.

Another character example is shown in Figure 5-5.

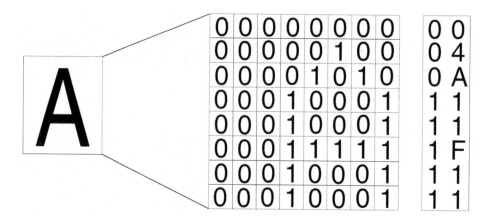

Figure 5-5 Uppercase 'A' bitmap

In the example bitmap in Figure 5-5 we are of course representing an uppercase letter 'A' along with the 8 bytes which can be used to describe this characters bitmap.

We now have the ability to describe our required characters as a series of numerical values and so we now need to determine how to send them out to the monitor in such a way that they form characters on the display screen.

We know that the electron beam scans across the entire screen one pixel row at a time so we must send data out for one row of each character as the full display line is scanned.

As the line of pixels is scanned the system must select the correct source for the bitmap data based on the character data stored in each screen location within the video SRAM.

In our example when the top row of the display is scanned we must begin by sending the top row of the uppercase 'H' bitmap. Once the first 8 bits have been sent we switch to the top row of data for the uppercase 'E' character and send the next 8 bits of data. This is followed by the top row for characters 'L', 'L' and 'O'.

Figure 5-6 shows how this would look.

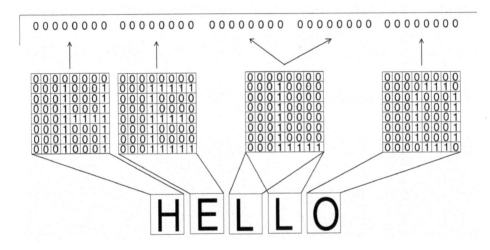

Figure 5-6 Scanning the First Line

As you can see the stream of pixel information is taken from the appropriate bitmap as each character space is scanned.

Notice that we only need to have a single copy of each bitmap and so in this case although the character 'L' is displayed twice there is only a single bitmap for the uppercase 'L'.

As each pixel space is crossed by the electron beam the system must use the information contained in the bitmap images to determine if the beam should be on or off (a '0' or a '1').

If the value in the bitmap is a '0' then the beam is turned off but if the value is a '1' then the beam is turned on.

As this all happens at very high speed the human eye will perceive the image as being static and we will simply see the result of the scanning process as if it was a fixed image.

Once the entire first line of the display has been scanned and all required character pixel data for the first row has been sent the electron beam will return to the beginning of the next pixel row down and the next line of pixel data will be sent.

This process continues line by line for the entire display area and Figure 5-7 shows how the display would appear after the third scan line has been completed.

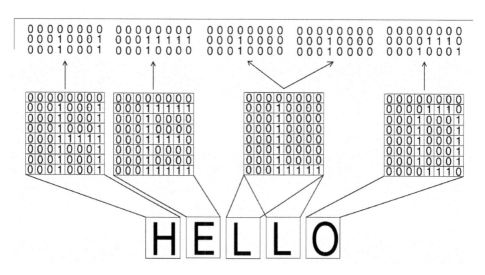

Figure 5-7 The First Three Lines Scanned

By the time the electron beam has reached the bottom right corner of the display the entire image will have been built up from over 200,000 individual pixels or dots.

The entire process is repeated approximately 50 times every second and so we see a static image on the face of the CRT.

It is finally time to start designing some actual electronics which will allow us to send this pixel data stream to the monitor and ultimately give our Z80 computer the ability to display text on the monitor screen.

Our circuit design must run without the need for constant attention from the Z80 so that our computer can focus its power on the software it is running.

The Z80 will however need to be able to write character data into the display system and also read data back from it.

The reason it needs to be able to read data back may not be obvious at this point but by the end of this chapter it should become clear why this is the case and also how it will be done.

It is important to understand the limitations imposed on our design by the nature of the type of display we are using and while it may seem tempting to simply replace it with a modern LCD display which can be implemented much more easily I will repeat that our goal is to design and build a computer using methods which were common when the Z80 was first released.

It is always very tempting to take short cuts when projects begin to get complicated but in my opinion you can learn far more by doing things the hard way. If you really want to you can always replace elements within the design with easier to handle equivalents but designing circuits such as those I will be presenting in this book can be a great deal of fun and will provide a 'feel' to the design which is simply missing from more modern versions.

After all the entire purpose of this book and project is to have fun in designing a computer system rather than to get it over with as quickly as possible.

We can therefore happily ignore the commercial pressures that designers are normally confronted with.

Having said that it is almost certain that the designers back in the 1970's and 1980's would have thrown their CRT's into the nearest skip and selected an LCD if they had been available but that is not what I am aiming for.

The Design Begins

From the description I have presented so far in this chapter it is probably apparent that the display system will need to be able to keep track of the location of the electron beam on the display and be able to select the correct pixel data to send to each location.
There are a number of different tasks which will be needed for our display system to work so I will break the system down into blocks and describe each one in turn.

The required building blocks of our display system are…

1)   Character Column Pixel Counter
2)   Screen Character Column Counter
3)   Character Pixel Line Counter
4)   Screen Character Row Counter
5)   Horizontal Drive Generator
6)   Vertical Sync Generator
7)   Blanking Signal Generator
8)   Video Mixer
9)   Cursor Generator
10) SRAM to store the screen data
11) ROM to store the character bitmaps
12) Address Multiplexer to allow the CPU RAM access
13) Bidirectional Data Buffer to allow the CPU Read/Write access
14) Read / Write control logic
15) Video blanking circuit
16) Data Shift Register and Latch
17) Display System Control Logic

That is quite a list of requirements so I shall describe each in turn but to help visualise the overall system architecture Figure 5-8 shows a simplified block diagram of the entire display design.

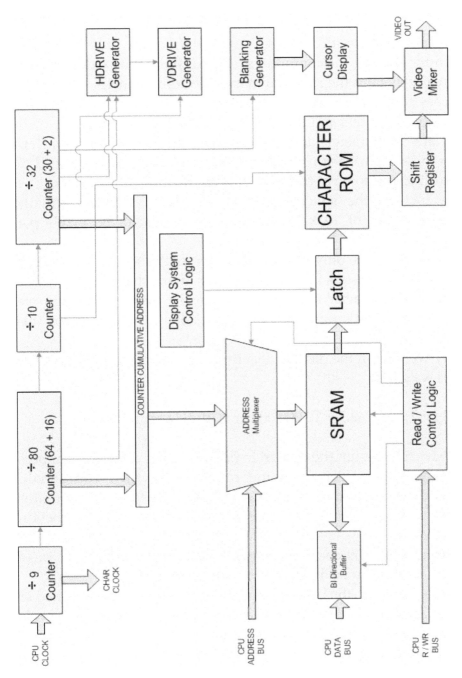

Figure 5-8 Simplified Display System Block Diagram

In this design I decided to use a 10.0 MHz clock. This is another reason for starting the computer system design at the video display as it really dictates the required master clock frequencies.

It is easy to explain where this frequency comes from if we look at the various counters and the pixel count that we are using.

There are 64 characters across the screen and 30 rows of characters down the screen. Each character is made up from an 8 x 8 grid of pixels although some of these are spacing pixels.

If we include the spacing pixels then each character actually occupies a grid of 10 x 8 pixels giving a total of 80 pixels per character.

Although there are only 64 characters across the screen we actually count to 80 for reasons I will explain later in this chapter.

We have 30 character rows going down the display although we count up to 32 rows and again I will explain the reason for this later.

Finally we refresh the display 48.5 times each second so using these values we get…

8 x 10 x 80 x 32 x 48.5 = 10,000,000 or 10.0MHz (rounded up)

If you wish to design the system to operate using different numbers of characters or rows or frame refresh rates then you should calculate the required clock frequency. If you try to run the monitor too far from its acceptable rates then it is unlikely to function correctly.

I selected a 64 x 30 character display and 48.5 Hz refresh because this will work very well with the monitor I am using.

While looking into the best column and row count to use I looked at quite a large number of alternatives but as I explained earlier in this chapter I selected 64 x 30 because it gave me the best compromise between line length and row count while also leaving some spare bytes in the SRAM which could then be used for non volatile data storage.

You should feel free to experiment with different screen layouts and resolutions but just bear in mind that you cannot simply increase the dot clock frequency in order to increase the number of characters on the screen. You will need to redesign a number of the counter circuits along with the monitor drive and blanking circuits should you wish to alter the design I am presenting here.
It is however a lot of fun to try different ideas in designs such as this so I highly recommend giving it a go.
It is probably fair to say that many of my design decisions were based on the actual CRT and drive circuit I selected so you may well find that different values are more appropriate for your own display.
As ever feel free to experiment and you may well find that alternatives work better for you.

At this point it is worth having a better look at the overall design of our video output system and then we can get started on the actual circuit design.

It is probably now apparent that the video display system is not a trivial design task although it is certainly a very interesting one and once broken down into separate blocks it is easy to understand.
The next obvious question is of course how to go about translating our theoretical design into practical circuits.
What we have outlined is a very complex sequence of data control which could easily result in unwieldy or unworkable circuit designs.
In this case we can simply begin at the start of the required counter sequence and develop a circuit which will provide the required outputs.

So let's get started.

Character Pixel Column Counter

This counter is at the start of the display timing chain and is clocked from the main Z80 CPU clock at 10.0MHz.
Figure 5-9 shows the schematic for this counter.

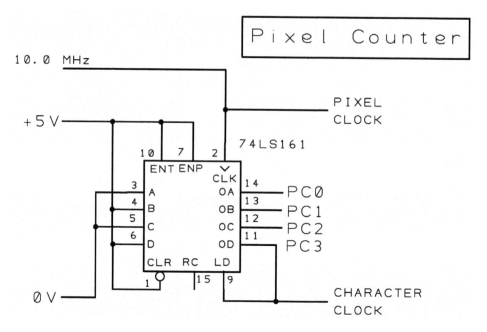

Figure 5-9 Pixel Counter Schematic

As you can see the pixel counter circuit is very simple although it will become increasingly useful as our Z80 computer development proceeds.
I mentioned earlier that I decided to start with the design of the video output system for a number of reasons and we now get to yet another reason for selecting this as the starting point for our project. If you examine the schematics of many computer systems using many different types of processors, including Z80 designs then you will see a very common design feature.

That design feature is a binary counter / divider circuit directly following the main clock generator circuit.

The reason that so many, if not all, computer designs include this is due to the way that a typical processor chip processes instructions and how the overall system design must work with the CPU.

If we look at our Z80 as an example then it actually processes individual instructions over a number of main clock cycles. Typically with the Z80 it takes a minimum of 4 clock cycles to complete an instruction although this can often be even longer.

This is because the processor must perform a number of actions in order to complete the execution of any instruction.

With the Z80 the first clock cycle is always used to fetch the next instruction from memory and the following clock cycles are used to complete the actions required by that instruction.

As it turns out this multi-clock machine cycle makes designing the computer very much easier as it gives us opportunities during each instruction clock cycle to perform the various tasks which the computer needs to complete in order to function correctly without the need to slow down the Z80.

A good example of this is allowing time to write data to its RAM or to the video display system.

By including a divider after the main system clock we can generate a number of clock phase signals which we can selectively use to perform various system tasks at the appropriate times during an instruction cycle. I will come back to this in a later chapter.

The system we are developing here is no exception to the need for multiple clock frequencies and we will need a number of clock phase signals in order to complete the system design.

We would normally need to add at least one additional device to generate these clock phase signals and although we do not need to make use of the divided output signals produced by the pixel counter in the display system they will be very useful later and save us the trouble of adding a separate clock divider. Just remember that they are here and we will make use of them later.

So as you see there is another good reason to begin our system development here.

Getting back to the pixel counter I said that we do not need all the outputs it generates but we do actually need one of them as it is a very important clock signal within the video system.

The output from pin 11 of the pixel clock is labelled as 'CHARACTER CLOCK' and will be used to time the counting of characters as we send them to the video display monitor.

The main 10MHz clock will be used as the pixel clock.

The operation of this circuit is very straight forward and is based on the load feature of the 74LS161 binary counter device.

When a clock is applied to pin 2 it starts to count up with the binary count value being output on pins 11 to 14 with pin 14 being the least significant bit.

Pin 11 (bit 3) is connected to the load input pin and so as soon as bit 3 goes high the counter is reloaded with the value set on pins 3 to 6. These pins are hard wired to provide an input value of 5 which means that each time the counter is loaded it starts counting from a value of 5. When it reaches a value of 15 the next clock cycle causes bit 3 to go high and this reloads the counter again with a value of 5. The counter therefore counts from 5 to 15 and then is reset to 5.

The result is that it effectively divides the pixel clock by 9 and the resulting clock is available from pin 11.

Note that this clock is effectively out of phase with the main dot clock and this is intentional as it allows each counter to complete count steps without entering any race conditions.

A race condition exists when any small delays in signal propagation could cause the circuit in question to fail to operate correctly or the entire system to crash.

This must always be avoided in digital systems and the easiest way to do this is to ensure that each device is allowed sufficient time to finish its operation before making use of its output.

We now have the two main video display system clocks.

The first is the Pixel clock which is running at 10.0MHz.

The second is the Character clock which is running at 1.1MHz.

The outputs labelled PC0 to PC3 can be used elsewhere in our computer system as main clock phase signals.

Screen Column Counter

The next circuit we need to create is one which will count the number of columns of characters on the screen.

I should point out here that many of the circuits I will be presenting are typical circuits used many times before. It is the overall system design that we are attempting to create so hopefully the various configurations for the devices we are using will be familiar.

Although the purpose of the column counter may at first seem simple there is a complication which I mentioned earlier.

If you recall I explained that the retrace time of the monitor electron beam is a fairly significant part of the overall line scan period.

In our design the time required to scan the beam from the left of the screen to the right is around 54 uS and the time required for the beam to retrace from the right to the left is around 11.5 uS.

We do of course need to allow time for the retrace portion of the scan otherwise the monitor display output will be out of sync with our pixel data stream and will therefore appear scrambled.

The pixel data for our 64 column display output is 54 uS and so we can calculate how much longer is required to allow for the retrace.

54 /64 gives us 0.84 uS per character.

11.5 uS will therefore require an additional 14 Character periods.

(11.5 / 0.84) and allowing a margin we will use 16.

As we already have a counter running to count the column positions we can use it to time the additional time for the retrace.

We do however still need the timer to provide an output signal after completion of character 63 (characters are numbered from 0) so that we can keep the pixel output data synchronised.

Remember that the 74LS161 devices we are using have a load function so we can make use of it again to give us the outputs we need by reloading it with an appropriate value at the right time.

Figure 5-10 shows the schematic for the Column Counter circuit.

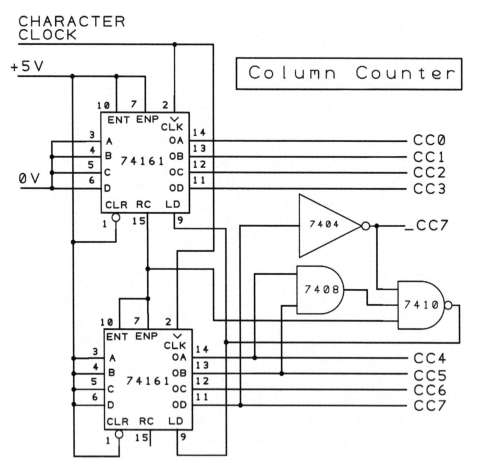

Figure 5-10 Column Counter Schematic

Although this circuit provides a number of functions it operation is very simple. It is clocked by the output of the pixel counter which we looked at earlier and the two 74LS161 counters are cascaded to form an 8 bit binary counter. The outputs are monitored by an inverter and a 3 input NAND gate along with a two input AND gate to detect when the counter reaches a count of 63. This signal is available to us at the output of the NAND gate and this signal is also use for the next function which this counter performs. The output of the NAND gate is used to load the two counters with a new value. The load inputs are hard wired to provide a binary value of...

11110000

This is of course a value which is 16 below the overflow count for an 8 bit binary counter so once this value has been loaded the counter will continue to count for an additional 16 clock cycles before overflowing back to zero.

In this way the counter counts from 0 to 63 and outputs the required end of line signal but continues to count up for another 16 cycles to provide the count required for the entire scan period including the retrace.

The outputs labelled CC0 to CC7 and _ CC7 will be used later to help select the required data stream bitmap.

This is a major advantage in using binary counters for this type of function because they not only provide the required timing functions but they also generate a binary sequence which is ideal for operations such as memory address selection.

The binary outputs also create accurate timing clock edges for every possible state within the overall circuit and so we can make use of them in other parts of our display circuits for operations such as drive pulse generation and video blanking but more on that later in this chapter.

It should be clear by now that this circuit can very easily be adapted to provide almost any combination of primary count output along with secondary timer output.

An important aspect of this counter operation is that the most significant bit (CC7) effectively has a value of 64 because it goes high when the counter reaches 63 and is reloaded. Once reloaded the output of CC7 goes high and remains high until the counter overflows back to zero. We can therefore use this output as a column overflow indicator.

If you decide to adapt this circuit for your own design then be aware that some count ranges in our system are used for specific purposes which may be disrupted if the counter is modified.

Character Pixel Row Counter

The next circuit we need to add is one to allow us to count the rows within each character bitmap which are required to display each complete full character row.

This is not the same as the character pixel row count because each character row is made up from 9 CRT raster lines.

Remember that the character bitmaps are 8 x 8 characters so we will need another counter which will count each of the rows in each character bitmap.

Once again we will use a 74LS161 to build this circuit and because this counter only needs to count from 0 to 8 it is even easier to design than the previous two counters because 8 is of course available directly from a binary counter so there is no need to load the counter with a specific starting value or to monitor its outputs for a particular bit pattern.

Figure 5-11 shows the schematic for this counter.

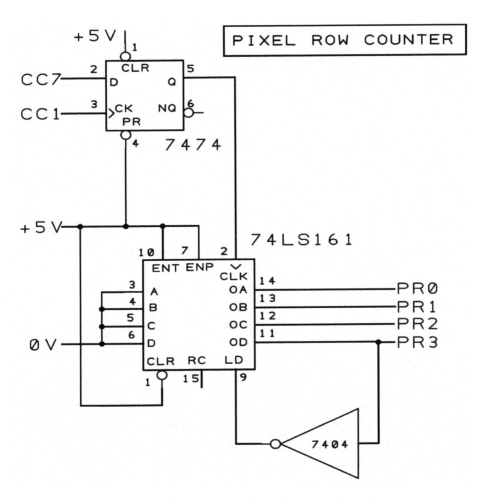

Figure 5-11 Character Pixel Row Counter Schematic

This counter is clocked at the end of each scan line and so it is used to count the rows of pixels in each character bitmap. It counts from 0 to 8 and as it counts it allows the system to select the correct row of pixels in the currently selected character bitmap within the character ROM. For example if the current count is 3 then the 4th row of character pixels in each bitmap is selected.

Each row of characters on the screen is built up from 8 rows of pixels and so each time this counter reaches a count of 8 it clocks the next count in the system which selects the first row of pixels in the next row of full characters.

The 3 least significant bits of this counter are used to select the least significant bits of the character ROM and so it selects the correct byte in each group of 8 bytes which describe each character.

Screen Row Counter

Figure 5-12 shows the Screen Row Counter and its function is to keep track of which row of full characters on the screen is currently being sent to the monitor.

This counter is another 8 bit counter although only the first 6 bits are actually used.

It is clocked from the output of the Character Pixel Row Counter and this occurs at the end of every 8th scan line.

In this way the system counts vertically through the scan lines which are used to create each row of screen characters.

I selected a screen character row count of 30 to give a total display of 64 x 30 characters but as with the Column Counter it counts beyond the required count in order to allow time for the vertical retrace of the electron beam.

This counter is loaded with a value of zero by having all the load input pins hard wired to 0V. It then counts from zero to 32 and then reloads the counter with a value of zero and starts counting again.

The reason it counts to 32 is to allow time for both the vertical and horizontal retrace to complete before it starts again.

Although it counts from 0 to 32 it is also used to provide a sync pulse at character 31 to trigger the monitor retrace.

We will look at the horizontal and vertical drive and sync signals later in this chapter.

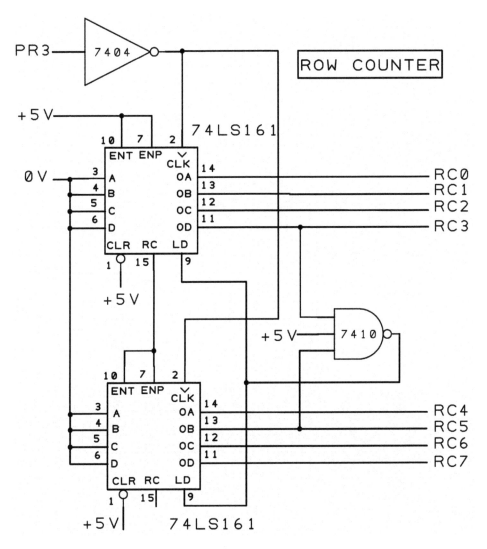

Figure 5-12 Screen Row Counter Schematic

We now have all the counters we need in order to generate the required data stream timing for character output to the monitor display.
Figure 5-13 shows the complete counter schematic.

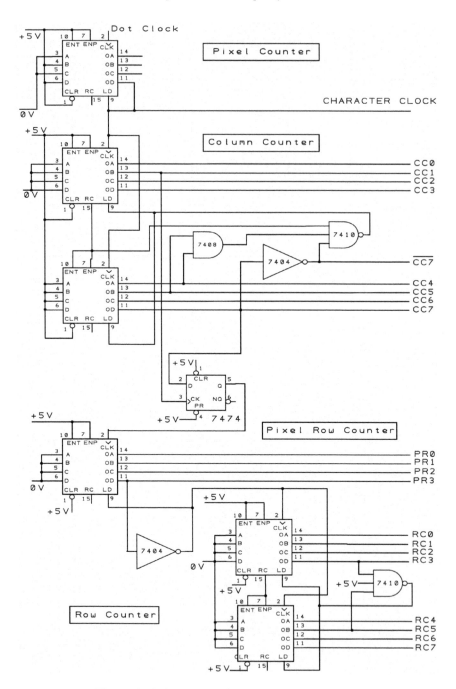

Figure 5-13 Complete Video Counters Schematic

So far we have designed the counters which we need to time the generation of the pixel data stream in order to correctly display our text data on the display.

The design I am presenting here produces a text display which comprises 64 columns and 30 rows of characters and a refresh rate of 48.5 Hz.

It would be perfectly possible to design a system with different numbers of columns and rows and different refresh rates if the counter values and clock frequencies were correctly organised but the design as presented here will suit our purposes very well.

Although we have all the counters we need to send pixel data to the display we still do not have any way of generating the horizontal and vertical drive and sync pulses.

These do of course need to be very carefully timed to produce a properly synchronised and stable display output.

The data stream also needs to be free from glitches as this would cause unpleasant artefacts on the screen.

I mentioned earlier that the first counter produces a series of division ratios for the main system clock and that this may be useful in other parts of the system.

We also need to keep a careful eye on all the clock edges to ensure that each of the system elements is clocked at the proper point in each cycle based on how it responds to the clock edges. That is if it responds to a rising or falling clock edge and by appropriate selection we can make good use of this to ensure reliable and stable operation of our system.

If you look at Figure 5-13 you will see that each of the counters has a series of binary output lines which are shown down the right side of the schematic.

We can now begin to make use of these binary outputs to generate the correctly timed signals which we require to drive our video display system.

Horizontal Drive Circuit

The monitor I have selected is typical of many monitors of the time in that is needs a horizontal drive signal to produce any horizontal scanning of the display and this is also used within the monitor to generate the high voltage required for the CRT to operate.

We will now design a circuit which can generate a properly timed HDRIVE signal. It should be noted here that if incorrect drive signals are sent to the monitor then it can be damaged so it is best to check the drive signal timing with a scope prior to connecting to a monitor.

Figure 5-14 shows the required HDRIVE output.

Figure 5-14 Required HDRIVE Output

The pixel data stream we send to the display must be properly timed and synchronised and to do this we simply need to select the appropriate outputs from our counters.

As the HDRIVE falling edge occurs at the end of each horizontal scan line then we can select the appropriate counter outputs although we do need to take a few things into account.

We will use the Column Counter outputs to generate the HDRIVE output because it must be timed based on the current character column which is being sent to the screen. This is of course controlled through the Column Counter circuit.

If you recall this counter counts from 0 to 63 and is then loaded with a value of F0 (hex) and it then continues to count until it overflows back to zero.

The point at which this timer is loaded is at the start of column 65 so we can simply use bit 7 of this counter going high as the starting point of our HDRIVE signal.

The HDRIVE signal must then remain constant until the timer reaches the end of the retrace period just as the timer overflows.

We can easily determine this point by monitoring a few of the output lines of this counter.

At the time it is reloaded the binary value is

11110000

The most significant 4 bits will then remain unchanged until the counter overflows back to 00000000.

If we monitor bits 3 and 4 we will see that they change state just as the counter reaches the last cycle prior to overflowing.

In addition we must ensure that the HDRIVE rising edge occurs in perfect synchronisation with the start of the next scan line.

An easy way to achieve this is to use the first bit of the counter to clock the reset of a latch. In this way the HDRIVE signal will start when the counter is loaded and it will end when the next scan line begins.

A simple bit of logic and a latch are all we need to generate this signal and this is shown in Figure 5-15.

These circuits may seem to be a little over complicated but unfortunately unless we include these additional features the display is very likely to be either unstable or totally corrupt.

It is surprising how sensitive video output circuits of this type are to artefact generation if the timing of the various signals is not absolutely correct and consistent.

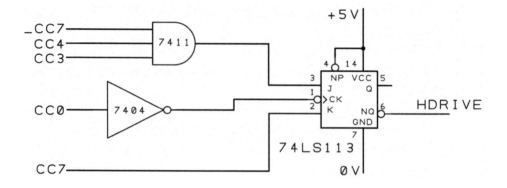

Figure 5-15 HDRIVE Generation Circuit

This circuit produces the output we need for the monitor horizontal HDRIVE input signal including a suitable delay for the retrace.

It is just a JK flip flop which is clocked using bit 0 of the Column Counter and the state to which it is clocked is determined by the states of the counter outputs required to provide the correct timing. The inverted CC7 input does not require any additional gates as _CC7 is already available in the Column Counter circuit (See Figure 5-13).

Now that we have the HDRIVE signal we can actually use it as part of the VSYNC generator in a very similar manner.

Vertical Sync Circuit

The VSYNC generation circuit is shown in Figure 5-16 and it works in a similar way to the HDRIVE circuit.

It uses a single output from the Row Counter along with the HDRIVE signal to generate a synchronisation pulse at the start of character line 31.

The HDRIVE signal is used to clock the flip flop so that the VSYNC pulse is accurately timed with the horizontal retrace.

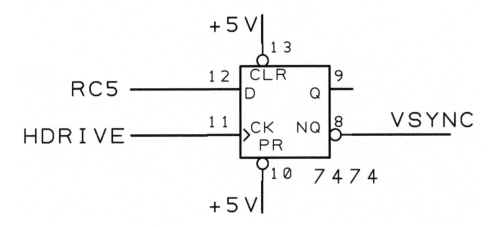

Figure 5-16 VSYNC Circuit

Note that the length of the vertical sync pulse is fairly long because it is active for the entire time that the RC5 output is high and it is not cleared until the following line starts.

This does not matter in our design as the monitor is only particular about when the pulse begins and not how long it lasts, unlike the horizontal drive pulse.

However if you prefer you could add a few additional gates to the vertical sync pulse generator circuit to detect when the next RC0 output occurs following RC5 going active. At that point you could reset the vertical sync output to produce a much shorter pulse but our monitor does not need us to do that so we will avoid the additional complication.

At this point we could connect our video control circuits to the monitor and assuming everything is correct we should be able to generate a raster on the screen of the monitor.

However it you try to do that at this stage then the display would most likely not look as you may expect.

Remember that we are effectively over scanning the display by counting beyond the last column and last row of the designed text output limits.

The display would therefore extend well beyond the area we wish to use for the display of our text. It will also show diagonal retrace lines which are created whenever the electron beam is returning to the left side of the screen.

If you look closely you may also be able to see large reversed 'ghost' characters which are produced when pixel information is clocked out during the retrace periods.

This is to be expected and we will now deal with this by designing a suitable video blanking circuit which will turn off the electron beam whenever we are outside the proper text display area. All the retrace artefacts such as retrace lines and ghost characters will also be eliminated. In addition the inter character areas will be blanked to avoid unwanted outputs.

Video Blanking Circuit

The video blanking circuit is a very simple arrangement which monitors a few of the counter outputs and when required it forces the electron beam to turn off and so prevents the display of unwanted artefacts.

Blanking is required for all scan areas which fall outside the intended text display area on the screen and also for retrace periods where the electron beam is moving across the face of the CRT from right to left.

Without this blanking the displayed image will look very messy and be almost unreadable. If you build this system then you will most likely find it very interesting to disable blanking as described on the next page to see what effect it has.

Figure 5-17 shows the video blanking circuit.

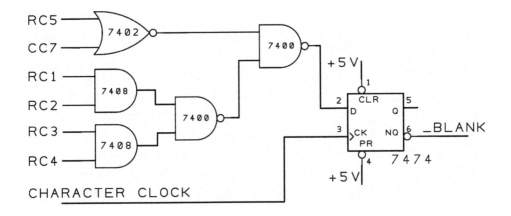

Figure 5-17 Video Blanking Circuit

If you want to see what the blanking circuit is actually removing from the display then you can temporarily connect the _BLANK output of the 7474 to pin 5 and the system will then display only the 'blanked' information.

This circuit is activated under the following conditions...

    1) The Character Counter output is greater than 63.
    2) The Row Counter Output is greater than 31.
    3) The Row Counter Output is greater than 30.

It may seem odd having separate detection of the last 2 cases in this list but this is needed because of the way in which the counters work.
When any of these conditions are true the blanking signal is latched by the CHARACTER CLOCK and then eventually cleared by the character clock when none of the conditions are true.
The character clock is used to clock the blanking signal to ensure that the blanking periods start and end at exact character boundary intervals and this prevents unwanted display artefacts.

The output from this circuit is a low level signal which is active whenever blanking is required and this signal is sent to the video mixer which we shall look at later in this chapter.

At this stage we could again connect the output of our video control system to the monitor and we should now get a good looking raster displayed on the screen if the video input is at a high (white) level.

At the moment it would just be a blank raster with no actual image information because we are not yet sending any pixel data to the monitor but this is still a good test because the monitor will only display a stable raster if the horizontal drive and vertical sync are within acceptable limits and this will only occur if all the counters are running correctly.

So how do we now make use of the counters and monitor drive signals to produce an image on the display?

We could simply set up some video memory and store all the bytes required to create the character images and send them in the correct sequence to the video input of the monitor.

However as I described earlier in this chapter this method would be a very inefficient way to store the video information and it would give the computer CPU a lot of work in order to maintain the video output. It would also cause a lot of display disruption if the CPU was busy.

This is because each character is actually built up from 8 bytes of information.

As an example if you recall from earlier in this chapter the uppercase 'H' character is built up from the following bytes...

00, 11, 11, 11, 1F, 11, 11, 11

It would be very RAM intensive to have to store and manipulate 8 bytes for every character we wanted to display and it would also require a lot of memory. In this case we would require 15360 bytes to store a full screen of text.

To resolve this problem we can us a 'Character ROM' in conjunction with a much smaller amount of video RAM.

In fact we can reduce the amount of video RAM required to just 1920 bytes and the CPU only needs to manipulate a single byte for each character it wants to display.

Not only does this save on the amount of RAM needed by the video system but it also reduces the amount of work that the Z80 needs to perform when writing text to the screen by a factor of 8.

This is a very significant saving and it does not actually need many additional components in order to make it work.

An additional advantage in using this approach is that we can very easily change the character set our computer uses to display text by simply swapping a single ROM.

We can even add additional graphics characters to create our own video display format but to begin with let us start by figuring out how to send the text characters to the display.

In the next few sections we will design a suitable video storage and display system which our counters and drive electronics can make use of to efficiently display text on the monitor screen.

Character RAM

The first thing we need is somewhere to store the character information in a form that our computer can easily access and manipulate. We only require a very modest 2048 bytes of video RAM and this will even include 128 bytes of non volatile RAM which we can use to store system information should we need this.

For this design I wanted to use a type of memory which was available at the time and is in keeping with the vintage feel of our project.

I therefore selected the HM6116 SRAM.

This is a simple 2048 x 8 bit RAM in a 24 pin DIL package.

If you are not familiar with computer memory from the 70's and 80's then you may be wondering why designers did not use this type of memory throughout the entire computer design instead of resorting to the use of much harder to drive DRAM memory.

The simple answer is cost.

SRAM is a lot more complex internally than DRAM and back when the Z80 was an infant SRAM was incredibly expensive.

Even a small SRAM such as the HM6116 was very costly but as only a small amount of this type of memory is required for our video RAM it would have been feasible to use it even back then.

The next question is how to go about storing the required character information in the SRAM.

We do not actually want to store the character bitmaps in the video RAM but instead we will store a value which indicates which particular character we want to display in each location on screen.

We already have a display Column Counter and Row Counter and so we can use the outputs of those two counters as screen coordinates and hence RAM addresses.

The actual values we store in the video RAM will be used to identify the required character and this is referred to as the character set.

For example we could assign the character values as follows…

A = 0
B = 1
C = 2
Etc

In this example if we wanted to display a 'B' then we would store a value of 1 in the SRAM location where this character is to appear.

For reasons I will explain later in this chapter we will need to limit the character set values to no more than 127 so we will use character values from 0 to 127 (0 – 7F hex) to represent the characters we wish to display.

You are free to make up whatever characters you choose by creating them from 8 x 8 bitmaps but there are widely accepted character sets already established and so we will adhere to convention and use a typical character set. I have however setup our character set so that it will work properly in our system.

If you decide to go ahead and design your own character set then it is best to test a few characters before gong too far as some detail is lost when the characters are sent to the video display and hence they do not always appear exactly as intended.

To a certain extent this will depend on the type of monitor and interface you are using because the limitations such as minimum pixel duration and scan frequencies vary considerably.

The character set and video circuits I am presenting in this book should work well across most monitor designs but as ever you should feel free to experiment.

You will notice in the circuits I show that the character data has been limited to just 5 bits but you could easily increase this by connecting the remaining ROM data outputs but remember to allow for character spacing on the display.

In fact I will be modifying the video output system in a later chapter in order to improve its functionality and part of this will be to create an alternate character set.

Each character will still be formed using a 5x7 pixel format within an 8x8 bit bitmap but the way in which the data is aligned within each bitmap will be modified.

I will describe this in more detail along with the purpose behind it in a later chapter but for now we will continue to use the character set I have described so far.

If you prefer you will have the option to continue using the original character set or even completely replace it with one of your own design.

Table 5-1 shows the character set we will be using.

Other ASCII Characters

Symbolic Name	Hex Value	Glyph	Symbolic Name	Hex Value	Glyph
commercial-at	0	@	grave-accent	20	`
A	1	A	a	21	a
B	2	B	b	22	b
C	3	C	c	23	c
D	4	D	d	24	d
E	5	E	e	25	e
F	6	F	f	26	f
G	7	G	g	27	g
H	8	H	h	28	h
I	9	I	i	29	i
J	A	J	j	2A	j
K	B	K	k	2B	k
L	C	L	l	2C	l
M	D	M	m	2D	m
N	E	N	n	2E	n
O	F	O	o	2F	o
P	10	P	p	30	p
Q	11	Q	q	31	q
R	12	R	r	32	r
S	13	S	s	33	s
T	14	T	t	34	t
U	15	U	u	35	u
V	16	V	v	36	v
W	17	W	w	37	w
X	18	X	x	38	x
T	19	Y	y	39	y
Z	1A	Z	z	3A	z
left-bracket	1B	[	left-brace	3B	{
backslash	1C	\	vertical-line	3C		
right-bracket	1D	]	right-brace	3D	}
circumflex	1E	^	tilde	3E	~
underscore	1F	_	del	3F	

Table 5-1 JMZ Character Set

I will explain later where and how this character set is stored but first we need to determine how to store the character values in the video SRAM in such a manner that they can be used by the system. Each character screen position will be treated as a single location in an imaginary coordinate system comprising a grid of 64 characters by 30 characters. Note that this is close to the maximum which this type of monitor can reliably display.

Figure 5-18 shows an example of how text can then be stored in this grid.

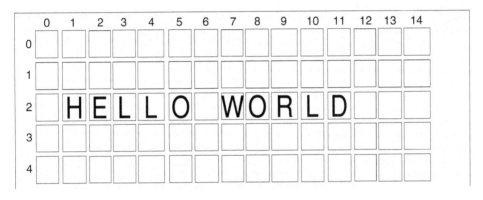

Figure 5-18 Video RAM Grid Example

This image shows an example of the top left corner of the monitor display. The numbers along the top represent the Column Counter values and the numbers down the left side represent the Row Counter values.

In this example the uppercase 'H' character is located in screen grid location 1, 2.

In this manner we can uniquely identify each screen location and store whatever character value we want to display in that location.

To map the screen locations to the actual SRAM address we will simply treat the grid as a series of rows of characters each of which is 64 characters in length.

In this way the SRAM addresses from 0 to 63 will store values for the top row of characters and addresses 64 to 127 will store values for the second line of characters and so on.

In our example here the uppercase 'H' will be stored at RAM address 129. It actually does not matter what order the characters are stored as long as it is consistent.

We now have a way to store text information in the SRAM and because we already have the Column and Row counters in place it is now a simple task to use these counters to select the required SRAM addresses as the monitor screen is scanned.

Figure 5-19 shows the circuit we will use to select the correct memory address for each screen character location.

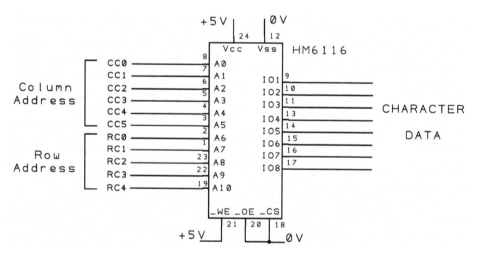

Figure 5-19 Video SRAM Character Mapping Circuit

This is a very simple arrangement because all we need to do is connect the address inputs of the SRAM to the appropriate outputs of the Column and Row counters.

The lower 6 bits of the address are taken from the Column Counter and the upper 5 bits are from the Row Counter.

In this way the memory addresses selected for a particular display location are consistent and easy to decode.

An important point to mention here is that we can only use the counter outputs directly because we have selected column and row counts which is an exact multiple of 2.

Had we selected a column count which was not a multiple of 2 then we would need to add additional circuits between the counters and the SRAM address lines in order to reconcile the counter outputs with the SRAM address.

As each memory location is selected then the data for the character at that location is available on the SRAM data output pins. In our current example if the Column address is 7 and the Row address is 2 then the data output pins of the SRAM would have the value for an uppercase 'W' character which referring to our character set table is 17 hex.

It is worth noting here that in order to bring the character set in line with the ASCII standard we would need to add 40 hex to the values shown in the character set table. For example the ASCII character 'A' is normally represented by a hex value of 41 but as we are only dealing with the hardware system here we can use whatever values are most convenient and our computer system software can map the values as required.

Now that we have the SRAM connected to the counters the data appearing on its output pins will be updated every time the counter values change and so will always represent the character at the current screen location.

The next thing we have to do is determine a method to convert the character values into actual character bitmap values and again this is now easy because we have all the counters we need to perform that task. We simply need to add a ROM memory with our character bitmap information programmed into it and connect it to the counters correctly.

Figure 5-20 shows the arrangement for connecting the SRAM to the character ROM which will perform the translation from current screen location data and character row to character bitmap data.

I have simplified this circuit somewhat to make the explanation easier but I will show the complete circuit later in this chapter.

At this point I will expand on something I stated earlier in relation to the timing of the various clocks and signals.

In a complex electronic circuit such as the one we are designing here it is important to take into consideration the way in which the individual components work. If we fail to do that then the system may well fail to operate as we expect it to.

In this case we need to remember that both the SRAM and the ROM take time to put data onto the data output pins when the required address is applied to their input pins. We must allow for any such delays when we design the circuits to avoid situations where the data output lags behind the circuit operation.

While it may not be evident in the circuits I am showing here I put considerable thought into organising the various parts of the system to ensure that all timing constraints were adhered to. It is beyond the scope of this book to go into depth regarding this but as we progress I would encourage anyone new to this sort of design to look carefully at the way the circuits are configured and to consider how the rising and falling edges of each clock and signal are timed relative to each other.

In particular it is worth examining the timing relationship between the address inputs of both the SRAM and character ROM and the data output pins of these two devices.

In terms of the clock speeds and required data rates any delays introduced in the timing of the various signals is important.

It will hopefully become clear that there are significant delays introduced by the SRAM and character ROM which would most likely cause improper character display if we did not take it into account in our circuit design.

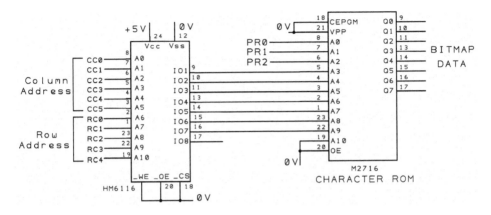

Figure 5-20 Video Character ROM Circuit

Once again the design of our counters makes this circuit very simple. The character value from the output of the SRAM is applied to the address inputs of a ROM.

The ROM is programmed with the bitmap information for each of the characters in our character set as described earlier in this chapter and so this is our character ROM.

Each bitmap is organised as a group of 8 consecutive bytes within the ROM.

If you look at the circuit in Figure 5-20 you will notice that the output from the SRAM is connected to the ROM memory address lines A3 – A9.

This is because each character bitmap comprises 8 bytes and so by connecting the SRAM to these address lines we effectively jump through the ROM 8 bytes at a time.

For example SRAM value 00 selects the address range 00 to 07 in the ROM and SRAM value 01 selects address range 08 to 0F (hex).

By doing this we automatically select the correct range of bitmap data within the ROM for each character value which is selected.

The next question is how to select the correct byte within each eight byte bitmap as each pixel row is scanned.

Yet again we already have what we need to do this and if you recall the display is scanned one bitmap line at a time and the current line being scanned within a specific character row is kept track of in the Pixel Row Counter. This counter counts from 0-8 and is used to keep track of which bitmap line of the characters is currently being sent to the display.

As you can see in Figure 5-20 the lower 3 bits from the output of this counter (PR0 – PR2) are connected to the lower 3 bits of the ROM address. This means that the required character bitmap is selected by the Column and Row counters while the correct byte within the bitmap is selected by the Pixel Row counter.

The result is that as the monitor display is scanned then at any instant the appropriate character and character bitmap line is presented on the data output pins of the character ROM.

Notice that data bit 8 from the SRAM is currently not connected but we will be making use of that later in this chapter when we look at how to generate a cursor on the screen.

While it is perfectly possible and relatively easy to generate a cursor in hardware I decide that this would be mostly done by the Z80 because it will be far less work for the CPU to carry out this task internally with just a bit of assistance from the video display system.

I will describe this 'assistance' in more detail later.

We are now making good progress but the data coming from the ROM is presented 8 bits at a time and we only have a single video input line controlling the video display.

Our next step is therefore to convert this 8 bit parallel data into a serial data stream which we can send to the monitor in such a way that the monitor can use it, along with the two drive signals, to generate an image on the screen.

Modern LCD displays often support parallel data input but our vintage CRT based display will only accept one bit at a time and so that is what we must provide.

Another important aspect of the way we send data to the video display is to avoid gaps in the data stream or glitches which would cause artefacts on the display output. Flickering and unwanted spurious output creates a very unpleasant looking display and so it is important that our video generation system can switch precisely from one bit to the next at exactly the right time even when loading new data bytes.

I mentioned earlier that each clock line throughout the system must be carefully considered to ensure that they occur at a time and phase which is appropriate in order to give the required circuit behaviour.

This is especially true in a video output system where any small errors will be clearly visible on the display. We therefore must design a circuit which can be loaded with the 8 bit bitmap values and then send this to the display without any delays or overlap.

Video Shift Register

As it turns out it is very easy to convert the parallel data from the character ROM into a serial data stream although we do need to make sure that the timing of the individual data stream bits is correct.

Figure 5-21 shows the circuit we will use to do this.

This circuit takes the parallel data from the character ROM and puts it into a shift register. This shift register then converts the data into a serial data stream which can be sent to the monitor. In fact we need to perform a bit more processing on it before it is finally sent to the monitor but we will come back to that shortly.

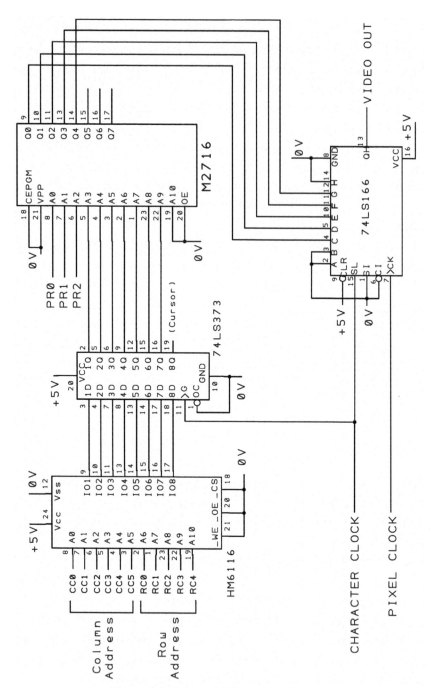

Figure 5-21 Video Shift Register Circuit

There are a few features in this circuit which are worth discussing. Firstly you will notice that there is now a latch between the video SRAM data output and the character ROM address inputs.

At the moment we do not really need it but its purpose will become apparent in a later chapter. For now you can just assume that data passes through it transparently as it did previously.

Next you have probably spotted that only 5 of the data lines from the character ROM are actually connected to the shift register. The shift register would accept all 8 bits and in fact by connecting all 8 bits we could use different width bitmaps for our characters. However I decided to limit the bitmaps to 5 bits wide to keep the explanations simple. The unwanted bits will always be zeros and so I have just connected these input pins on the shift register to 0V. This means that the shift register will always shift out zero values for these bits.

In the final design all 8 data bits from the character ROM are connected to the shift register inputs (See the schematic in appendix B).

Also notice that bit 7 of the SRAM data is now labelled (Cursor) and this probably gives a clue as to what we will use this for but I will save that explanation until later in this chapter.

I mentioned that the timing of the serial data stream bits is very important and because of the way the counters have been designed we can simply use the Pixel Clock and Character Clock to time the latching of the parallel data and the shifting of the serial data. Had the counters not been designed to have their data outputs synchronised with these clocks then this may not work but this is of course why the counters had latches between some of the stages.

We are getting close to having a fully functional video text display output but any self respecting computer will need to display a cursor so that the user knows where the next character they enter will appear on the screen.

Cursor Generation

There are many different ways in which a cursor can be generated and the method selected will often depend on the specific function of the machine and the architecture of the circuits employed.

One method is to maintain a second set of Column and Row counters which are updated whenever the cursor is moved. The current values in these counters is compared to the current display scan Column and Row counters and if they are the same then the display is at the cursor location so the video output can be inverted for that character to display a cursor.

This method works well but requires the addition of quite a few components such as counters and magnitude comparators along with the glue logic required to make it all work.

As our design is using an 8 bit SRAM to store the video information but we are only use 7 of those bits we can actually make use of the 8th bit to store the required cursor information.

What I decided to do was use this spare bit by setting it to a '1' for the character position which was at the cursor location but setting it to a '0' for all other locations.

The CPU will need to keep track of where the cursor is and maintain this bit but as it will need to do that whatever the method we use it gives us an easy solution for the cursor creation with very little overhead.

There is an addition we will need to make to the system for this to work but this is again something we would need anyway so it is a zero cost solution. I will come back to that later.

For now let's focus on how we can use the spare SRAM bit to create a cursor on the screen.

It is worth mentioning here that this method also allows us to selectively display inverse characters anywhere on screen should we wish to which makes the video system even more flexible.

Figure 5-22 shows the circuit we will use to add the cursor along with the ability to display full screen inverse the video.

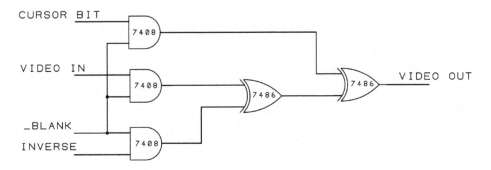

Figure 5-22 Cursor Generation Circuit

The cursor generation circuit is deceptively simple and once again it can be this simple because of the way the previous circuits have been arranged. I should add at this point that this is not actually the way the cursor will be generated in the final version of the system but we will use this circuit for initial testing as the principle is the same.

This circuit takes the spare data output bit from the SRAM (here called 'CURSOR BIT') and it uses that bit to invert the video if it is set. As this bit is only set with a value of '1' for the current cursor location character then only the character at that location is inverted. This causes the display of an inverse character at the cursor location which is exactly what we want.

Unfortunately there is one complication in that simply inverting the video would cause an unwanted side effect.

If you recall the scan counters actually count well beyond the text output area of the display and the over scanned areas are blanked to prevent characters from being displayed during those parts of the scan.

If we now just invert the video output then we will end up with a 'ghost' cursor which will appear whenever the cursor falls within the over scan repeat areas.

To avoid this we gate the cursor display using the blanking signal as this will force the display to be off when outside the intended text display area even if the video signal is inverted.

This circuit also has an input which will allow the CPU to invert the entire text display area under software control and this also must be gated using the blanking signal to ensure that only the text area is inverted.

It is always a good idea to add any such features as early in a design as possible because attempting to add them later can create complications. On the other hand if you include a feature which turns out not to be needed you can always just ignore it but I have included the features which I intend to make use of. As with all development projects it is very easy to get bogged down trying to decide if you need a particular addition and I have found that in such cases where the addition is easy then it is best to just go ahead and include it.

OK that's it we now have a fully functional video text output display system which can send character data stored in its video SRAM to the monitor display using a character generator ROM in order to provide the character set.

If you now connect this to the monitor and switch it on you will most likely see a screen full of garbage comprised of random, but nice looking, characters.

As I just said we have a video text output system but we currently have no way to write character data into it or read character data from it.

To make use of this system we must now add some additional components which will allow our CPU to write data into the video SRAM. The CPU will also need to be able to read data from the SRAM as well due to the way we are generating the cursor.

The cursor is generated by setting an otherwise spare bit in the video SRAM for the character at the cursor location.

However this also means that it will need to be able to read the current character value from the cursor location and update it for this to work.

Fortunately adding both read and write functions to our circuit is a relatively simple task.

Video RAM Read and Write

At the moment the outputs from the scan counters are connected directly to the address inputs of the video SRAM memory. In order to write to a specific memory location in this SRAM the CPU must be able to select the address it wants to access. The same is true when it wants to read data from the SRAM, it will need to be able to select the required address.

The easiest way to allow both the counters and the CPU to control the video SRAM address bus is to insert a two port multiplexer (MUX) at the input to the SRAM with one set of inputs to the multiplexer coming from the counters and the other input coming from the CPU address bus.

This will of course also require us to add some additional control circuitry and also deal with the impact this may have on the video display but you may remember that I added a latch between the output of the SRAM and the character ROM and this is actually the reason I added it.

Once the data from the SRAM has been stored in this latch we will have around half a character pixel row time to do whatever we want with the video SRAM.

While this is only a few clock cycles it is still long enough for us to write new data into the SRAM without interfering with the next video RAM access from the scan counters.

We also have the video blanking input to the display system which the CPU can use to totally blank the display if it wants to carry out a lot of updates without generating unpleasant video output effects.

Figure 5-23 shows the circuit for adding the address multiplexer.

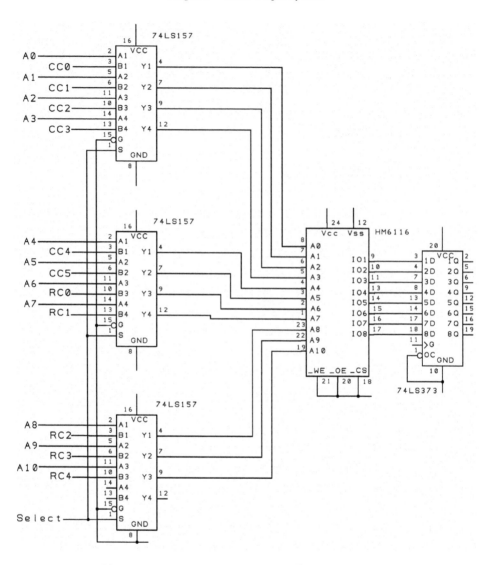

Figure 5-23 Video RAM Address Multiplexer Circuit

This is just a simple 12 bit two port multiplexer although we only use 11 of the available bits. This circuit will now allow both the scan counters and the CPU access to the video SRAM address bus but the CPU will also need to be able to both send and retrieve data to and from the SRAM.

We can give it this ability by adding a bidirectional buffer between the SRAM data and the CPU data bus as shown in Figure 5-24

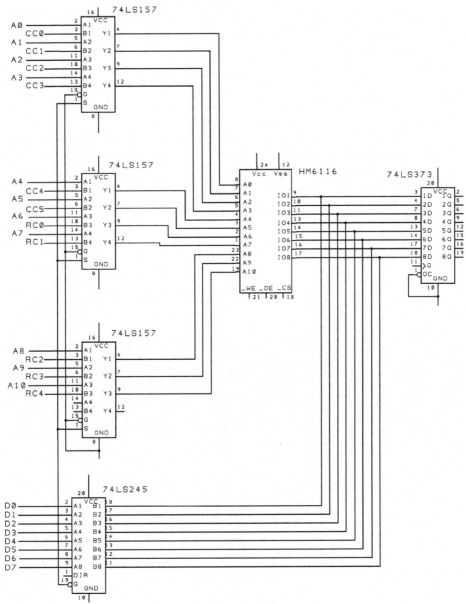

Figure 5-24 Video Data Buffer Circuit

The final piece in our puzzle is to put in place some Read / Write control logic to make sure that the SRAM, MUX and Buffer play well together and do not all try to fight over control of the address bus or data bus. The circuit in Figure 5-25 will provide this logic.

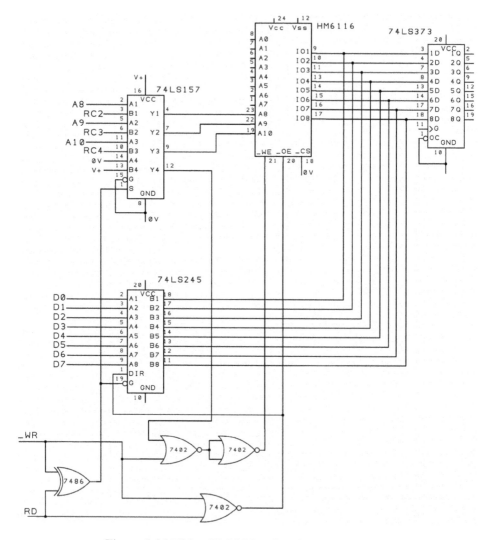

Figure 5-25 Video SRAM Read-Write Logic Circuit

So with just the addition of a few gates we have our read write control logic which operates in the following manner.

Video Output Scanning

In this mode the _WR input is high and RD is low.
This sets the buffer direction for video SRAM to CPU BUS although the buffer is also put into tri-state mode so the direction is not really important in this mode.
The video SRAM is in read mode and its output is enabled while the MUX selects the scan counters.

CPU Data Write

In this mode the _WR input is low and RD is low.
This sets the buffer direction for CPU BUS to video SRAM and also enables the buffer output.
The SRAM _OE pin goes high to disable the SRAM output although this is not strictly needed.
The multiplexer selects the CPU address bus input and after a short delay created by the two NOR gates the SRAM _WE line is driven low which causes the SRAM to write the data from the buffer into the selected address.
Notice that there is also a control line which is derived from the 12th output of the address multiplexer. This is to prevent a race condition occurring when the _WR line from the CPU is taken low to enter the SRAM write mode. Without this control the _WE pin on the SRAM would be driven low before the new address supplied by the CPU had propagated through the multiplexer and had time to be set up by the SRAM. The result would be that both the address sent from the CPU address bus *AND* the current video counter address locations within the SRAM would be updated with the character value supplied from the CPU.

This is because the video counter address would still be present on the SRAM pins when the _WE line first goes low resulting in the data value being written to this address and a few nS later the new address supplied from the CPU would appear on the output of the multiplexer and this address would then be used to write the data value into the SRAM.

We would therefore end up with both the intended video SRAM location being correctly updated but also a random SRAM address being written to as well.

The control output from the multiplexer prevents this by not allowing the SRAM _WE input to go low until the multiplexer has finished switching to the CPU address bus and at the end of each write cycle it will also cause the rising _WR signal to propagate to the SRAM _WE pin before the multiplexer changes back to the counter address.

The result is that only the intended CPU supplied address in the video SRAM is written to which is exactly what we want.

CPU Data Read

In this mode the _WR input is high and RD is high.

This sets the buffer direction for video SRAM to CPU BUS and also enables the buffer output.

The SRAM _WE pin is high and its _OE pin is low which enables its output.

The MUX selects the CPU address bus.

The video SRAM outputs the data from the selected address which the CPU can now read.

The design of our video system means that all the Z80 needs to do in order to read or write to the video memory is to simply execute a memory read or write instruction to the required video memory address.

The control logic we have just implemented will ensure that the correct data is either read from the video SRAM or written to the video SRAM during the instruction cycle.
We do however still need to design a memory mapping circuit so that the video SRAM is selected whenever an address within the intended video memory block is accessed and we will deal with that in a later chapter.

There is also another issue we must deal with before we can call our video system complete.

Video Artefact Blanking

If you build the circuits as I have shown in this chapter then they should work as intended to allow the correct output of the video data stream. The circuits also allow the Z80 to read data from the video SRAM and write data into the video SRAM. This does however result in a video display problem which we will now address.
As I have described the video output data stream is generated by the video counters consecutively reading the video RAM contents and using that data to determine which part of the character ROM bitmaps to send to the display. This process is very dynamic and we cannot stop and start it because that would lead to odd display outputs so the video output process must continue undisturbed.
This leads us to a potentially tricky problem because each time the Z80 wants to read or write data from or to the video RAM it must take control of the address inputs of the video RAM which is the purpose of the video address multiplexer. However when it does this the video counters and output circuits continue to run but they momentarily do not have control of the video RAM address and so the data selected for the next output of the shift register will most likely be taken from the wrong memory address.

This will result in short flashes appearing on the video display as it outputs the incorrect video information. It will do this every time the Z80 takes control of the video RAM address and you can see this as artefacts on the video screen. As I mentioned above we cannot simply halt the video scanning circuits during a read or write operation as this would cause incorrect synchronisation of the various counters and the entire display would look very odd.

Luckily there is a very easy solution which once again is made simple by considering this issue from the start of the design and including control logic signals which we can now use to eliminate the video artefacts.

What we need to do is blank the video output during a character row output cycle if a Z80 read or write operation occurred.

Detecting the read or write of the video RAM is of course very simple because the memory decoder circuits have a dedicated _VRAMCE control line which will go low whenever the Z80 attempts to access the video RAM. Unfortunately we cannot use this signal alone to blank the artefacts because it is a short duration signal and will end before the current character row output has been completed. I will describe the memory decoder in a later chapter.

For example if the Z80 reads the video RAM and the video shift register is loaded from the SRAM then the data loaded into the shift register will be incorrect because the address it was loaded from was provided by the Z80 and not the video scan counters. The shift register is unaware of this so will continue to shift out the data that was loaded into it until all 8 bits have been shifted out. Exactly how long this will take is ambiguous because the Z80 memory read and memory write operations are not synchronised with the display counters and so we must determine when to un-blank the video signal.

Once again there is a very simple way to determine the optimum time at which the video signal should be released.

Remember that what we are trying to do is ensure that the video is blanked until all 8 bits of the current character have been shifted out of the video shift register if the Z80 performed a read or a write operation during the current cycle.

The solution to this is to add a flip flop which is set when the Z80 performs a read or write operation on the video RAM and is cleared by the shift register load control signal which occurs after all 8 bits have been shifted out of the shift register.

The output of this flip flop can be used to blank the video output and this blanking will begin if the Z80 access the video RAM and will continue until the current shift cycle has ended and this is exactly what we need.

Figure 5-26 shows the circuit we can use to remove the display artefacts.

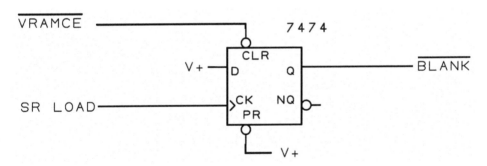

Figure 5-26 Video Artefact Blanking Circuit

This very simple arrangement will largely remove the video artefacts and make the display output much nicer.

On many early computers the video output may have included a number of unwanted or spurious characteristics and I was initially tempted to leave the artefacts to make our computer feel more authentic.

I decided to remove them by adding this circuit because I recall that using computers which had display artefacts becomes irritating after a while so despite the authenticity they may provide I decided that they had to go.

If you decide to build your own version of this system then you could try disabling this circuit in order to get the complete vintage experience.

Figure 5-27 shows the signals produced by this circuit.

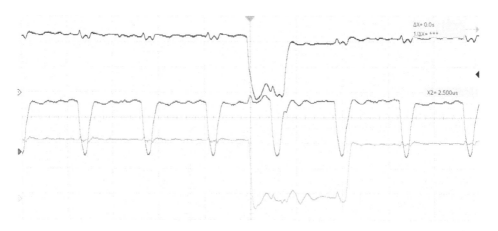

Figure 5-27 Video Artefact Blanking Signals

The top trace in this image is the _VRAMCE control line and as you can see it is a short duration signal.

The second trace down is the shift register load control line.

The lower trace is the blanking output from the flip flop but it is important to remember that the shift register load signal is asynchronous relative to the _VRAMCE line so the actual point at which the flip flop is cleared will vary.

The result is that the blanking period will be automatically adjusted to span the exact period required based on where in the video scan cycle the Z80 tries to access the video RAM.

The blanking pulse will always begin on the falling edge of the _VRAMCE signal but it will wait until the shift register has finished its current cycle before allowing the video output to resume.

This does not interfere with the video scan counters and so there is no impact on the video synchronisation with the result that the display is very stable and totally free from any spurious artefacts.

In operation the artefact blanking works by turning off the CRT electron gun to suppress the display of any unwanted or spurious output so there may be a question here for anyone who is not familiar with the operation of scanning display systems.

That question is how does the system handle artefact blanking on a white background?

For example if half of the display was a solid white then surely there would be 'dark' artefacts caused by the electron gun being turned off.

The simple answer is that this does not usually cause any problems and so we do not need to distinguish between light and dark screen artefact blanking and I will now briefly explain why this is the case.

Display Persistence and Persistence of Vision

As the CRT electron beam is scanned across the face of the display it will cause the phosphor coating it impinges on to start glowing brightly as long as the electron gun is turned on.

The electron beam is moving rapidly across the display and so it is only in any particular position for a very brief time on each pass. As I explained earlier the display is formed by this beam following a zig zag pattern across the entire screen area and it does this around 50 times each second.

This means that the display is refreshed once every 20mS and although this is a relatively short period of time we would be aware of a very annoying flickering of the display if the phosphor stopped glowing as soon as the electron beam moved on. The display would also be very dark and difficult to see and so to avoid this problem the phosphor has a property which is referred to as 'Persistence'.

Persistence is where the phosphor continues to emit light for some time after the electron beam is no longer exciting it.

In the case of our display this persistence lasts for a number of mS and tubes used in displays of this type have specially selected phosphor coatings which minimise the appearance of flicker while providing a reasonable display response. We do not want the persistence to be too long as this would tend to make the display look smeared whenever anything was changed such as a new text character being added.

The rate at which the emitted light decays is not linear and looks something like that shown in the graph in Figure 5-28.

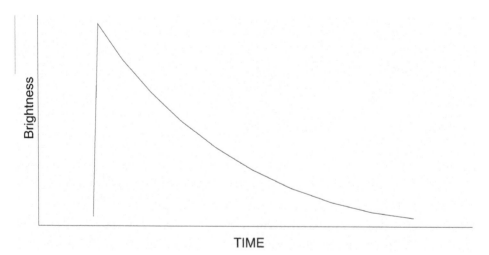

Figure 5-28 Phosphor Persistence

As you can see the light output of the phosphor rises very quickly when it is struck by the electron beam but it takes quite some time for the emission to subside. This property has the tendency to even out the display light output and it greatly reduces flicker.

In addition to the persistence of the phosphor our eyes also have an appreciable amount of persistence to light and when the two are combined we perceive the display on a CRT as being at a very steady light output although in reality it is still flickering. This is also the reason why we need to scan the display quickly and why we use a frame rate as high as fifty cycles per second.

So how does this help us with the artefact blanking?

If the screen background is dark where the artefact would have appeared then forcing the electron beam off will cause that area of the screen to remain dark and so the artefact is suppressed.

On the other hand if the area of the screen where the artefact is about to appear is bright then cutting off the electron gun does not result in a dark artefact flashing into view.

The reason is the persistence which I described above.

In the persistence decay graph shown in Figure 5-28 you can see that given enough time the display will return to dark after it has been excited by the electron beam. However we are refreshing the screen at intervals which are short compared to the persistence and so the screen will take a number of frames to return to dark once excited.

When an artefact is produced it is only present for a few hundred nS at most and so it only occurs during a single display frame. The display phosphor at the location of the potential artefact is effectively skipped for a single display frame (1/50 second) but the screen does not go dark in that area because of the screen persistence and our own eyes also contribute in minimising any possibility of dark artefacts becoming visible.

There is no possibility of the same screen location containing consecutive frame artefacts because of the way the screen is scanned.

It is really only because of the display and our eye persistence that the artefacts are a problem in the first place because in reality they are so brief that we would otherwise most likely not notice them. Luckily this same persistence also makes artefact removal simple because we only need to concern ourselves with removing bright on dark artefacts and we can simply ignore dark on bright artefacts because the persistence hides them.

This sort of thing may seem a bit counter intuitive at first but it is the basis for how images are displayed on a CRT display and as long as we understand how it works then we can simplify our system design.

While the artefact blanking method I have shown here works well for simple text output it is not really suitable for more complex video display as it will only be able to blank artefacts under certain conditions. Early PC's used a similar method in their BIOS routines but they also supported video blanking synchronisation which allowed the output of data to the video system to be performed at very specific times during the display scanning and this could be used to totally eliminate artefacts at the expense of limiting the video output bandwidth.

I decided to include similar support in this system although I will not be using it during development. The basic idea is to transfer data to or from the video RAM only during either vertical or horizontal retrace periods of the display output. This means that the artefacts are totally removed because they only occur when the display is blanked during the retrace intervals. Because I designed the circuits with this in mind it is once again very simple to implement this. All you need to do is connect either the vertical or horizontal sync pulse outputs to one of the spare interrupt inputs and then add a suitable interrupt handler. For example if the vertical sync is used to generate an interrupt then an interrupt will be triggered at the start of each vertical retrace period and so you would have a few uS to send your data to video memory 50 times every second.

Alternatively you could use the horizontal retrace period but generating so many interrupts would have a significant impact on the system performance so unless you really need the video bandwidth then it would be best to use the vertical retrace period instead. You could of course send more than one character to the video RAM during each interrupt as long as you were careful to send all the required data before the retrace period ends.

You could of course use both methods and for operations such as clearing the screen you could send the data directly without waiting for the retrace and then for slow text output you could write the data to a buffer and have the interrupt handler send any buffered data to the video RAM at the next retrace.

There are many options and which you select is entirely up to you but by designing the system in this way it gives you many choices and you are free to select whichever best suits your purpose.

The video system for our computer is now complete.

It can scan the video SRAM and display the stored character data on the monitor screen and it also allows the CPU to read or write data out of or into the video SRAM.

In addition it is also able to display a cursor and the CPU can blank or inverse the entire display if required or inverse any individual characters.

We may need to come back and make some additions to this system as our computer design progresses but this is a good starting point and it also now gives us some tools for the rest of the design.

A point for consideration as we progress through this project is that as I was developing each circuit and deciding which discrete devices to use my first stop was not the component bin.

My first stop was the list of spare gates already present in the circuits I had designed so far. This helped to minimise the number of devices that would be required in the final design.

ℒ ℴ𝒳ℰ

Chapter 6 – The Basic Z80 Circuit

In this chapter we will put together a very simple but functional Z80 CPU circuit to get the computer processor design under way. We will begin with a circuit which is about as simple as we can get but will still provide a functional Z80 processor.
This circuit is shown in Figure 6-1.

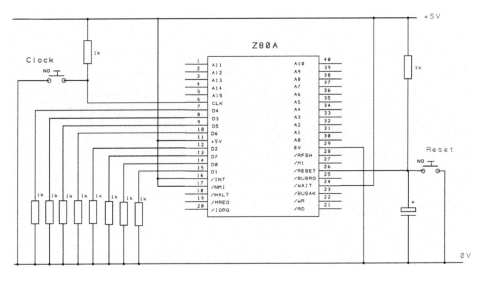

Figure 6-1 Very Simple Z80 Circuit

Yes, believe it or not that is all that is required to get a Z80 processor to run and as you can see it takes very little to bring a Z80 to life.

Of course this circuit cannot really do anything useful and it will not run any actual programs as there is nowhere to store them and there is also no way for it to output any data but this processor circuit will actually run.

We have provided a clock, of sorts, and power and set the various control lines as required to enable the processor to run.

The clock is provided by pushing the button and the Z80 will require a minimum of 4 button presses for each instruction cycle to complete.

In normal operation a Z80 is expected to execute millions of cycles each second but this circuit goes to demonstrate how easy the Z80 is to get started with and also the static nature of its operation.

If you build this circuit and try running it then it will do no more than continually fetch an instruction with a data value of 00000000b because all the data lines are connected to 0V.

The resistors are only needed to prevent CPU damage if it tries to output any data onto the data bus.

The OPCODE represented by 00000000b is a NOP, or no operation, instruction and this is a valid Z80 instruction.

If you build and power up this circuit and put a scope on the address lines and control lines you will see that the processor is actually running and internally it is operating as it would in a more complex system. The address will increment on completion of each instruction cycle and all the control outputs will be doing their thing.

If you have never experimented with a microprocessor before then it can actually be quite interesting to spend some time observing the behaviour of a processor in a circuit like this because its operation is not obscured or modified by external circuits.

For anyone new to working with microprocessors and who jump directly into a complex computer system it can often be difficult to figure out which operations are provided by the processor and which are functions of the peripheral circuits.

For those familiar with microcontrollers but not discrete microprocessors it may come as a surprise how little system functionality a device such as the Z80 will provide but providing this additional detail is my intention in this book.

Now that we have a basic Z80 circuit we will continue by adding some of the elements which our computer system will require.

Initially we will limit the circuit to the absolute basics in order to get it up and running but we will add a few additional features before the end of this chapter which will begin to give some idea of how complex this design will become.

I will try to keep each stage and module of the project separated but there will inevitably be some cross over between the various parts of our design.

Simple Z80 Circuit

In order to do anything useful we must feed the Z80 with a suitable clock signal and the frequency of this clock is a fundamental aspect in designing any computer system.

The JMZ is no exception and we must begin by selecting a clock frequency which will meet the design goal of our final computer system. You may be tempted to simply run the Z80 as fast as it can possibly operate on the assumption that this will give the maximum potential performance.

While there may be some merit in that assumption there are also other considerations which must be included when selecting a clock frequency for a system. In our design we must select a clock frequency which will allow us to incorporate all the required support circuits which we will be adding to our computer.

Luckily we have already managed to establish the required master clock frequency in the previous chapter when we designed the video output system for our computer.

We can therefore design a very simple clock circuit and this is shown in Figure 6-2.

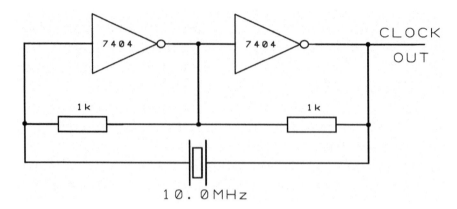

Figure 6-2 Clock Circuit

This circuit is a basic ring oscillator based on a couple of 7404 invertors and the frequency is controlled by a 10.0 MHz crystal.

This will provide the required clock output at the frequency which we determined when we designed the video system.

This circuit also has relatively good start up characteristics which will help to minimise any potential boot up problems.

I will point out here that this oscillator circuit will only work with certain types of 74 series devices and crystals so it you build this circuit and the clock fails to start up then you should check that you are using a 7404 and not one of the alternate 74 family devices such as a 74LS04 which will not work well, if at all, in this mode.

The next item we need to add to our design is a good reset circuit because the Z80 has some specific requirements to ensure that it starts up correctly. If you simply apply power and clock pulses to a Z80 processor it may well fail to operate as you expect it to because its' internal circuits are not properly initialised.

In particular the reset line must be held in a low state for a number of clock cycles when power is first applied otherwise it may start up improperly and fail to function as it should.

The circuit in Figure 6-3 provides a start up reset delay of around 15mS which allows plenty of time for the oscillator to start up and then send some clock cycles to the Z80.

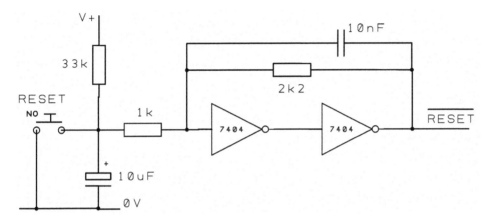

Figure 6-3 Reset Circuit

This circuit holds the reset output low until the 10uF capacitor charges and then the output is driven high. The 2k2 resistor and 10nF capacitor provide strong hysteresis to ensure a rapid and clean transition of the reset line.

It is important that the reset line changes state quickly because if this occurs too slowly it can put the Z80 into an unknown state.

Pressing the reset button will discharge the capacitor and cause the reset cycle to restart. There is no need for any specific capacitor discharge for the 10uF capacitor because once power is removed the top end of the 33k resistor is effectively connected to 0V and so the capacitor will rapidly discharge. When power is removed the reset circuit will be rearmed in approximately 80mS which is perfectly adequate for our application.

If you would prefer to speed up the rearming of the reset circuit then you can add a reverse biased diode across the 33k resistor.

The reset line will be connected to the Z80 RESET pin (pin 26).

While we are on the subject of reset you may have noticed in the video output system that I simply connected all the reset pins of the various IC's to V+.

This is perfectly acceptable in this case because I designed the overall circuit in such as way that irrespective of how the individual parts of the circuit start up they will all fall into line by the end of the first full cycle of the system.

If you power up the computer with the monitor already running then you may notice a very brief flash of garbage on the screen prior to the Z80 starting up.

This lasts less than 20mS and as the video RAM will be full of garbage anyway it makes very little difference.

During a normal power up it will take the CRT a number of seconds to begin displaying anything at all as it takes a while for the tube heater to get to temperature. This means that in normal operation the Z80 has started up and the video RAM has been cleared and the video circuits are running normally before anything ever appears on the screen.

However if you prefer you can bring all the reset pins together into a dedicated reset line and have all the circuits start up in a specific state by simply adding a buffer to the reset circuit.

Additionally if you find that your system does not start up reliably following a power on reset then you can try extending the reset time by increasing the value of the 33k resistor.

It is also sometimes a good idea to add a delay at the beginning of the boot up code sequence in order to allow time for all peripheral circuits to complete any reset requirements.

The next thing we need to add to our design is a divider circuit for the main clock although you may recall that we actually already have this available in the video circuits.

I will however reproduce the circuit here to make the explanation clearer and also to help demonstrate how the various parts of the system will come together. You could of course decide to keep each part of your circuit design completely separate rather than combining functions across them.

Figure 6-4 shows the clock circuit with the first clock divider connected which you may recognise as the Pixel Counter from the video circuits.

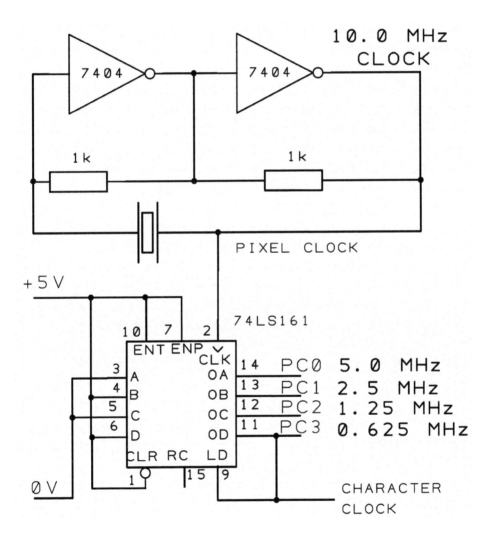

Figure 6-4 Clock and Divider Circuit

The four outputs from this counter are labelled PC0 to PC3 and they provide a series of clock frequencies with each output being divided by 2 from the previous counter stage.

As you can see this gives us a range of frequencies and we will be connecting the clock input of the Z80 (pin 6) to the second of these clock outputs. The Z80 will therefore be running at a clock frequency of 2.5 MHz.

The importance of dividing the primary clock in this way and running the Z80 at a lower frequency will become increasingly apparent as the design of our system progresses. Once again I hope that the reason for designing the video system first in order to determine the required system clock frequencies is becoming clear.

If not then it will become very much more apparent when we get to the chapter on adding Dynamic Ram to the design.

We now have the CPU clock and reset circuits in place so we can move on to some more interesting aspects of the design.

As with any microprocessor system things begin to get much more interesting when we can actually run some code and we are surprisingly close to being able to do that. Of course we will also need to create some actual code so that we can test our circuits.

Adding a ROM

Like the vast majority of small computer systems the JMZ will need to have a small operating system which will be responsible for the start up of the computer along with some of the fundamental functions of the system such as hardware interfacing.

This code will be stored in none volatile memory normally referred to as Read Only Memory or ROM.

Although the details of our design will change a great deal as the project progresses we will develop it in small steps in order that I can attempt to explain its operation as clearly as possible.

We will therefore add a ROM to our design which will contain a very simple test program and which will then allow us to test some of the basic Z80 operations.

I will not complicate things by adding any memory mapping at the moment although we will implement some simple address mapping later in this chapter.

We will also need a test program to allow us to determine if the Z80 is able to fetch instructions from the ROM and also if it is able to address memory.

If you are not familiar with the way a microprocessor fetches instructions from memory and then decodes and executes them I strongly recommend that you have a look through the Zilog Z80 user manual as understanding this mechanism will really help to clarify the purpose behind the test programs.

It is also important to appreciate that instructions are not processed in a single step within the Z80 but are in fact executed in a number of discrete steps and as each step in this process is started or ended the control outputs from the Z80 change state to reflect its progress.

A computer system will make heavy use of these control signals in order to control its various hardware circuits and this is exactly what we will need to implement as our design takes shape.

To begin with we will mostly ignore these control signals and I will only connect the bare minimum required to get each circuit to work.

I will however come back and explain the purpose and function of each of the Z80 control signals as we need to make use of them.

The Z80 includes some very clever memory handling features which are aimed at making efficient use of system RAM but for our first test we do not need to connect any RAM at all so we will start by adding just a single ROM. We will go on to add some system RAM later in this chapter.

Our test program will however still try writing to this non existent RAM because the Z80 has no way of knowing if RAM is actually present at all so we can still observe the bus signals during this test.

I should say here that it is very much easier to see what is going on in systems like this if you have access to a logic analyser. While you can use an oscilloscope for much of the basic testing it is often easier to understand what the circuits are doing if more than a few channels of data can be observed at the same time.

During the development of this computer I made extensive use of a logic analyser to test that the various signals were all performing as they should and at the correct times during each instruction cycle. You do not need to go to such lengths if you are following the design I am presenting here although I would still encourage the use of a logic analyser as it is not only interesting but it also makes a great learning tool.

While it is not possible to directly observe much of the inner circuit behaviour of the Z80 what we can observe are the states of the various control line outputs that it provides.

As each instruction cycle proceeds and the instructions are decoded and processed the Z80 control lines will change state to give a continual indication of the internal state of the Z80.

Indeed we will need to make use of these control lines later in order to control the overall operation of the different circuits which we will be adding to our system design.

Efficient operation of a complete system is heavily dependant on understanding what each of the control lines indicate and how to make best use of the Z80 machine cycle clock phases.

Although it may be possible to design and construct a computer system around a Z80 while ignoring the clock phases it will almost certainly be very inefficient and quite possibly very unreliable.

Once again I would recommend spending some time studying the Zilog Z80 user manual as this gives a lot of very useful information as to the internal operation of the Z80.

Figure 6-5 shows the Z80 CPU circuit with a ROM added.

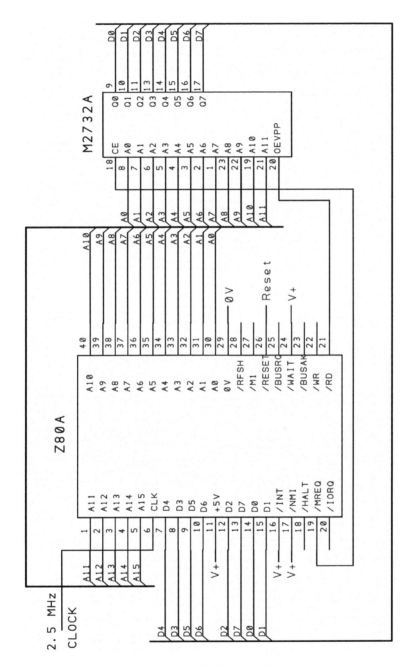

Figure 6-5 CPU with ROM

The circuit shown in Figure 6-5 should now be capable of running code from the ROM but we do of course need to write a test program so that we can check to see if it is actually working.
I started by programming the ROM with the following test code.

Test Program 1

```
START:    LD       A,45h
          LD       B,05h
          LD       HL,4000h

LP1:      LD       (HL),A
          NOP
          NOP
          NOP
          LD       A,(HL)
          INC      HL
          DJNZ     LP1
          JP       START
```

When converted to machine code this is (Hex byte values)

3E 45 06 05 21 00 40 77 00 00 00 7E 23 10 F8 3C 00 00

These values are written to the ROM starting at address 0000 because the reset vector of the Z80 is of course 0000H.
This program is very simple. It writes a value of 45H to address 4000H and then reads the value back and then it increments the address by 1 and writes 45H to the next address. It does this for the 5 addresses starting at 4000H and then it loops back to the start and repeats the program. This continues until it is stopped.
Assuming everything is correct then you should be able to use a logic analyser, scope or even a logic probe to test its operation.
Although the Z80 is attempting to write a data value to the memory address at 4000H it cannot of course do that because there is not yet any RAM in our test system but we will now go ahead and add some. Figure 6-6 shows the circuit with some RAM added.

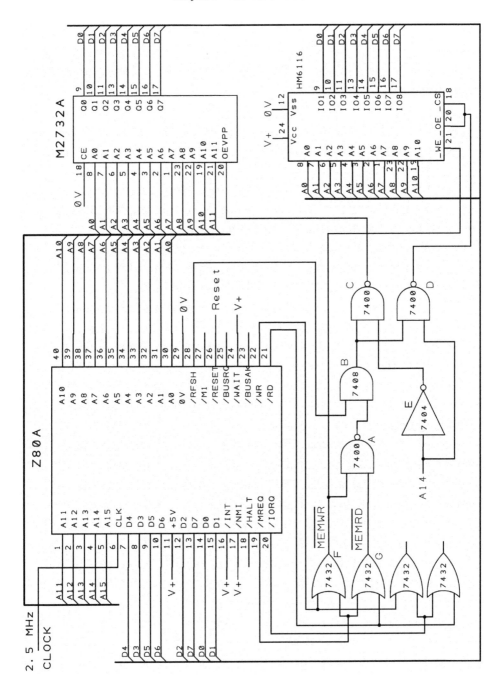

Figure 6-6 CPU with ROM and RAM

This circuit also includes some very simple memory mapping to map the ROM to a starting address 0000 and the RAM to address 4000H upwards.

Notice that in the previous circuit the ROM output enable pin was connected directly to the Z80 but is now connected via some logic.

The circuit in Figure 6-6 is still very simple but it is the basis for the rest of our CPU logic control design and we will expand this circuit design later as we add additional functionality.

Note that in this circuit I show the RFSH line as being connected directly to the control logic but it actually needs a bit of additional decoding before it is used and I will show this later.

In order to be able to selectively write to and read from individual devices in our system the Z80 must be able to enable them individually in response to the execution of particular instructions.

For example if it wants to read a data value from main RAM then it must be able to select this RAM separately from the ROM or video RAM. It must also be able to differentiate between writing to the RAM and reading from the RAM.

If you look at the data sheet for the Z80 you will see that in addition to the 16 bit address bus and 8 bit data bus and power / clock and reset pins it also has a number of control inputs and outputs.

You may have noticed that some of them have been connected to either 0V or V+ in the circuit shown in Figure 6-6. This is to allow proper operation of the Z80 for our test but I will not distract us at this time by describing their function. I wish to keep our attention on the RAM and ROM access which is what the additional circuits in Figure 6-6 are for but the control lines must still be connected.

To begin with the Z80 needs to be able to access memory in either 'Read' mode or 'Write' mode.

It should be noted that while we can read from the ROM we cannot of course write to it for obvious reasons.

Whenever the Z80 executes an instruction which results in one of these two operations then it will lower the output on the MREQ pin and if the operation is a read then the voltage on the RD pin will also be lowered but if the operation is a write then the WR pin voltage will go low instead.

So for a read both the MREQ and the RD lines go low and for a write the MREQ and WR lines go low.

The two gates in Figure 6-6 (F and G) decode these states and produce two new signals which indicate if the memory access is a read or a write.

They have been labelled as MEMRD and MEMWR in the diagram.

We can now use these two lines to further determine what action is required when accessing memory.

The MEMWR output from the decoder circuit is connected directly to the _WE pin of the RAM chip but nothing will happen unless the RAM chip is enabled.

Gates A and B work together to enable or disable memory based on the state of the RFSH output from the Z80.

This output is only used when the system contains DRAM and our system currently only contains SRAM and so we could simply ignore the RFSH output but we will be adding DRAM later and so I included these gates now to simplify later explanations but for now you can just ignore them.

Gates C, D and E are used to create a very simple memory mapping circuit and they cause the ROM to be selected when the Z80 outputs an address from 0000 to 3FFF and the RAM is selected from address 4000H and above.

Notice that the ROM output enable line (Pin 20) is no longer connected directly to the Z80 but is now controlled through the memory mapping circuit.

The two OR gates at the bottom left of the circuit are for IO control operations and I will come back to those later. I added them here in order to make the testing easier.

If we run our test program again we should find that the Z80 can now successfully store and retrieve the data values from the RAM. We now have a working Z80 based computer but we still have a great deal of work to do before it can do anything useful. In fact this is where it starts to get much more exciting.

We are currently using a very simple SRAM arrangement but as I stated in a previous chapter I will be designing a system much more in keeping with early Z80 designs and so it is time to delve into the mysteries of Dynamic RAM.
In the next chapter we will replace the SRAM currently fitted in our test system with 64k of dynamic memory (DRAM) and while this will certainly add a great deal of complexity to the design it is not as hard to understand as it may first appear.
As with most aspects of electronic design the most important step in any design is to get a firm understanding of the way in which the devices we want to use actually function. Once we have this knowledge then designing them into a system becomes very straight forward or at least a lot less daunting.
Our next step is therefore to investigate how dynamic memory works and what we need to do to in order to incorporate it into our computer system design.

In the next chapter we will modify our basic Z80 circuit design in order to implement the control circuits required for DRAM.

॒౿ఠ

Chapter 7 – Adding Dynamic Memory

Memory is easy to add to computer systems these days but that has not always been the case and in this chapter we will delve into the mysteries of the so called Dynamic Memory.

In the history of computers one of the areas which has been a major factor in the development and scale and cost of systems is memory. Almost every computer requires some way to store information in a form that it can easily access and modify.

Not surprisingly this part of a system is referred to as memory because it is used to store and recall data much like our own internal biological memory although hopefully more reliably.

Creating a mechanical or electronic device to store small amounts of data is relatively simple but where things get difficult is when there is a need to increase the amount of storage capacity.

The main focus for the development of computer memory has been in the attempts to bring the size and cost per bit down while increasing the storage capacity and operational speed.

It is probably fair to say that as much time and effort has gone into the development of memory systems as for actual microprocessor design.

Many different types of technology have been developed to try to keep up with the ever increasing demand for more memory and lower cost. As with the development of processors some of the ideas tried were more successful than others.

These include purely mechanical storage methods through electro-mechanical to acoustic to magnetic and on to electronic systems.

Today for a very small outlay you can easily purchase a memory storage device no bigger than a postage stamp which can store many Giga Bytes of data so it can be hard to appreciate how hard won large scale computer data storage systems has been.

When the Z80 processor was first available memory of more than a few thousand bytes was incredibly expensive and this will go a long way to explain why the schematics of early computers are so complex in the way that they needed to add multiple devices.

If you want to design and build a Z80 using modern components then it can actually be very difficult finding memory with capacities as small as the limit which a Z80 can access.

This limit is 64k for a single bank system but early in the life of the Z80 it would usually require many memory chips to construct a system with a full 64k of random access memory.

This amount of memory was deemed to be huge for a small computer back then but today there is frequently much more memory than that inside a small microcontroller device.

Memory technology has changed a great deal over the decades since the Z80 was designed and modern systems use electronic memory almost exclusively as the other memory technologies have fallen by the wayside except for niche applications.

Early in the migration to newer memory technologies there were two main options available for standard types of electronic memory which was commercially available.

The first of these is the Static RAM device or SRAM.

These devices store data bits in circuits similar to flip flops and a separate circuit is needed to store each individual bit along with decoding and driver logic circuitry. This results in devices which are fabricated with huge numbers of active transistors and this in turn makes the integrated circuit chips very large and so extremely expensive.

This is less of an issue in modern microchip fabrication facilities but decades ago the cost of such devices increased very rapidly as their size and complexity increased.

In fact early static RAM devices had a fairly low capacity and bit for bit they were more expensive than systems such as core memory.

To a certain extent the cost issue was partly addressed by the introduction of the second major type of electronic memory technology.

This type of memory is called Dynamic RAM or DRAM.

This type of memory works in a fundamentally different way to SRAM in that the data bits are stored in banks of tiny capacitors which are fabricated onto the integrated circuit itself. This method of storing data vastly reduces the number of active transistors which are required for a given size of memory chip which in turn makes them very much cheaper to manufacture.

While the complexity of the internal circuitry is very much less complicated for DRAM than it is for SRAM there is a penalty to pay for this simplicity.

Data can be written to DRAM memory and read from DRAM memory in much the same way that it can for SRAM but unfortunately the data will be lost a few thousandths of a second (mS) after it has been written unless steps are taken to prevent this from happening.

The reason that the data is lost is because the small capacitors which are used to store the data will discharge shortly after they have been charged when data is written to them.

Fortunately the DRAM devices are designed in such a way that there is a means by which this data loss can be prevented.

Each data bit in a DRAM in stored in a memory cell which consists of a small capacitor along with some simple active devices which allow the charge on the capacitor to be modified in order that the required bit state can be saved. It will of course be storing either a '0' or a '1' in order to represent the bit value.

Figure 7-1 shows a typical DRAM memory cell circuit compared to an SRAM and as you can see the DRAM only requires a single transistor compared to the 6 which are required for the SRAM cell.

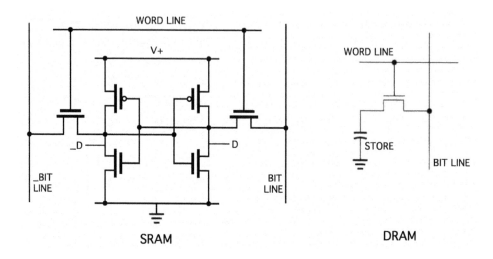

Figure 7-1 DRAM Compared to SRAM

The access control circuitry in the DRAM cell also allows another function to be performed and this function is normally called 'Memory Refresh' or just 'Refresh'.

It works by performing a read operation on the cell and because of the way the circuit is arranged this operation results in the capacitor being recharged if the cell is storing a '1' or leaving it discharged if the cell is storing a '0'.

The end result of this is that every time a DRAM memory cell is read its storage capacitor is 'Refreshed' and this will prevent the cell from losing its bit value.

This may all sound very elaborate and over complicated but the huge saving in fabrication costs make it worth while.

The major complication when using a DRAM in computer systems is in ensuring that each DRAM memory cell is refreshed frequently enough to prevent data from being lost.

While the required refresh interval varies depending on the type of DRAM in use the maximum interval is typically in the order of just a few milliseconds (mS).

The DRAM devices utilised in early Z80 system would therefore need to have each memory cell refreshed around 500 times each second if data loss was to be avoided.

It we considered carrying out the memory refresh cycles using software then this would imply that a 64k system would require as many as 32,000,000 refresh cycles each second and even if this only took a few instructions then there is no way that a Z80 could perform this task.

Naturally it would be impractical to refresh a DRAM under software control so it is almost always carried out using some form of hardware circuit.

The DRAM memory chip designers also structured the devices in such a way that the refresh burden could be greatly reduced.

If you take a look inside a DRAM memory then you would find that the actual memory cells are arranged in arrays of rows and columns to form a memory cell grid.

For example in a typical 64k memory the cells are arranged in an array which is 256 x 256 cells giving a total of 65536 cells (or 64k).

A single refresh cycle actually refreshes an entire row of cells and so only 256 individual refresh cycles are required to refresh the entire memory array.

This reduces the total refresh burden to just 128,000 refresh cycles each second although this is still way beyond the ability of the Z80 to perform the refresh task in software.

The vast majority of computers which do not use the Z80 include a simple binary counter circuit which is used to keep track of which memory row should be refreshed next.

This counter just cycles round continually ensuring that every row of the DRAM is refreshed within the allowable time before data is lost.

The Z80 has a unique feature which can assist us in the DRAM refresh process and this feature is the internal 'R' register.

This register is the refresh address counter register and it is automatically incremented during each refresh cycle.

The Z80 also has a Refresh (RFSH) output pin which is driven low by the Z80 when a memory refresh should be carried out.

At the same time as the RFSH pin goes low the Z80 places the current contents of the internal refresh counter onto the lower 7 bits of the address bus pins and this ensure correct timing of the cycle.

The refresh pin goes low during clock phases 3 and 4 of the M1 instruction cycle and because the Z80 is busy at this part of the cycle carrying out internal operations (instruction decode) then the refresh can be carried out in what would otherwise be idle time.

The Z80 cannot perform any external tasks such as memory reads or writes while it is decoding an instruction and so the refresh is a transparent operation which does not utilise any processor time.

This is a very useful feature of the Z80 which can help to simplify the design of our computer circuits.

As with so many things in electronics (and life in general) there are always complications which we need to deal with.

I gave a clue to this a few paragraphs ago when I stated that the Z80 puts the refresh counter value onto the lower 7 bits of the address bus. This was not a typo and I did not intend to say bits 0 to 7 which would of course be 8 bits.

It really does only put 7 counter bits onto the address bus.

I mentioned earlier in this chapter that when the Z80 was designed 64k of memory was though to be far more memory than would ever be needed in a small computer system and at that time 16k was considered to be the maximum required.

For this reason the internal refresh register is only a 7 bit register and so can only provide a 7 bit refresh address.

This is fine for any memory devices which have a maximum array row count of 128 as this can be fitted into just 7 bits and so 128 x 128 is 16384 bits (16k). While some memory devices are available with rectangular cell arrays which allow larger memory capacities to be utilised with just 128 rows most memory chips use square arrays and so devices with capacities over 16k require 8 bit refresh addresses and hence 8 bit refresh counters.

Yet another complication is that many chip designers selected small packages with a limited number of pins and this led to the adoption of Row and Column addressing which leaves us with two options.

    1) Design an 8 bit refresh counter circuit
    2) Add an 8th bit to the Z80 refresh counter.

One of my goals when I began this project was to showcase many of the features available to us in the Z80 processor and for that reason I will be selecting option 2.

It is very easy to add an extra bit to the Z80 refresh counter and Figure 7-2 shows the circuit for this.

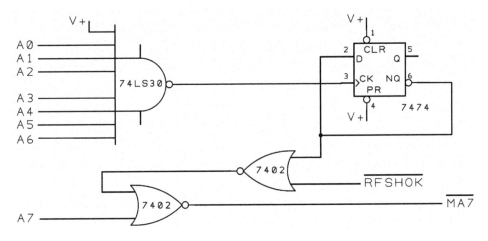

Figure 7-2 Adding bit 7 to the Refresh Counter

Note that this circuit has a flaw which I will correct in a later chapter but we will ignore it for now to keep the explanations less complicated.

The operation of this circuit is very simple and it works in the following way in order to add the 8th refresh counter bit.

The lower 7 address lines from the Z80 are connected to the inputs of an eight input NAND gate and address bit A7 is connected to one input of a two input NOR gate.

The spare input of the eight input NAND gate is connected to V+ at the moment but we will be using this for another purpose later.

Each time the refresh counter value is put onto the address bus the 7 bits applied to the eight bit NAND gate will increment and at some point they will all be set to a '1'. This will cause the output of the gate to go low and when the value is taken off the bus the output will return to the high state and this rising edge will clock the 7474 flip flop. The 7474 is wired so that it will simply toggle its outputs each time it is clocked and so its outputs are effectively the clock divided by 2.

When the Z80 refresh cycle is inactive its _RFSH pin is high and this pin is connected to a second NOR gate input (Shown as _RFSHOK). This gate allows the output of the 7474 to control the output of the gate which the A7 address line is connected to.

In this way the A7 state from the CPU is either allowed through the gate or the output of this gate is controlled by the state of the 7474 output.

The effect of this is for the gate to act as a simple single bit multiplexer and the _MA7 line is either taken from the CPU A7 line when refresh is inactive or is taken from the 7474 output when refresh is active.

During the refresh cycle the output of the 7474 is effectively the 8th bit of the binary refresh counter.

There are a few issues worth pointing out here.

Firstly the 7474 will toggle whenever the appropriate values appear on the address bus even if a memory access is not intended and this could lead to the skipping of some refresh cycles.

In order to prevent this we will slightly modify this circuit later in the design to effectively gate it so that it only responds during actual refresh cycles.

Secondly the _MA7 is an inverted version of A7 but this does not actually matter in our design as long as it is consistent.

As long as we are consistent in the way we address memory then it does not matter which particular memory cells are used for which memory address.

The third and most important point is that we cannot use the RFSH output from the Z80 on its own to control the RAS input to the DRAM during a refresh cycle. If we tried to do this then it is almost certain that we would lose data from the memory due to improper refresh addresses being applied to the DRAM.

The reason for this is clear if you go back and look at the Z80 timing diagrams and in particular the M1 cycle.

As I mentioned previously the M1 cycle is 4 CPU clock cycles in length with first two of these clock cycles being used to fetch the next instruction from memory and the second two are then used internally by the Z80 to decode that instruction.

At the start of the third M1 clock pulse the Z80 starts placing the refresh address value from its internal refresh counter onto the lower 7 bits of the address bus but as with the fetch part of the M1 cycle it takes some time for the address to appear and stabilise on the address bus output pins of the Z80.

When the RAS input to the DRAM is lowered this falling edge is used to latch the currently applied address bits into the internal DRAM row select register.

Because the Z80 address pins are not stable when the RFSH pin voltage initially drops then if it is used to immediately latch the address bus value into the DRAM then the wrong address would most likely be latched.

The result of this is that incorrect memory address locations would be refreshed. This would in turn result in data being lost for the addresses which were 'skipped' and missed their refresh.

The solution is fairly simple because if we again look at the Z80 M1 timing diagram we can see that on the second clock edge of the M1 T3 cycle the MREQ pin voltage drops to indicate that the address pins contain a valid value. The Z80 also uses the MREQ pin for this purpose in the T1 phase.

We can therefore use both the RFSH and MREQ lines to determine when to lower the RAS input to the DRAM and by waiting until the MREQ pin goes low we can be sure that the correct address is being applied to the DRAM address pins when it is latched.

It is very simple to add this feature to our design as we only need to add a single OR gate with one input connected to the RFSH pin of the Z80 and second to the MREQ pin.

The output of this OR gate will then only be at a low level when the address is stable during a refresh cycle and this is the best time to lower the RAS input to the DRAM.

In our schematics I call this line _RFSHOK.

We now have an 8 bit refresh counter but we still need a way to send its count value to the actual DRAM and we also need a way to selectively send the Row address and Column address to the memory chips.

Like many DRAM devices of the time the chips we are using are 64 x 1 bit but they only have 8 address lines labelled A0 to A7.

If you have never encountered this before then you may be wondering how we can address 64k of memory space using just 8 address input bits.

If you recall I mentioned earlier that the memory is internally arranged as a square array and in this case the array is organised as 256 rows by 256 columns.

To access a particular address in this array we must supply the required 16 bit address as two 8 bit bytes.

The first 8 bits we send is the Row Address and the second 8 bits we send is the Column Address.

Although we will be sending an address to the DRAM as two separate bytes you should remember that as far as the Z80 is concerned the address is a single 16 bit value.

When the Z80 wants to access memory it puts the 16 bit address onto its address bus and it is up to us to determine how to pass it on to the DRAM as two separate 8 bit values.

In practice it is very simple as we just select the lower 8 bits of the address bus for the first byte and then we select the upper 8 bits as the second byte. All we need in order to accomplish this is a two channel, 8 bit multiplexer and some control logic.

DRAM Addressing

In order to send the 16 bit address from the Z80 through the 8 bit address input pins of the DRAM chip we must divide the address into two 8 bit values.

We then send these two 8 bit bytes to the DRAM in turn but there are some specific timing constraints which we must adhere to while doing this if the DRAM is to successfully latch the correct address into its internal buffers.

The DRAM has two strobe inputs called 'Row Address Strobe' or RAS and 'Column Address Strobe' or CAS.

Both of these inputs are active low so we refer to them as _RAS and _CAS respectively.

To select a specific address within the DRAM we must perform the following actions for a memory Read...

1) Apply the low 8 bytes of the address to the DRAM
2) Lower the _RAS input
3) Apply the high 8 bytes of the address to the DRAM
4) Lower the _CAS input

As soon as we lower the _CAS strobe input the DRAM responds by enabling its data output and outputting the bit value stored at the 16 bit address we have just supplied to it.

Notice that unlike the SRAM chip the DRAM does not have any chip select or output enable control pins because these functions are controlled by the _RAS/_CAS sequence.

In fact the DRAM write enable line is also used as part of the overall timing sequence in order to determine the way in which the device controls the data output pin but we will come back to that detail a little later.

If you are using a different type of DRAM to those I have selected for this project then you may need to change the exact sequence of control signals although the approach I am showing in this book is very common across many types of dynamic memory devices.

If we want to perform a write to the DRAM then we must perform the following actions…

   1) Apply the low 8 bytes of the address to the DRAM
   2) Lower the _RAS input
   3) Lower the _WR input
   4) Apply the high 8 bytes of the address to the DRAM
   5) Lower the _CAS input

In this case the DRAM takes the value which is currently applied to its data input pin and it stores it at the internal address which was supplied in steps 1 and 4.

An important point to make in this sequence is that I am using a write method referred to as 'Early Write' which I will describe below but you can modify the design if you wish to use a more conventional mode of DRAM operation.

However the early write mode simplifies the system design and reduces the number of components required as I will now explain.

Early Write

I mentioned above that the active state of the DRAM data output pin is controlled by the _RAS/_CAS sequence and by lowering the _WR pin before we lower the _CAS strobe input the output pin of the DRAM remains in its high impedance state.

This means that it will not try to output any data while we are trying write to it as its data output pin will remain inactive.

This allows us to connect the DRAM input and output pins directly together and this therefore eliminates the need for a separate buffer to control access to and from the CPU data bus and of course it also eliminates the need for separate logic to control this buffer.

We will add a buffer to the CPU busses later for other purposes but we will not need an additional buffer for the DRAM memory.

We now know the sequence of events needed to send an address to the DRAM but we need to add a circuit to control this sequence in order to make this work.

The 16 bit data bus from the CPU must be split into two and the easiest way to do this is to use a multiplexer.

There are of course many other ways to achieve this operation but for our purpose a two port 8 bit to 8 bit multiplexer is ideal.

These devices act in a similar way to a bank of switch over relays and allow us to select either of two 8 bit inputs and connect the selected input to the output pins. They are however very much faster than mechanical relays which is fortunate because we only have a few tens of nS to switch between inputs.

I actually decided to use two 4 bit by two channel multiplexers and combine them into a single 8 bit circuit to form the required 8 bit multiplexer but you can use an alternate configuration if you prefer as long as it meets the required time constraints.

The importance of a fast switching multiplexer is due to the fact that this multiplexer sits between the CPU address bus and the memory address bus inputs.

It must therefore enable the memory address selection while avoiding propagation delays which could cause incorrect addresses to be latched by the DRAM.

This multiplexer must also allow the current refresh address to be sent to the DRAM during the Z80 refresh cycles.

Address Multiplexer

Figure 7-3 shows the circuit for our DRAM address multiplexer.

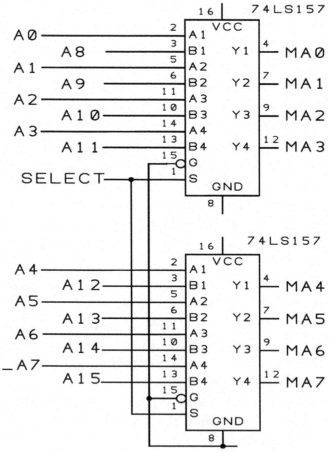

Figure 7-3 DRAM Address Multiplexer

You could easily use a series of discrete logic gates in place of these multiplexer devices but as they were readily available in the design period I am aiming to follow I decided to use them here.

An important feature of these components is that they must have a short propagation delay so that the values applied to the inputs appear at the outputs in 20nS or less. This is required because they are in the path between the CPU and the DRAM and we must send two separate addresses through this multiplexer at the beginning of each RAM access cycle so lengthy delays would almost certainly prevent proper RAM operation.

The two sets of inputs to the address multiplexer are connected directly to the Z80 16 bit address bus except for bit 7 which is shown in Figure 7-3 as _A7. This input is taken from the output of the refresh counter extension circuit which was shown earlier in this chapter in Figure 7-2.

The SELECT input allows either the lower 8 bits of the 16 bit address to be sent to the DRAM or the upper 8 bits.

For the next piece of the puzzle we need to design some control logic which can control this multiplexer but it must also provide the required control sequence for the _RAS, _CAS and _WR inputs of the DRAM.

In addition this logic must accurately time these events to satisfy the timing constraints of the Z80 CPU during its read and write cycles. It must also be able to allow the memory refresh address to be sent to the DRAM without actually enabling the memory chips and either causing unwanted reads or writes or creating data bus contention. It must do all this transparently as far as the Z80 is concerned so that the Z80 read and write instructions work correctly.

This sounds like a very complex set of requirements and is very frequently the point at which the idea of incorporating DRAM into a design is abandoned in favour of the much simpler SRAM.

However once the general principles are understood then the design task is not as daunting as it first sounds and the required control logic circuits can be made quite simple.

Another possible approach you could take here is to drop in a large scale DRAM controller device but as already stated my goal is to keep all the core circuits as discrete as possible and so I wish to avoid the use of such devices.

As much as possible I have structured this book and the JMZ project in order to make the circuit explanations as clear as possible although many of the circuits are inevitably fairly complex.

DRAM Control Logic

As I go through the following explanation it will rapidly become increasingly apparent why I have included a clock divider immediately following the main system clock generator.

Before I begin it is important to understand that what I am describing here relates specifically to DRAM and even more specifically to DRAM in small packages which was the type commonly available when the Z80 was first made available.

Modern DRAM operates very differently and although many of the principles are the same they are generally handled in a totally different manner.

It is also worth pointing out that it was not long before DRAM controller chips became available and these greatly simplified the implementation and design of systems which employed DRAM.

However I am hoping to give a feel for what it was like to develop systems without these safety nets and I also believe that building systems from discrete components is a lot more informative and interesting and fun than simply connecting together a few large scale devices.

If your goal is to get a commercial system up and running as quickly and cheaply as possible then it would of course be prudent to use the most time and cost effective solution. If like me you are more interested in learning about the inner workings of such systems then please read on.

Just remember that the large scale integrated circuits utilise very similar techniques and it never hurts to have a comprehensive understanding of the internal operation of devices being used.

So the first thing we need to consider when designing a system which will include DRAM is how accurate will the timing constraints be that we will need to adhere to.

With SRAM we can simply connected it directly to the Z80 with a minimal amount of control and decoding logic and it will most likely work first time.

Unfortunately we cannot do that with DRAM and one of the major difficulties in designing a DRAM control system is that you need to get a number of issues dealt with before you can move on to start testing your design.

In any system like this we should start by investigating what it is we are aiming for and so let's take a look at what the Z80 actually does during a memory read and write cycle.

If you are designing a system using a different processor then this will still apply although the specific timing requirements may well be very different.

Figure 7-4 shows the basic Z80 timing for a read or write cycle.

Note that this cycle relates to the operation of the Z80 itself and not any particular type of memory.

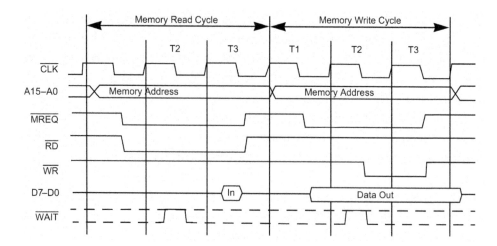

Figure 7-4 Z80 Read / Write Cycle

This diagram is taken from the Zilog Z80 handbook and it shows the timing of the control signals generated by the Z80 when it is executing a Read or Write part of an instruction cycle.

These cycles look fairly similar and they both follow on from the 4 cycle M1 instruction fetch part of the machine cycle and they are both three clock cycles in duration.

In the first two Z80 clock cycles of each instruction cycle the Z80 reads the data value which is pointed to by the address currently in its Program Counter register.

This is always the case and this part of the cycle is identical for all instructions. After all how does the Z80 know what the instruction is until it has read it. The Z80 stores the fetched instruction in its internal instruction register. The first 4 Z80 clock cycles are referred to as the M1 cycle and the 3rd and 4th clock cycles of M1 are used by the Z80 to decode the current instruction.

It then continues processing the instruction and then decides what to do next such as in the example shown in Figure 7-4 above.

This may be a memory read or a memory write which occurs in the second part of the instruction cycle.

A clever feature of the Z80 is its inbuilt support for DRAM and to help us with this it makes use of the second half of the M1 cycle by placing the contents of the internal refresh counter on the lower 7 bits of the address bus and lowering the voltage on the RFSH pin.

We will come back to the refresh cycle later in this chapter.

If you look closely at Figure 7-4 you will see that the WR line is driven low half way through the T2 clock cycle and the data must be written to the memory before this line goes high one clock cycle later. This means that if we take the write cycle as our tightest time constrain operation then we only have half of one Z80 clock cycle to decode the operation and send both the high and low address bytes to the DRAM.

The DRAM requires a number of discrete steps to be carried out in a timely fashion and if we look at the timing diagrams for the DRAM we can figure out how long we have to complete these steps but either way they must be completed to satisfy the Z80 timing.

In a write operation for example we must send the DRAM a 16 bit address in two bytes and this will require us to switch from the lower 8 bits of the address to the upper 8 bits of the address and provide latching pulses at the correct time whilst also allowing sufficient time for the address to make it through the latch and in addition we must allow the DRAM itself long enough between each step otherwise it will not behave correctly.

Looking at the timing diagrams in Figure 7-4 we can see that we only have half a Z80 clock cycle in order to complete the entire sequence required by the DRAM.

This is where we must start making some decisions as to how our system will be structured and what methods we will use to provide the complex sequence of signals required by the DRAM.

Some basic methods are to use delays following the Z80 read or write indications but this can be tricky as setting up analog timing within a high speed digital system is very unpredictable.

A second method is to design a simple shift register circuit which is clocked from the high speed main clock and which will generate a series of accurately timed pulses in sequence. These pulses can then be used to clock the various stages of the DRAM cycle.

A third method and the one I will be using here is to install a clock divider following the main system clock and then clock the Z80 itself from one of the divided outputs.

This is where we will begin to make full use of the clock signals we have made available in the master clock divider circuit.

In our case we are clocking the Z80 using a clock which is derived from the main 10MHz clock divided by four and is therefore running at 2.5 MHz.

This means that for each Z80 clock period we actually get 4 main clock cycles and if we make use of both rising and falling clock edges we can actually divide each Z80 clock period into 8 time slots. This is easily enough for us to design a DRAM control system and as you recall we already have the clock divider which we designed as part of the video output system.

Now that we have decided on the general method we will employ to control the timing of the DRAM control logic we had better get started actually designing the circuits which will carry out the work.

DRAM Cycle

If we now take a look at the DRAM timing we can determine the exact steps required in order to properly drive the DRAM.

You should be aware that different DRAM devices have slightly different requirements but I have selected a typical type of DRAM for our system and this design should therefore work will almost all DRAM types.

Figures 7-5 and 7-6 show DRAM read and write cycles respectively. These diagrams are taken from a DRAM specification sheet.

Read Cycle

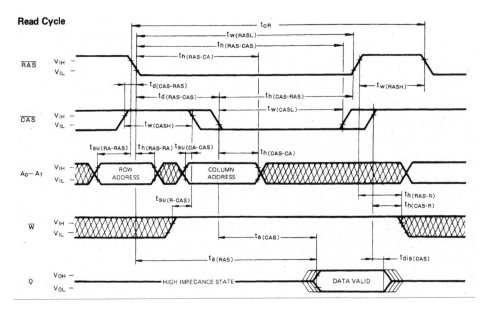

Figure 7-5 DRAM Read Cycle

Write Cycle (Early Write)

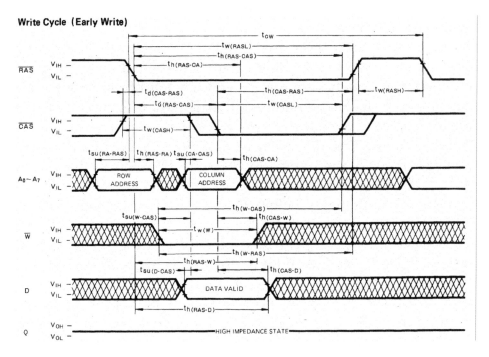

Figure 7-6 DRAM Early Write Cycle

DRAM timing requirements

In Figures 7-5 and 7-6 the general sequences for providing the 16 bit memory address to the DRAM device are the same.

It begins with the Z80 setting up the data output on its 8 bit data bus and 16 bit address on its address output pins and it then lowers the memory access pin signals depending on the type of memory access that is required. These are the _MREQ, _RD or _WR outputs of the Z80.

For a read cycle the _RD line goes low on the falling edge of the T1 phase of the cycle and for a write the _WR lines goes low on the falling edge of the T2 cycle.

If we therefore take the timing constraints of the write cycle as our target then we can be sure that we can meet the read cycle timing requirements.

As soon as the _WR line is driven low by the Z80 our control logic must kick into action.

Once it has decoded the memory write operation it continues by lowering the _RAS input of the DRAM device and as the address multiplexer is already selecting the lower 8 bits of the address bus then lowering _RAS causes the low byte of the address to be latched into the DRAM.

After a delay of 45nS the address multiplexer is switched to send the upper 8 bits of the 16 bit address to the DRAM and the system must then allow sufficient time for this address to propagate through the multiplexer before it lowers the _CAS input of the DRAM. It therefore waits for 50nS and then drives the _CAS line low which causes the upper 8 bits of the 16 bit address to be latched into the DRAM. The full 16 bit address has now been latched into the DRAM device.

As the Z80 had already set up the data on its data bus prior to lowering the _MREQ line then the data is already available for the DRAM to store in the selected address.

There is an additional complication which is created due to a choice I made in the way I was going to connect the DRAM data input and output pins.

Looking at the DRAM specification sheet you will notice that it does not have a chip enable or output enable pin. This is because its tri-state output is controlled by the _RAS/_CAS sequence of inputs. If we repeat the above process for a read cycle then when the _CAS input is driven low the DRAM will respond by enabling its output pin and driving its data onto the data bus. The DRAM output will remain enabled until the _CAS line is raised.

The same thing will happen during a write cycle unless we use a feature of the DRAM called 'Early Write'.

By using this early write feature during a write cycle the data output pin of the DRAM remains in its high impedance state throughout the entire write cycle.

This means that we can avoid the need for a separate buffer between the DRAM output pins and the CPU data bus and so we can simply connect the DRAM input and output pins together and then connect them both directly to the CPU data bus. It also avoids the need to design any additional control logic for this buffer and anything that reduces the complexity of the system logic is generally a good thing.

In order to utilise the early write feature all we need to do is lower the _WR input to the DRAM before we lower the _CAS input. Normally the _WR input is lowered following the latching of the upper part of the address when _CAS is lowered and this causes the DRAM data output pin to become active. By dropping _WR prior to dropping _CAS the DRAM enters its early write mode and the data output pin is left inactive in its high impedance state.

This requires that we add a step to the sequence I indicated above and we need to lower the _WR input to the DRAM shortly after lowering the _RAS input.

Figure 7-6 shows what this sequence looks like.

Figure 7-7 shows the outputs needed from our DRAM control logic circuits in order to properly control the DRAM devices.

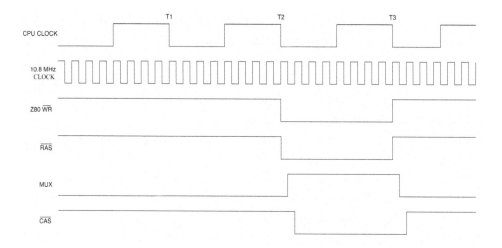

Figure 7-7 DRAM Control Logic Timing

As we can see in this diagram the sequence of drive signals for the DRAM occur in rapid succession following the _WR signal from the Z80 which occurs on the Z80 clock falling edge in the T2 phase of the instruction cycle.

The _RAS line is lowered approximately 12nS after the _WR pin on the Z80 goes low. This is how long it takes the decoding logic to propagate the signal but this delay has no impact on the system operation. At this point the low 8 bits of the address are latched into the DRAM.

After a further delay of around 10nS the DRAM _WR signal is lowered and this puts the DRAM into its early write mode.

Around 45nS from the Z80 _WR line dropping the address multiplexer is switched to send the upper 8 bits of the address to the DRAM.

Around 45nS after the multiplexer changes the _CAS line is driven low and this latches the upper 8 bits of the address into the DRAM but the DRAM output pin remains in its high impedance state because early write mode has been enabled.

The Z80 raises the _WR output half way though the T3 phase of the cycle and that allows plenty of time for the control logic to 'unwind' the DRAM control signals and return the device to its idle state so it is then ready for the next cycle and the Z80 data and address bus are freed up.

Each step in the logic timing is controlled by the 10.0 MHz main system clock and this demonstrates why it is so useful to drive the processor from a divided clock as it allows plenty of scope for tight control of other devices in the system.

By using alternate edges of the main system clock in the DRAM control logic we are able to control the timing of each event in 50nS steps.

If we need shorter duration delays then we could add a few buffers where the delays are needed although by careful use of the gates in our system we have already allowed for this as part of the logic circuit design. For example the delay from _RAS to _WR was achieved using the gate which controls it and so no further delays were required.

The timing in our control logic allows around 250nS for the DRAM to respond to the read requests and as we are using 150nS devices then this is more than sufficient for reliable operation.

RAS only Refresh

There is another function which our control logic must take care of and that is the DRAM refresh cycles. I should point out here that there are of course easier ways these days to drive DRAM memory systems but as I stated earlier I am hoping to show the basics of such a system and how it can be achieved without the safety net of modern integrated control devices.

The requirements I am describing here may sound very complicated but they are surprisingly easy to accomplish with a little though and just a few logic gates.

Earlier in this chapter we looked at a circuit to increase the Z80 refresh address counter from 7 to 8 bits although the devices I will actually be using support 7 bit refresh addressing.

While they are 64k the internal arrangement is such that the memory array is divided into 4 banks and a row in each bank is refreshed during each refresh cycle so in theory we would simply use the 7 bit refresh address directly. However not all 64 DRAM devices support this refresh mode so I included the 8th bit in the refresh address to support other DRAM types and sending the extra bit to devices which do support 7 bit refresh address does not do any harm.

With that said we now need to add refresh logic to our DRAM control circuits but we do not actually need to make any further changes. You may remember that I had added some additional gates to some of the circuits I showed earlier and the refresh control is specifically what those gates are for.

They take care of gating the memory access in such a way that when the refresh output of the Z80 is low the memory control logic only generates the _RAS signal but it does not go on to complete a full memory access cycle.

The DRAM is provided with each refresh address in turn during each refresh cycle and the _RAS input is driven low for the duration of the refresh phase of the M1 cycle.

The refresh address performs a complete count every few hundred uS and this is all the DRAM needs to retain the stored data.

In fact the DRAM is being refreshed almost 10 times faster than it really needs but this does not matter and will ensure that it will operate reliably even as it ages.

Alternatively you may want to add additional banks of DRAM and due to the generous timing allowances you could do this with very little effort.

Figure 7-8 shows the DRAM control logic circuit and as you can see it is no where near as complicated as you may expect although this is largely due to the circuit designs we have already put in place.

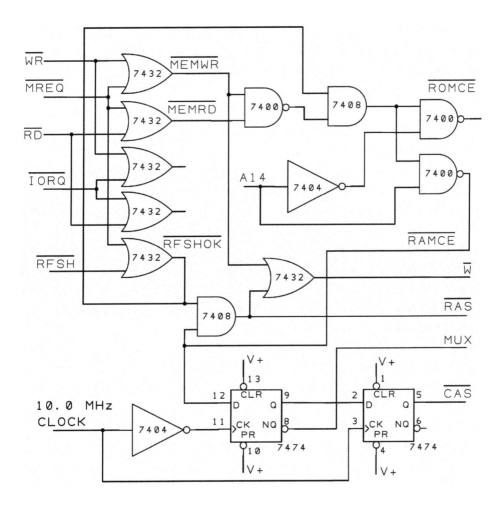

Figure 7-8 DRAM Control Logic Circuit

175

We will of course need to modify the memory mapping part of this circuit later in order to connect the video RAM and also to arrange the memory banks and blocks as we want them but this will not have any impact on the DRAM control logic.

Despite the seemingly complex set of design requirements I indicated earlier in this chapter I hope you can see that the resulting control logic circuit is relatively simple and easy to follow.

Not only does this circuit take care of the complex task of controlling the DRAM but it also forms the basis for our entire memory mapping control system which we will look at shortly.

The top section of this schematic is the same decoding circuit we saw previously but the lower section now shows the DRAM control logic which operates as follows.

During a refresh cycle the Z80 drives the _RFSH input low and this enables the gate which controls the _RAS output. This is gated through an OR gate using the _MREQ line to ensure that the Z80 address bus output pin voltages have stabilised.

If no other memory access lines are low then only the _RAS signal is lowered and the DRAM is refreshed using the memory address which the Z80 has put onto the address bus. The address multiplexer will be selecting the low byte of the address because no memory access cycle is in progress.

In a read cycle the decoder section of this circuit detects the memory access by the Z80 through the _MREQ and _RD lines and either the _RAMCE or _ROMCE line is lowered depending on the output from the memory address decoder.

If _ROMCE is low then the ROM is enabled and the Z80 can read data from it but none of the DRAM access circuits are activated.

If _RAMCE is low and _RFSH is high then _RAS goes low and the DRAM access sequence starts.

In a read cycle the OR gate keeps the _W (DRAM write enable) line high which prevents the DRAM from writing data.

The _RAMCE line is now low and is connected to the data input pin of a flip flop and after 45nS on the next falling edge of the 10.0 MHz clock this data value is latched to the Q output of the flip flop which then goes low.

At the same time the NQ output of the flip flop goes high and this is used to control the address multiplexer which is changed to select the high 8 bits of the address and so the DRAM now sees the high order byte of the 16 bit address.

The low Q output of the flip flop is connected to the data input of a second flip flop and on the next falling edge of the clock this data value is latched to the Q output of the flip flop which then goes low. This output is the _CAS drive for the DRAM and so the memory has now latched the entire 16 bit address into its internal address buffer and it responds by enabling its output pin and outputting the data value at the selected address.

If the current operation is a write cycle then approximately 10nS after the _RAS line drops the DRAM _W control line is driven low.

This delay is produced by the OR gate which drives the _W line and it is sufficient to allow the DRAM to enter early write mode.

The rest of the DRAM control logic cycle is the same as for a read except that the early write prevents the DRAM from enabling its output pin which is exactly what we require.

Towards the end of the memory access cycle the Z80 raises the memory access control lines (_MREQ, _RD, _WR) and the DRAM decoder logic responds by raising the _RAMCE line which also raises the _RAS control line.

This causes the first flip flop to clock a high value to its output on the next falling edge of the clock and this resets the MUX to connect the low order byte of the address to the DRAM so it is then ready for the next refresh cycle. On the next falling clock edge the second flip flop clocks a high value to the _CAS control line and this completes the required DRAM access cycle.

The overall timing which this circuit provides gives more than adequate timing conditions for the DRAM and in fact it should operate correctly even if the Z80 clock frequency was doubled.

As each memory chip we are using is a 64k x 1 bit device we require 8 of these to make up our full 64k x 8 bit array.

The circuit for this is very simple as most of the DRAM pins are simply connected directly together. Also note that the input and output pins are also connected together which is possible due to our decision to use the early write feature of the memory.

Figure 7-9 shows the full circuit for the memory chips.

If you decide to go ahead and build this system then you should be sure to check that the memory devices you use support the early write feature.

Memory devices which do not support early write should not be used in this configuration as they will enable their output pins during each write cycle and this will conflict with the data being pushed onto the bus by the Z80 and most likely the results will not be good. The vast majority of DRAM devices support this feature so it should not be difficult finding suitable parts. The speed of the DRAM should also be unimportant and I have tested this circuit using devices from 100nS access time up to 250nS and they all worked without any issues.

If the devices you decide to use in your design do not support early write then you will need to add a buffer between the DRAM output pins and the Z80 data bus and also some logic to control that buffer.

Figure 7-9 shows how the DRAM chips are connected.

Later in the book I show a small prototype DRAM board that I designed during this project which was intended to make it easier to build the Z80 circuits onto bread boards. The circuit on this board is essentially identical to that shown in Figure 7-9.

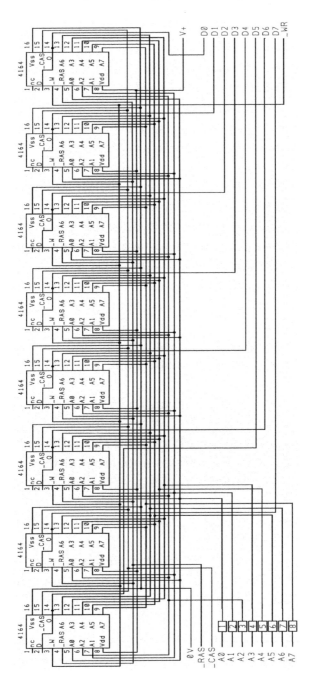

Figure 7-9 DRAM Circuit

Now that we have the DRAM system designed we should really test it before we proceed with the rest of the computer design because if the memory system is not reliable then further tests will be very difficult and also pointless.

We already have a very simple test program in the test ROM and we can start by making use of it to look for any obvious flaws in our design.

A scope should be connected to the 10.0MHz clock and also the _RAS, _CAS and MUX control lines.

If the system is then powered up you should see the control lines toggling as the test program loops around continually writing and reading the 5 address locations at 4000-4004 hex.

You will find this testing much easier if you have access to a logic analyser and all the CPU pins and DRAM control pins are monitored.

The analyser should be set to state mode and the 10.0 MHz clock used as the analyser clock with both rising and falling edges triggering.

Assuming that everything appears to be working then you should be able to see the correct data value being written to the correct address range and then read back. You should also see the correct refresh and data access addresses appearing at the DRAM address pins as the read and write cycles are performed and the refresh cycles complete.

This simple test program is however not really very through in its memory testing capability.

It is only trying to test a very limited range of addresses but more importantly it is always reading and writing the same data value and it is repeating this very quickly with just a few uS between each read cycle.

Because we are always using the same data value there is no easy way to determine if we are actually accessing the intended memory addresses because the data value give no indicated if this is the case.

In addition the very short repeated memory access to the same memory locations means that the tests will be successful even if the refresh cycles are completely inoperative.

This is because the process of reading the DRAM causes it to refresh the memory cells we are accessing and so they are effectively being refreshed by this test every few uS.

We need to write a new test program to provide a more meaningful test and this is shown below.

Test Program 2
```
START     LD        A,00h         ;Load register start values
          LD        B,FF
          LD        HL,4000h
LP1:      LD        (HL),A        ;Write values to RAM
          INC       HL
          INC       A
          DJNZ      LP1

          LD        A,00h         ;Reload register starting
values
          LD        B,FF
          LD        HL,4000h
LP2:      CP        (HL)          ;Check RAM values
          JP        NZ,ER
          INC       A
          INC       HL
          DJNZ      LP2
          JP        START

ER:       NOP                     ;Wait here if error
          NOP
          JP        ER
```

This code should be programmed into the ROM starting at address 0000. The byte values are (hex).

3E 00 06 FF 21 00 40 77 23 3C 10 FB 3E 00 06 FF 21 00 40 BE
C2 20 00 3C 23 10 F8 C3 00 00 00 00 C3 20 00 00 00 00 00 00

This program loads 256 memory locations beginning at 4000H with unique data values and once they have all been loaded it then goes back to each address and checks that the stored value is correct.

If the value read back from memory is incorrect for any location then the program halts otherwise the test loops back to the start and repeats until it is stopped.

This test has a number of improvements over the previous program. Firstly it is writing unique numbers to each memory location so it can detect simple memory address errors (but no memory decoding errors).

It also takes around 4mS to complete the loading part of the test which means that if the refresh cycles are not working the data will be lost and the test will fail.

If the memory control logic is working correctly then this test will continue indefinitely but will halt if not.

It will be apparent immediately if the test fails as all the DRAM logic control activity for the read and write cycles will stop and only the refresh cycles will continue, if they are working.

During development of this system I wrote quite a number of programs to help with the testing but I will not bore you with them all but one of the fun aspects of designing and building a system such as this is using it to develop code and this includes the system test programs.

I hope that this chapter has demystified the implementation of DRAM into a system and may have encouraged you to ditch the SRAM and give it a go.

There is actually no real cost benefit to selecting DRAM over SRAM these days but if you really want to get a feeling of accomplishment then putting together a functioning DRAM based memory system is certainly a good way to go about it.

In the next chapter we will expand on the memory mapping circuit and add bank switching to the design.

ℒ ℴℱ

Chapter 8 – Memory Mapping

The Z80 processor has a 16 bit address bus and this means that it can directly access up to 65,536 individual address locations or 64k.

For any systems based on the Z80 where more address space than this is required some kind of memory bank switching must be created. For our computer I wanted to include the possibility of running existing software applications such as the CP/M operating system and while this will easily run with just 64k there are some prerequisites which make running it without bank switching difficult.

CP/M requires 100 hex bytes of memory space starting at address 0000 but the Z80 reset vector is also 0000.

Each time the Z80 is reset it sets its program counter to a value of 0000 and then this address is used to load the first instruction from memory which is usually a ROM containing some kind of bootstrap code or a monitor program or even a full operating system.

However if we wish to load and run any program which needs RAM accessed at the bottom of the memory space then measures are needed to allow this to function correctly.

While there are several methods available for accomplishing this, a relatively simple method is to add some bank switching circuits to the design and place the boot ROM in a separate bank from the main system RAM.

A simple bank switching system could map the boot up ROM to bank 1 and then select this bank whenever the computer is reset.

The main system RAM can then be mapped into bank 0 so that the full 64k is available to user programs all the way down to address 0000.

This is the method I intend to use in this project but there are some issues which need to be handled when implementing a solution of this type.

If the only executable code is in a ROM which resides in bank 1 and the computer switches to bank 0 then it will no longer have access to the ROM code and will most likely crash.

One solution is to make an area of RAM common across all banks and copy some code from the ROM to this area during the start up process and then hand control to this area of code or include functions in this common RAM which allow transparent bank switching for the system.

The same cannot be done with the ROM area if a system such as CP/M is expected to run because mapping the ROM to the bottom of all banks would mean that CP/M would not be able to write to the first 100 hex bytes which is what is needs to do.

The solution I decided to adopt in this design is to create a memory map as shown in Figure 8-1.

You will notice that the top 8k of the memory space in both banks is common and of this the top 2k is reserved for the video RAM which will actually be the 2k SRAM in the video system.

We will of course lose access to the upper 2k of main system DRAM but being able to access the video RAM from either bank will make writing applications much easier.

The common RAM area will be part of the main system DRAM and the memory mapping will allow access to this irrespective of which bank is selected so it will effectively be a 'ghost' RAM area of the DRAM from 56k to 62k.

Mapping an area for I/O purposes will also make the computer much more versatile and as this area is otherwise un-used it does not get in the way.

Note that we could also use this space for additional ROM code.

Using this method of mapping means that during system start up the boot ROM is able to copy any critical code into the common RAM area and it can then be accessed from all banks.

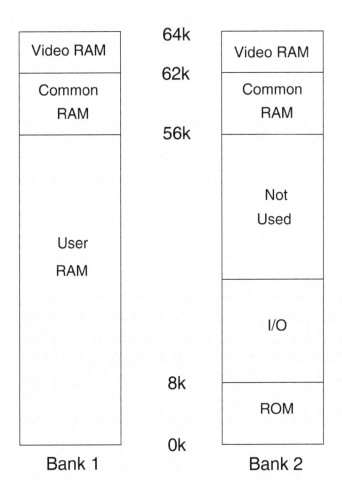

Figure 8-1 Memory Map

Now that we have decided on our memory mapping strategy we need to modify the simple test memory mapping circuit which we put in place in order to reflect the required map and also design a suitable bank switching circuit.

Although the area above I/O in bank 1 is shown as not used I do not fully decode it so this area is technically part of the I/O block.

We will now continue our design with the bank switching circuit as this may well have an impact on the way we design our memory mapping circuit.

Bank Switching

There are a few things we need to consider when designing our bank switching so that we can avoid complications in the future.

Our first consideration is in how the system is intended to start up because if the wrong bank is active following a reset then the Z80 will be unable to access the ROM and as this contains the boot up code then the system would fail to start.

The next decision we need to make is if our system is intended to handle certain types of interrupt. During an interrupt the system will branch to a specific vector and this memory location must contain a suitable handler to prevent the system from crashing. If the handler happens to be in a different bank than the one currently selected then nothing good is likely to happen so we must ensure that the Z80 is able to locate any such handler correctly.

This also applies to RAM areas such as the stack and interrupt vector table.

The Z80 also needs to be able to switch banks at will under software control in an efficient manner.

When I was considering these requirements it was clear that if I wanted the computer to be able to switch banks but also make function calls and handle interrupts then certain areas of the RAM would need to be in common RAM blocks and also the bank switching would need to be available from any bank.

Deciding on a method of actually switching banks was easy because there is only really one sensible option for this on a system like ours and that is to use an I/O port to control the bank switching circuit.

While we could use a memory mapped solution this could get messy as we would need to have an I/O memory mapped block in each memory bank which is not very efficient so it is not a method I would use for this function.

I decided to use port 0 for this and we will simply write a value of '0' to the port to select bank 0 and a value of '1' to select bank 1.

Following a reset then bank 1 will be selected as this is the bank which will contain our boot ROM and an interrupt will be able to select bank 0 if required.

However as I have already mentioned my system software will place both the stack and the interrupt vector table along with the interrupt handlers into common RAM blocks.

Now that we know what the circuit needs to do we can go ahead and design it. Figure 8-2 shows the bank switching circuit.

This circuit also provides the decoding for the non memory mapped IO circuits which I will come back to in a later chapter.

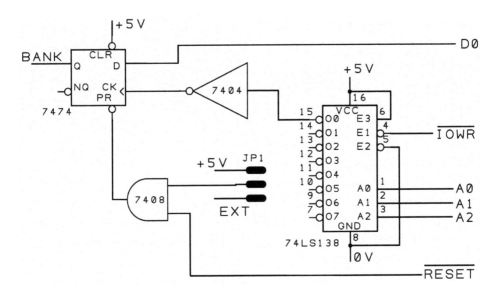

Figure 8-2 Bank Switching Circuit

This circuit works as follows…

The 74LS138 decoder is used to select one of 8 possible outputs and the particular output selected is determined by the three input lines which are labelled A0, A1 and A2.

The output of this decoder is latched when the _IOWR control line is taken low and this line is one of the outputs of the memory decoding circuit which I describe later in this chapter.

This allows the Z80 to select any of the decoder outputs by simply executing an 'OUT' instruction to the required address port.

In this case I decided to use port '0' to control the bank switching and so we connect the bank switching circuit to the '0' output of this decoder.

This line is inverted and used to clock a 74LS74 flip flop which has its data (D) input connected to the Z80 D0 line.

This will cause the Z80 D0 bit to appear on the 'Q' output of the flip flop whenever we execute an 'OUT' instruction to port 0.

We can therefore set the Q output of this flip flop to either a '0' or a '1' by writing a '0' or a '1' respectively to port '0'.

The flip flop output is used as the bank control line and we will use this later in this chapter to control the memory mapping bank select function.

One additional feature we need to add to this circuit is the ability to default the bank selection to a specific value during a processor reset. This is required because the computer system must be able to access its boot ROM following a reset and so we will ensure that the bank switching output is used to select the bank which contains the ROM when it is reset.

In order to provide the proper reset function we simply connect the preload pin of the flip flop to the processor _RESET line and this will cause the bank select circuit to always select the desired bank when the system is reset.

Notice that I have also included a select jumper which will allow us to force the starting bank if required by applying an external signal.

I included this as we may need to allow the system to select ROM based code in response to hardware operations or interrupts.

I did however remove this from the final design as the same function can be achieved in other ways.

Memory mapping circuits can appear to be complicated when you see them in schematics because they are generally the result of a number of layered circuit operations. In addition the designers normally simplify the circuits in order to reduce component count or meet timing constraints which can make the circuits difficult to follow.

The memory mapping circuit we will design is no exception to this but I will try to keep it as simple as possible and to help with the explanations I will show it one section at a time.

Memory Mapping Circuit

The first time you start to consider a memory mapping circuit it may initially seem very simple but as the circuit starts to develop it can rapidly turn into a convoluted maze.

To avoid this it is often best to start by reducing the complexity of the problem as much as possible by eliminating anything which is not really required.

In this case if we look at our intended memory map there are two items we can take care of immediately.

The first of these is the area which is identified as 'Not Used' in the area above I/O memory mapped addresses in bank 1.

In this case we can simply not fully decode this area and allow it to fall within the I/O space or the common RAM. In our case I decided to allow this area to fall into common RAM as this may prove to be useful.

The second thing we can consider is that the smallest block of memory which we wish to decode is 2k (2048 bytes) or 11 bit chunks of the address space.

As the Z80 uses a 16 bit address then this means we only need to decode the upper 5 bits of the address space because these 5 bits determine which 2k block we are addressing.

If we write this as an address it looks like this.

11111XXXXXXXXXXX

Where 11111 are the bits we need to decode and XXXXXXXXXX are the bits in each of the 2k block which we do not need to decode.

This makes the task of decoding the memory map much easier.

The decoder circuit works closely with the memory control circuits and so we will design both of these into a single group of circuits.

So far in our design we have been using a very simple memory map which we now need to replace although we will still use the same memory control design.

We should also keep in mind that some areas in separate banks do not overlap each other and so we can avoid the need to fully decode these areas outside of the current bank.

Do not worry if this does not make sense just yet as it will hopefully become much clearer as our decoder system develops.

As long as we end up with a design which can reliably select the required memory mapped device then that is all we need to concern ourselves with. Adding additional decoding for situations which cannot arise is a complication we can avoid.

We will require five output signals from our memory mapping and control circuit because we have five memory devices which we wish to control.

      1) DRAM   (Main system dynamic RAM)
      2) CRAM   (Common system RAM)
      3) ROM   (System Read Only Memory)
      4) VRAM   (Video RAM)
      5) IO   (Input / Output)

Actually item 5 in this list may comprise a number of separate devices which will need further decoding but for now we will consider them to be a single item.

The items in the list require separate outputs from the mapping circuits so that only one is ever enabled at once. This is important because each will attempt to put data onto the common Z80 data bus and if more than one device becomes active at the same time then damage is the likely result. This is where the need for good design of the memory mapping circuits is important.

The memory map diagram can be converted into a table of memory address ranges and this is shown in Table 1 below.

Memory	Bank	Address Bits
VRAM	All	11111 XXXXXXXXXX
CRAM	All	11100 XXXXXXXXXX
DRAM	0	00XXX XXXXXXXXXX
DRAM	0	01XXX XXXXXXXXXX
DRAM	0	10XXX XXXXXXXXXX
DRAM	0	11XXX XXXXXXXXXX
ROM	1	000XX XXXXXXXXXX
IO	1	00100 XXXXXXXXXX
IO	1	01000 XXXXXXXXXX
IO	1	01100 XXXXXXXXXX

Table 1 – Memory Mapping

I will now describe each part of the design in turn starting with the VRAM decoding and going on to the ROM and RAM decoding.

As you can see in Table 1 the VRAM is selected when the most significant 5 bits of the memory address are all equal to '1'.

All we need to do to produce a valid logic value for this is to use the circuit shown in Figure 8-3.

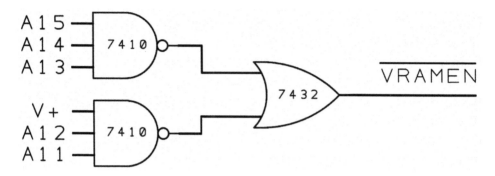

Figure 8-3 VRAM Address Decoding

This simply provides a low output (_VRAMEN) if bits 11 to 15 of the address are all set to '1'.

Next we need to decode the DRAM memory but as this is all the remaining memory below the VRAM in bank 0 then we can simply invert the VRAM signal and use it as the DRAM control but there is a complication we must consider.

While I have shown the CRAM memory space as being separate to the DRAM it is of course still part of the main system DRAM.

We will therefore need to allow the system to selectively enable the CRAM block of this memory when required and so I will include an extra logic gate to control the DRAM enable output and we will then use this as both the DRAM and CRAM enable signal. After all it is actually enabling the same memory device. Later I will show how this extra gate is used to select either the main DRAM or the CRAM block within this memory block.

As you can see by progressing through the memory mapping circuit design in a logical manner we can simplify its design.

Figure 8-4 shows the additional gate required to provide the _DRAMEN output signal.

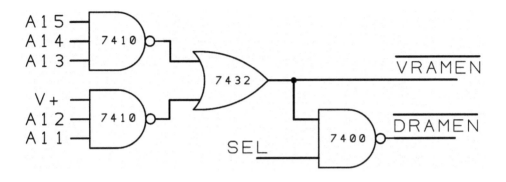

Figure 8-4 DRAM Address Decoding

The additional gate will not only invert the _VRAMEN signal but will also allow us to select when to enable this signal.
I will describe the function of the SEL input later in this chapter.

We now need to decode the ROM and IO memory spaces but as these occupy ranges lower down in memory then the decoding is slightly more complex but not excessively so if we choose not to fully decode the memory space above the IO block.
The circuit shown in Figure 8-5 can be used to decode both the ROM and IO memory blocks.

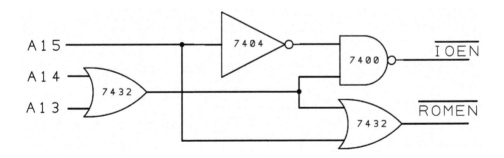

Figure 8-5 ROM and IO Address Decoding

This circuit produces a low output signal (_ROMEN) if the current memory address falls within the ROM memory space and a separate low output signal (_IOEN) if the current memory address falls within the mapped IO memory space.

The circuits I have shown so far only provide basic address decoding so we now need to add the bank switching control and also the bank override function for the memory blocks which are intended to be available in both banks.
In our design these are the VRAM and the CRAM memory blocks and the bank switching must be masked from these two blocks of memory in order that they can be accessed from any bank irrespective of the decoded address.

This may sound a bit complicated but with a bit of thought we can easily add these two features with the addition of just a few extra gates to the circuit we have already designed and this is shown in Figure 8-6.

This circuit includes all the decoding plus the bank switching and works as follows…

The control input labelled 'BANK' is used to select one of the two possible banks and this signal of course comes directly from the bank switching latch which we put in place earlier

. Applying a '0' to this input selects bank 0 and applying a '1' selects bank 1.
You could of course select any value for selecting the banks by changing the IO decoding but I felt that the approach I have shown here keeps things simple.

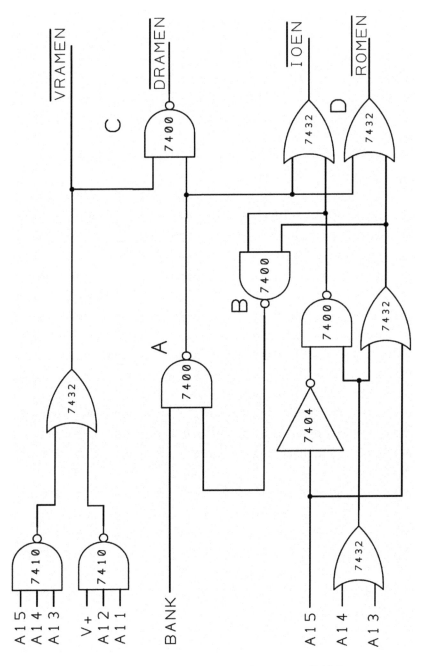

Figure 8-6 Bank Switching and Common RAM

BANK 0

When BANK is low the output of gate 'A' will always be at a high level and this is used to prevent the two gates 'D' from producing low outputs and so it effectively disables the _ROMEN and _IOEN outputs.

This means that the two banked memory blocks which are in bank 1 are both disabled.

With the output gate 'A' high then gate 'C' is enabled to invert and pass the value of the _VRAMEN line on to the _DRAMEN output.

In this mode the value on _VRAMEN and _DRAMEN are complimentary outputs and _DRAMEN is forced high if _VRAMEN goes low. This means that when bank 0 is selected the only possible outputs are _DRAMEN or _VRAMEN and the address decoding logic at the top left of the schematic detects when the top 5 bits of the address bus are all 1's and so it goes low only when the upper 2k of memory in bank 0 is selected. For all other addresses in bank 0 this output is high and so the _DRAMEN output will be low (DRAM enabled).

As this includes the common RAM address range we do not need any further address decoding for bank 0 because both areas cannot be selected at the same time as they occupy different address blocks.

This saves a few gates and simplifies the decoder but adding this extra decoding if you wanted to use a different memory map is not difficult. You simply need to add some additional logic to force the required output low (or disable the unwanted outputs) based on your required memory address mapping.

This means that the BANK 0 memory space mapping is now exactly as we want it to be.

BANK 1

Bank 1 is selected by applying a value of '1' to the BANK input control line.

Decoding bank 1 is somewhat more complicated than bank 0 because it has more address blocks and we must also ensure that both the common RAM and the video RAM are addressed when the applied address falls within the range of these two blocks.

We start by decoding the two lower address blocks for the ROM and IO using the four gates at the bottom left of the schematic.

The ROM address range is 0000 to 1FFF (hex) and the IO address range is 2000 to 7FFF (hex) and one of the two outputs from these gates goes low if the current address is within the specified range.

These memory address ranges do not overlap the common RAM or video RAM blocks so no additional decoding is required.

Everything from address 8000 (hex) and above is deemed to be common RAM or Video RAM.

In order to allow the common RAM or video RAM to be enabled when we have selected bank 1 we must add a few additional gates.

This is the function of gate 'B' and is why gate 'A' was included.

If both outputs from the ROM and IO address decoder part of this circuit are high then the output of gate 'B' is low. This is the state of these two outputs if the applied address is above the ROM and IO address blocks.

As we are in bank 1 the upper input of gate 'A' is already high and if the lower input from gate 'B' is low then the output of gate 'A' will be high.

The result is that gate 'C' is enabled to pass the inverted value of the _VRAMEN line and so if the current address while in bank 1 is above the ROM and IO address range but below the VRAM range then the _DRAMEN output will be low.

If the address is within the VRAM range then the _VRAMEN output will be low and the _DRAMEN output being the inverse of this will be high.

As with bank 0 the VRAM address range does not overlap the ROM or IO address range and so no additional decoding is required.

This arrangement provides all the memory address decoding we require along with bank switching and common system RAM and common video RAM.

We have achieved all this using only 12 gates but as ever these savings are partly due to the original planning of the system.

You can make the memory map for your system as complex as you wish and because it can be treated as a separate sub system of your computer it is generally fairly easy to design.

If you have never designed a computer memory mapping system before then a technique which is simple and fun and which may help is to build a simple binary counter with as many output bits as you need to decode.

Connect an LED to each of the binary counter outputs and an LED to each of your decoder circuit outputs.

If you then apply a very slow clock of around 1Hz to the counter clock input you will clearly see the operation of your decoder and being able to visualise it in this way will quickly show up any issues. For example only one of the output LED's should be on at any time. If more than one of the decoder output LED's illuminate at the same time then you have data bus 'contention' and your design requires further refining.

You can also use the same method using a logic analyser but for those without such a luxury piece of test equipment a few LED's can save a lot of frustration.

Once you have completed a few designs you can simply figure out the required circuits as you progress but this can be confusing if you are new to such designs and you may end up with a more complicated circuit than you really need.

The design of the memory mapping circuit is now complete as far as decoding the addresses is concerned but we cannot simply connect the output of the decoder circuits to the memory devices because they need to be accessed only when the Z80 needs them.

We therefore need to add the circuit we saw in an earlier chapter in order to allow the Z80 to enable the devices exactly when it needs to. We also need to ensure that the DRAM control circuit is used only when accessing the DRAM and not for any other type of memory mapped device.

If for example the _RAS and _CAS inputs to the DRAM are inadvertently taken low then this will cause the DRAM to enable its output pins and if other devices are using the Z80 data bus at that time then the system will most likely crash and some devices may even be damaged. We can provide control of the individual memory enable lines with a few simple gates and these are in turn controlled from the memory strobe control circuit.

We designed a version of the required circuit in the chapter in which we added DRAM to our system but the circuit we added then was simplified in order to allow us to more easily test the DRAM memory logic circuits. The decoding we used simply monitored the A14 address line and used it to decide if the CPU was accessing the DRAM or the ROM.

We now need to make this more sophisticated and connect it to the decoder we have just finished designing.

The memory strobe control circuit must output a low level signal whenever the Z80 wants to communicate with any memory device irrespective of the memory address in which that device resides.

We only need to make a very minor change to the circuit we used previously (which is why we used it in the first place) and the new version of this circuit is shown in Figure 8-7.

Note that this circuit also includes the input and output control for non memory mapped devices. This should not be confused with the memory mapped IO address space which uses a different method for external device access.

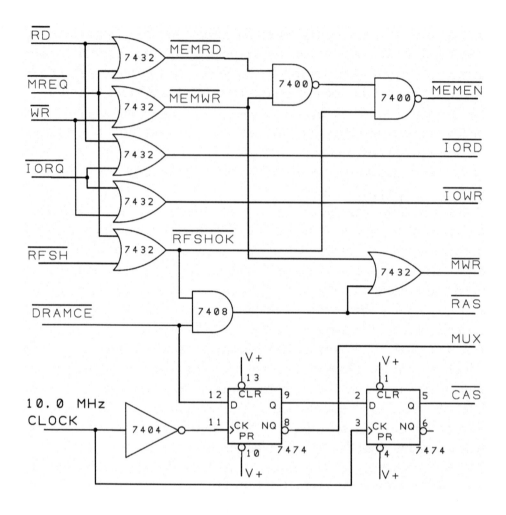

Figure 8-7 Memory Strobe Circuit

The only difference between this version of the circuit and the previous version is that it now outputs a signal I have called _MEMEN which is an active low signal.

This signal goes low any time the Z80 is ready to read data from a device or write data to a device so it is our global enable signal.

We now need to use that signal to control the output of our memory mapping circuit so that the correct device is enabled at the correct part of the Z80 cycle and if that device requires a simple strobe or the DRAM access sequence of signals.

As with the previous version of this circuit it also controls the refresh cycles required by the DRAM.

To make use of the _MEMEN signal we require a simple gating circuit to control the device chip select inputs.

Figure 8-8 shows the circuit for the memory chip select control.

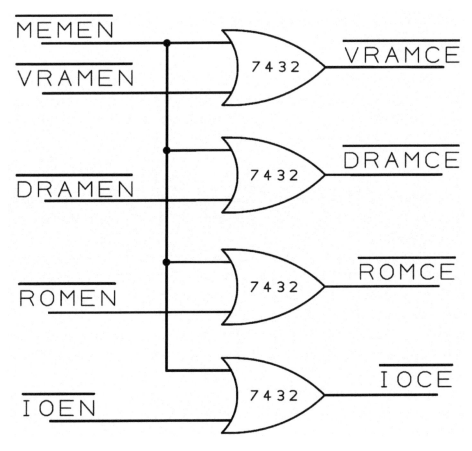

Figure 8-8 Memory Chip Select Control

The circuit in Figure 8-8 takes the memory enable outputs from the memory decoder and under control of the memory strobe output circuit the required memory device chip enable line is driven low.

The _DRAMCE output is used by the DRAM control as you can see in Figure 8-7 and the other outputs are connected to the appropriate inputs of the various memory devices.

The circuit in Figure 8-8 is a simple series of gates which are all controlled by the _MEMEN line. When _MEMEN goes low then any memory select output which has a low input is driven low for the duration of the _MEMEN pulse.

The duration and timing of this pulse is in turn controlled by the Z80 memory access control signals and so memory access is properly synchronised.

We now have the memory control circuits we require and once they are all connected together our computer will be able to access any of the memory devices it wants to. Each device will be mapped to the required address range and all control timing will be correct for each type of device.

As I stated previously the computer will switch to bank 1 following a reset so that it can access the boot up ROM code starting at address 0000h.

This also means that if required the computer can be used as a simple single bank machine because half of the RAM address space is non banked and so memory from 8000 hex upwards can be accessed without actually switching to bank 0.

We do lose 2k of DRAM at the top of the address space because this is occupied by the video RAM but 62k should still be enough RAM for most purposes.

If you decide to build this computer you could easily modify it should you wish in order to add more RAM by simply including additional banks.

Before I finish this chapter we need to make a small change to the refresh counter circuit which I showed in chapter 7.

As I stated when we designed this circuit it has a flaw which would cause the bit 7 flip flop to be toggled when address bits 0 to 6 were all '1' even if the Z80 was not in a refresh cycle. This could cause this counter to skip large chunks of the DRAM when counting the refresh address and this would of course lead to data loss.

The solution to this is very simple but I did not include it earlier because we have only just added the circuits we need to best deal with this problem.

This is always something worth considering when designing systems and rather than adding additional circuits which would increase the overall system design I knew that the solution to this particular problem would be less complicated if I waited until other things were in place.

In order to prevent the flip flop from being clocked by a matching address which occurs outside a refresh cycle we do of course need to use the refresh cycle itself to gate the clock to this flip flop.

As with the other refresh controlled circuits we cannot simply use the _RFSH signal from the Z80 on its own because the value on the address bus may not be correct when this signal first goes low.

As you may recall we overcame this issue earlier by combining the _RFSH and _MREQ signals from the Z80 to guarantee that the refresh address was correct before we made us of it.

We can do the same thing here and because we now already have a suitable signal we can make use of it.

If you look at the circuit in Figure 8-7 you will see that the _RFSHOK signal is active low when we have a valid refresh address available to us.

If you now go all the way back to Figure 7-2 in the previous chapter you can see that we have a spare input to the 8 input NOR gate which we previously tied to +5V.

We can now disconnect this input from +5V and make good use of it to allow us to gate the operation of the bit 8 refresh counter.

All we need to do now it to invert the _RFSHOK signal to give us RFSHOK and connect this to the spare input of the NOR gate. Figure 8-9 shows the revised refresh counter circuit arrangement.

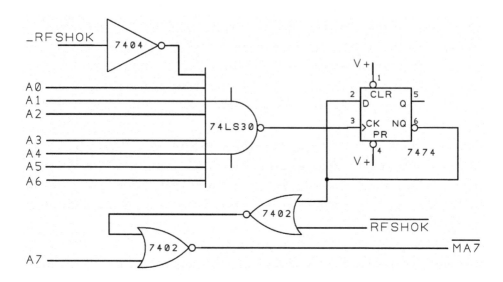

Figure 8-9 Revised Refresh Counter

This improved circuit now behaves exactly as we need it to and only clocks the flip flop when address bits 0 to 6 are high and the Z80 is in a refresh cycle with a stable refresh counter value on its address bus.

This will ensure that our bit 7 for the refresh counter will only toggle at the correct times and it will ignore non refresh cycle address bus values.

By waiting until now to add this feature we have avoided the need to include additional decoder circuitry and only needed to add a single inverter. I did of course use a spare inverter from one of the 74LS04 devices already in the design so this change was effectively free.

We now have all the circuits we require in order to allow us complete access to all of our memory devices but naturally we now need to test that this works.

I will describe the code we require in our boot ROM in much more detail in a later chapter but for now we will create a simple test program to allow us to test the bank switching and access to the non common areas of the main system RAM.

There is of course a complication we need to deal with before we can switch memory banks.

When we reset the system the bank switching circuit is designed to ensure that the bank containing our boot ROM is selected.

The Z80 CPU can therefore access the code in the ROM and execute the required instructions accordingly following a system reset.

However if we simply switch to a different memory bank then the system will crash because the ROM occupies the lower section of bank 1 from address 0000h to 2000h and this area in bank 0 is just RAM. Following a system reset this area of RAM will most likely contain nothing more than random garbage and so we cannot expect the CPU to run if we direct it to that area.

This is where the common RAM block comes into play and is specifically why I included it in our design.

As its name suggests the common RAM block is available to the CPU irrespective of the selected bank and so anything it contains will also be available to the CPU in all banks.

What we must therefore do prior to switching to bank 0 is to copy some code from the ROM into the common RAM block and then hand control of the system to the copied code. This code can then safely switch between banks without any problems because any code in that block will remain accessible whichever bank we select.

When we develop the code for our boot ROM we will need to include several features to enable the system to successfully boot up and run and so I have included a few of these features in the next test program.

They are of course very much simplified at this point but hopefully you will see how the general structure of the code will work.
The test code show below can now be programmed into a ROM and it should enable us to test the bank switching capability of our design along with the memory mapping.

Test Program 3

```
JP  START                              ;Jump to start of code

TEXT1    DB 'H','E','L','L','O'    ;Text

START
         LD      hl,BLOCK1         ;Copy code to RAM
         LD      DE,9000h
         LD      BC,30h
         LDIR
         JP      9000h            ;Jump to copied code


     ;ORG 9000h

         BLOCK1
         LD      A,00             ;Switch to bank 0
         OUT     (00),A

MEMTEST  LD      A,00             ;Test RAM 0000 - 00FF
         LD      B,FFh
         LD      HL,0000h

LOOP1    LD      (hl),A
         INC     HL
         INC     A
         DJNZ            LOOP1

         LD      A,00
         LD      B,FFh
         LD      HL,0000h

LOOP2    CP      (hl)
```

```
            JP        NZ,ERROR
            INC       HL
            INC       A
            DJNZ      LOOP2
            JP        MEMTEST

ERROR       NOP
            NOP
            JP        ERROR
END
```

This code should be programmed into the ROM starting at address 0000. The byte values are (hex).

C3 08 00 48 45 4C 4C 4F 21 16 00 11 00 90 01 30 00 ED B0

C3 00 90 3E 00 D3 00 3E 00 06 FF 21 00 00 77 23 3C 10 FB

3E 00 06 FF 21 00 00 BE C2 22 90 23 3C 10 F8 C3 04 90 00

00 C3 22 90

This program is very simple but is now starting to take on the structure which we will need to use in our system boot ROM.

It begins by jumping over a block of data which at the moment is simply some dummy text but this is where we will place our text strings etc in a later version.

It then copies a block of code from the ROM up into the common RAM block.

Once the code has been copied it hands control to this block of copied code and program execution then switches from ROM based code to RAM based code (we have loaded our first program).

Because the code which is now running resides in common RAM it can switch to bank 0 which is what it now does.

Once bank 0 has been selected the code proceeds to test the block of RAM which is in bank 0 at address 0000h to 00FFh.

If any bytes it reads back are incorrect then the test stops.

If you do not have a logic analyser you can use a scope or even a logic probe to monitor the CPU _RW line and if the test fails then this line will become inactive.

If everything is working as it should then the test will continue to repeat until the power is switched off or the reset button is pressed.

This is a big step in our system development as we now have the ability to access all areas of our memory space and we can also switch between banks and run much more complex test programs.

From this point in our project we can use the system itself to help us carry out further tests.

Note that in the circuits I have shown so far we have been using 32k EPROM's for both the main system ROM and the video character ROM.

The way in which the circuits have been designed allows the use of either a 32k or 64k EPROM for the main system ROM and for the character generator we can use either a 16k or a 32k EPROM.

I will explain why I have selected such a large EPROM for the character ROM in chapter 11.

The initial design for our computer memory system is now complete and we can move on to the next phase of development.

Once we have these circuits on a prototype board we can come back and look at the exact signal timing to make sure that everything is operating as is should be and if required we can then make modifications but for now we will continue.

Chapter 9 – Initial Testing

The design of our Z80 system is progressing well and so the next step is to translate the various circuits which we have created so far into a prototype board.

As I have been designing each circuit I built them up on breadboards although for practical reasons some of the circuits were simplified when put onto breadboards.

While this approach can be very useful for testing individual circuits it becomes increasingly less practical as the circuits grow. This is especially true where high speed digital circuits are being tested or where accurate measurement of critical signals is required.

One approach to designing systems is to design the entire system on paper, or more usually these days in some form of CAD system, but to help with the explanations and demonstrations in this project I decided to create circuit boards at each major step in the project.

These boards could then be used to accurately test the overall timing and interaction between each sub system to ensure that all the required timing constraints were acceptable.

In a later chapter I show each of the breadboard layouts and the resulting circuit boards but in this chapter I will just show the first main board design.

Naturally it was important to design these boards in such a way that they would behave in a very consistent manner as each new version was designed.

Figure 9-1 shows the first version of the JMZ CPU laid out on bread boards and ready to run some test code.

Figure 9-1 JMZ CPU on Breadboards

You can also see the small DRAM board which I designed as part of this project at the lower right of this image.

I could of course have use additional breadboards to make up the DRAM circuits but due to the large number of interconnections and the sensitive nature of the DRAM timing I decided against this as it is way too easy to waste a great deal of time investigating apparent faults that only exist because of the way the circuits are laid out.

Putting all the DRAM chips onto a small daughter board in this way eliminated many of the potential problems which could easily hamper effective development.

Several years ago I built a full microprocessor from discrete transistors on a huge set of breadboards and I probably spent most of the development time chasing poor interconnections.

In addition to the breadboards themselves I was also attaching a logic analyser to the circuits as part of the testing and the combination of bread boards and the loading created by the logic analyser leads would most likely make life difficult.

Once the breadboard version of the CPU was basically up and running I then translated it into a printed circuit board which is shown in Figure 9-2.

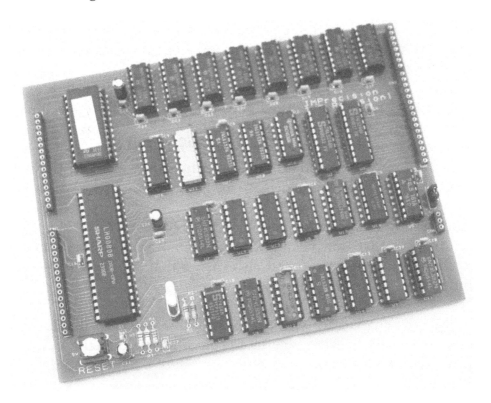

Figure 9-2 JMZ Main Board Version 1

Using this board I was able to easily attach a logic analyser and I could be reasonable sure that the results I was getting were indicative of those I would get from later designs.

I spent quite some time running many tests on this board to ensure that the timing for the Z80 CPU and the DRAM along with the memory decoding circuits was exactly as I had intended when designing the circuits.

The connectors along the edges of this board provided access to the various busses and control signals to enable me to attach this board to the next circuits which I wanted to design.

This incremental approach is much more time consuming and expensive than a direct approach to a final design but for the sake of clarity when writing this book it has hopefully helped to make the overall process easier to follow.

Fortunately this board worked very well and all the circuit timing and decoding worked exactly as expected.

The DRAM timing in particular was working exceptionally well with sufficient overhead to allow much higher main CPU clock speeds if I ever wanted to increase the performance of the system.

After testing this board we now have the basics of a working Z80 computer but we now need a way to communicate with it in order to simplify future testing and also ensure that the development is progressing in the right direction.

In the next chapter we will therefore add a keyboard interface to our system which will allow us to communicate directly with the JMZ rather than having to resort to the use of a remote terminal as required by so many simple Z80 designs.

Attaching a keyboard and having the Z80 handle incoming key stroke data will also enable us to check the efficiency of certain aspects of our overall design.

ౙ৯ౌ

Chapter 10 – Keyboard

It is beyond the scope of this book to go into the design of a computer enclosure and the various pieces of hardware which are required to complete the physical design of a computer system.

My goal is to keep this project focussed on the electronic design while also making it possible for anyone reading this book to build their own version of the system. It would be way beyond most hobbyists' budget to cover the cost of tooling and manufacture of a computer case or even some of the smaller assemblies which would be required. They are also not really needed as part of the electronic system design although there is one particular piece of hardware that creates a bit of problem as it is really a piece of hardware but we need it to create a working machine.

I am of course referring to the keyboard and I spent a considerable amount of time during this project weighing up the various pros and cons of the various options with respect to this.

There are a number of ways I could add a keyboard to our system and although my intention is to design a vintage style system I do not really consider the keyboard to be an integral part of the electronic design. It is however a fact that most system designers back in the 1970's and 80's needed to design their own keyboards as standard units were not available at that time.

There were keyboards around but they tended to be designed specifically for larger computer systems and they were very expensive and so unsuitable for use in a low cost computer.

The issue for us is one of cost because actually designing the keyboard hardware is relatively simple but the unit cost would be very high and I did not want to prevent anyone from building one of these systems because a single component was prohibitively expensive. On the other hand I did not want to start adding Bluetooth modules or something similar to our design as that would be going totally against the design philosophy I have laid down for this project.

Many keyboards of the time used very simple scanned arrays to implement the keyboard interface circuits and this would be in keeping with our design feel but without the actual keyboard hardware it would be fairly useless.

After a great deal of thought I finally decided on the approach which I would take as I believed it would not detract or distract us too much from our vintage design path but would also be a solution which is available to anyone who wishes to build one of these JMZ computers.

The option I selected was to use a PS2 keyboard and design a discrete logic interface for it which would be at home in our JMZ system.

I appreciate that a PS2 keyboard is a relatively modern unit but as it is not an integral part of our design and does not need modern drive electronics it should not be too far out of place.

While I was considering my options I did look briefly at making use of the inner workings of a PS2 keyboard and creating a matrix style scanning interface. This would be simple as most PS2 keyboards use a membrane key switch panel and rubber key plungers.

It would be fairly easy to make a simple interface board and scan the keys in much the same way as a vintage keyboard design. However this requires some tricky reworking of the keyboard and as I already pointed out this project is not really about the hardware so I decided against this approach.

There are also many different designs of PS2 keyboards so I could not really describe a universal way to modify the keyboard which would work for everyone.

Instead I decided on a logic gate design which would allow direct connection of a PS2 without the need to modify it.

We would not need to contaminate our design with modern microcontrollers or similar and we would end up with a fully functional keyboard which would allow us to make full use of our computer system. It would also allow the use of almost any PS2 keyboard without needing to search for a specific model.

This project is not really intended to be about relatively modern devices such as the PS2 keyboard but I will describe its general operation and interface in this chapter so that the design I am presenting for the interface will make more sense.

PS2 Interface

The PS2 keyboard interface is actually very simple although it has been complicated in more recent years by the added support of USB adaptors and USB device connection.

For the sake of this discussion I will limit the description to the basic PS2 serial communication protocol as this is what we will be making use of in our project.

If you look at the original connector for a PS2 keyboard you will see that it has 6 pins and many older computer systems have two of these connectors. One connector is coloured green and is normally used to connect a serial mouse to the system but the one we are most interested in is the purple connector which is for connecting a keyboard.

The PS2 protocol is very similar to the original IBM AT keyboard protocol but it has some additional features which were added to enable better operating system support.

Although the connector has 6 pins most keyboards only used 4 of these but sometimes the keyboard and mouse connections were combined into a single connector.

Figure 10-1 shows a simplified image of the PS2 connector.

The pins are connected as follows…

1) Data
2) No connection
3) 0V
4) +5V
5) Clock
6) No connection

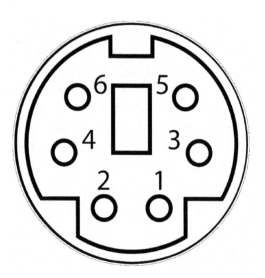

Figure 10-1 PS2 Connector

The PS2 Protocol

The PS2 port is normally a bi-directional serial data port where data is transferred in either direction synchronously using a clocked handshaking protocol. Despite the port being able to transfer data in both directions it is designed with a bias for sending data from the device (mouse or keyboard) to the system host which is usually a computer.

This makes sense as the data transfer for both of the supported devices is most frequently from device to host rather than the other ways around.

For a device such as a keyboard the host may wish to send data to perform such tasks as turning on the 'Caps Lock' light or sounding a beeper if the keyboard supports such features.

For our purposes we will ignore the ability of the PS2 device to receive data and only use the device to host mode of transmission.

The PS2 port has two power lines which provide power for the device and the ground connection also serves as the system signal ground.

It also has two signal lines which are defined as the 'Data' and 'Clock' lines and both operate in a bi-directional mode which is typically implemented through the use of open collector line drivers.

When the device wishes to transmit to the host it sends the data in an 11 bit serial data frame which consists of a start bit followed by 8 data bits and then a parity bit and finally a stop bit.

The start bit is always low and the stop bit is always high.

The protocol uses odd parity and the data is sent starting with bit 0 and ending with bit 7.

When sending data the device sets up the required bit value on the data line with the clock line at a high level and then it lowers the clock line and after a short delay it raises the clock line and sets up the next bit value. It continues to repeat this sequence until all 11 bits of the frame have been sent. The data bits are read by the host on each falling edge of the clock.

The host can stop the device from transmitting data by pulling the clock line low for a period of time and the device will see this as a command to wait at which time it will release both the clock and the data lines so that the host is then free to use them.

The device will wait until the host releases the clock line before it commences transmission. In this way the host can control the direction of the data flow and this is how the host takes control of the data line at which time it can send data to the device.

It is worth pointing out here that the device to host mode of the PS2 port is very similar to the original IBM AT keyboard protocol and with a few small modifications you could use an AT keyboard if you prefer although these are far less common than the PS2 version which I intend to use.

Figure 10-2 shows a typical example of PS2 data transfer signals.

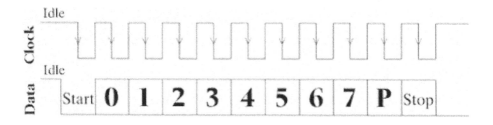

Figure 10-2 PS2 Protocol Signals

If you are interested the host to device mode of data transfer is a little more complex than the device to host and it woks in the following manner.

1) The host pulls the clock line low and waits for a few uS.
2) The host pulls the data line low (The device has halted).
3) The host releases the clock line.
4) The device toggles the clock line.
5) The host outputs a data bit as each clock pulse is received.
6) The device reads in each bit on the rising edge of the clock.
7) After the last data byte the host releases the data line.
8) The device will pull the data line low to acknowledge.
9) After a short idle time the device resumes transmission.

As I mentioned earlier we will not be using this mode of operation but you may want to implement it if you wish to control your keyboard LED's.

An advantage of the way in which the PS2 port favours device to host data transfer is that in the idle state the port is ready for data to be transferred from the device to the host and so we do not need to concern ourselves with implementing any logic to gain control of the port. We can simply start reading data after power up when the keyboard transmits it but there are a few things we need to be aware of.

If you attach a scope to the data and clock pins of the keyboard with power applied and then press a key you will see more than a single data packet being transferred each time you press and release a key. This is because a PS2 keyboard will send the key scan code in the fist data packet as soon as you press a key, assuming that the host has not taken control of the port.

If you keep the key held down then after a short delay the keyboard will start repeating the transmission of the key code packet in what is known as 'Typematic' repeat.

The keyboard will continue to resend the data packet until you release the key.

However as soon as you release the key the keyboard will send a special data value packet containing a data value of F0 followed again by a packet containing the key code data value of the last key that you pressed.

Therefore the keyboard will always send at least three data packets each time you press and release a key.

If you release the key prior to the typematic repeat starting then the three data packets will contain the following information…

1) Key scan code
2) Special code F0
3) Key scan code

Also note that if you press the Shift and another key then this is sent as separate data packets for each of the two keys.

The first is the code for whichever shift key you pressed and the second is the code for the key that you have also pressed. This is again followed by the F0 and repeat scan code as with normal single key presses.

Each key, including the two shift keys have unique scan codes which do not change when a key such as shift is pressed.

This means that the scan code for the 'A' key is the same if you have the shift key pressed or not.

That is the scan codes from the keyboard for the character 'A' is identical to the code for the character 'a' and it is up to the host machine to determine if the shift key, or other modifier key, was pressed and held prior to the character key being pressed.

Note that both the shift key and the character key must be pressed at the same time otherwise the shift key up code is sent.

Luckily our interface circuit can ignore most of this and leave the key code interpretation up to the Z80.

All the circuit will need to do is figure out how to extract the actual 8 data bits from the transmitted data packet and avoid getting 'lost' in the data stream.

It would be perfectly possible to implement a PS2 port interface by connecting the data and clock signals to the Z80 through some sort of memory mapped buffer or I/O port and then convert the data stream using software. However this would require giving up a fair amount of processing power so that the Z80 could accept keyboard input on a bit by bit, or bit bashing, basis but it is generally better to design a hardware solution if this will reduce the load on your system processor.

In this case a hardware circuit which only flags the receipt of complete character scan codes will greatly improve overall system performance with relatively little circuitry and so that is the option I selected.

PS2 Interface Design

As ever there are many ways in which we could create a circuit for reading input from a PS2 keyboard and there are also a few short cuts we could take if we wished.

The first option we have is to simply ignore the key down and special 'F0' data packet and only return the key scan code when a key has been pressed and released.

This has a few advantages but just as many disadvantages and it really comes down to what you require from your system design.

To further explain this we will look at two different ways we could read in the data from a keyboard.

The circuit shown in Figure 10-3 shows a circuit which will only return the scan code when a key is released and ignore the first two data packets.

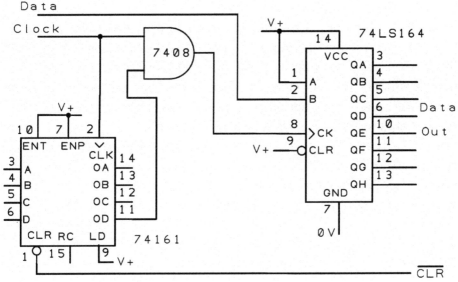

Figure 10-3 Simple PS2 Interface

This circuit is very simple and it works by counting the number of clock cycles it receives from the PS2 device following a clear signal being applied to the _CLR input.

The 'D' output on pin 11 of the 74LS161 will go high just before the first bit of the third data packet is received from the PS2 device.

This will enable the clock to the 74LS164 shift register which will then begin to clock in the data bits and it will then stop after the last data bit has been received. The Z80 is then free to read this data byte and rest the counter ready for the next transmission.

This has the advantage that it does not require any special code in the Z80 to determine which particular packet in the sequence it has received and so it can simplify the operating system requirements.

It does however suffer from a few drawbacks.

Firstly the circuit will not operate until a key is either released or held down and if held down the code produce by this circuit will be ambiguous although this can be resolved by disabling the circuit as soon as the first data byte is received.

Secondly it does not differentiate between a key being pressed and a key being released which is actually one of the major benefits in the PS2 (and previously the IBM AT) keyboard protocol. This distinction allows for complex key handling and as long as the operating system is written to take advantage of this feature it really helps to make the most of the keyboard.

For these reasons we will avoid the over simplification that this circuit provides and design a new version which will return all the keyboard scan codes to the Z80.

We will begin with the same shift register which we used in the circuit shown in Figure 10-3 and also the 74LS161 counter and we will use them as the basis for a more intelligent PS2 interface.

In order to capture all incoming device data packets we need to have a system which can determine where a data packet starts and when all the data bits have been received.

Anyone who has spent time working on vintage computer systems will be well aware that they frequently contain hardware which is designed specifically to meet some requirement of the particular computer. This was common back when the Z80 was a new device because most electronic functionality needed to be designed using discrete electronics rather than an off the shelf large scale integrated circuit which would most likely be used today.

The design of our PS2 interface will be a hardware solution specifically for our computer so it is in keeping with our goal.

It is an option to read and check the parity bit and stop bit and although this would be simple to implement in hardware I have decided to leave that to the Z80 should we decide it is needed.

We already know that each packet begins with a start bit which is followed by 8 data bits and so all we need to do is count up to 9 and the circuit shown in Figure 10-4 will do exactly that.

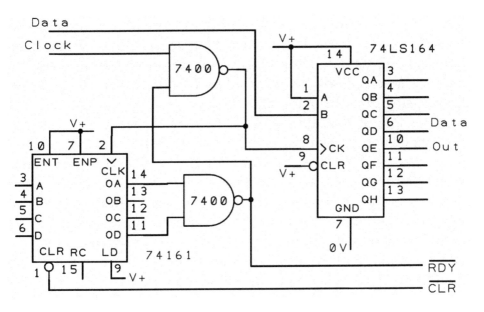

Figure 10-4 An Improved PS2 Interface

This circuit is very similar to the previous one but it works very differently and will return all the keyboard scan codes.

Following a clear applied to the _CLR input it will begin counting incoming clock pulses and also clocking the incoming data into the shift register. Notice that the shift register itself is not cleared because it will always receive 9 bits of data which will cause it to effectively overflow but the final 8 bits it receives are the required data bits. Following the 9th clock pulse the output of the NAND gate which is connected to the 'A' and 'D' outputs of the counter will go low and this will in turn disable the clock being applied to both the counter and the shift register. It will also hold the clock at its current level and prevent the data already captured by the shift register from being shifted out of position.

The output from this gate can also be used to inform the Z80 that a keyboard input has been received and that a scan code is ready.

Because the incoming clock has been disabled the remaining bits from the PS2 device will be ignored.

You may prefer to add some additional circuitry to detect and check the parity bit and stop bit and then use this to either reject the data if an error is found or just ignore the erroneous data packet.

Both of these options are relatively easy to incorporate into this design using discrete logic components.

A device such as the 74LS180 or 74LS280 parity generator / checker IC could be used to determine if the parity bit is correct.

To capture this bit you could add a flip flop such as a 74LS74 which would be reset when the _CLR signal from the Z80 is applied and its data input pin could be connected to the incoming data line. You only then need to use the output of the clock control gate to enable it and it would then capture the state of the incoming parity bit.

All you would then need to do is feed the output of this flip flop into the parity checker and its output could then be used as an error indicator to send to the Z80 or just reset the circuit in order to simply reject the data packet.

A very similar mechanism could be used for the stop bit except in this case you would enable the flip flop from the output of the first flip flop and then handle its output in the same way. The stop bit should always be high so if a low stop bit is detected then your circuit could respond as it did for a parity error and either flag up the fault or reject the data packet.

I decided against either of these approaches for error checking because there is a more fundamental check which can be made and which is probably required anyway.

As each group of three data packets is received by the Z80 it will needs to keep track of which particular packet was last received.

In my design the Z80 keyboard handler stores the scan code which is received in the first PS2 data packet and when the key is finally released it checks that the release scan code matches the key down scan code.

The Z80 can therefore determine if an error has occurred and respond accordingly.

This is not as effective in detecting all errors as the bit level errors but for our system it is more than adequate.

Naturally you can make your error checking as robust as you feel is appropriate for your own system.

Retrieving Keyboard Data

So we have now captured the PS2 scan code from the incoming keyboard data packet but the Z80 must now be able to read it.

The 74LS164 does not have tri-state output pins and so we cannot connect it directly to the CPU data bus as it would cause bus conflicts so we need to insert a suitable data buffer between it and the data bus.

Figure 10-5 shows the circuit with a data buffer added.

Notice the order of the data bits with D0 from shift register bit 7.

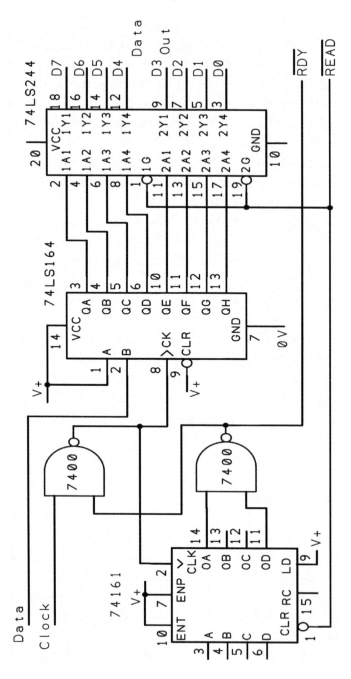

Figure 10-5 PS2 Interface with Data Buffer

The circuit shown in Figure 10-5 now includes a data buffer and so it can be connected directly to the Z80 data bus.

You may recall that I included a number of extra outputs in the bank switching circuit which I showed in Figure 8-2 in chapter 8.

We can now use one of these spare outputs to control the PS2 interface circuit.

Notice that the _CLR input has been renamed to _READ and this input is now used to enable the data buffer when the Z80 wants to read the key scan code value from the interface and this signal is also connected to the counter _CLR input and so the action of reading the scan code also resets the counter which re-enables the circuit ready for the next keyboard input. This avoids the need for the Z80 to explicitly clear this circuit following a read of the data.

Also notice that the _RDY output can also be used to inform the Z80 that a new keyboard scan code is ready to be retrieved and we will use this later to generate an interrupt whenever a key is pressed. This will make our system very responsive to keyboard input without the need to over burden it.

We have created a suitable PS2 interface with just a few logic IC's which will allow us to attach a PS2 keyboard to our system and it is still, in my opinion, keeping us close to a vintage design.

This interface can now be used to create a comprehensive keyboard input module within our system boot ROM and monitor program.

We can also create a BIOS module which can be copied to the common system RAM area by the start up code but I will come back to that later.

The design of our interface lends itself very well to providing an interrupt driven key stroke handling method because the data ready output can be used to either directly or indirectly generate CPU interrupts. The combined read and reset control line will minimise processor overhead when reading incoming keyboard data and this will also ensure that we are able to process all key strokes without slowing down the Z80.

We have even taken the burden of handling the individual data packet bits away from the Z80 which will now only be required to handle complete data bytes and it is not involved with the low level bit operations. This is the sort of functionality which is normally added by the inclusion of large scale integration devices but as you can see we have created a good balance of simplicity and functionality while using just a few simple logic devices.

I also believe that this approach is not only more interesting than resorting to large scale devices but it also gives a much better insight into the inner workings of such devices which perform the same fundamental tasks.

Another advantage we gain by avoiding the need to process each data bit as it arrives is that we relax the time constraints associated with the keyboard serial data stream. Like any serial interface the PS2 protocol has some timing restrictions for each data bit in each frame which our operating system would need to be careful to adhere to but only having to handle complete data bytes removes this issue. Or at the very least it greatly reduces the timing constraint because the Z80 will have fairly long intervals, relatively speaking, between each data byte and this will most certainly be a lot easier to program than it would be if we needed to respond to every bit at relatively short intervals.

Now that we have a working keyboard interface we need to test it and the best way to do this is to create a keyboard handling module which we can use as a starting point for keyboard operations within our operating system.

Actually I say that we have a working interface but it does have a potential flaw which we may need to deal with.

Possibly you have already spotted this but if not I will explain it in depth in the next chapter when we begin designing the computer interrupt controller circuits.

For now I will just include the schematic of a revised design for the PS2 interface and I will describe its purpose in the next chapter.

Figure 10-6 shows the revised PS2 Interface circuit.

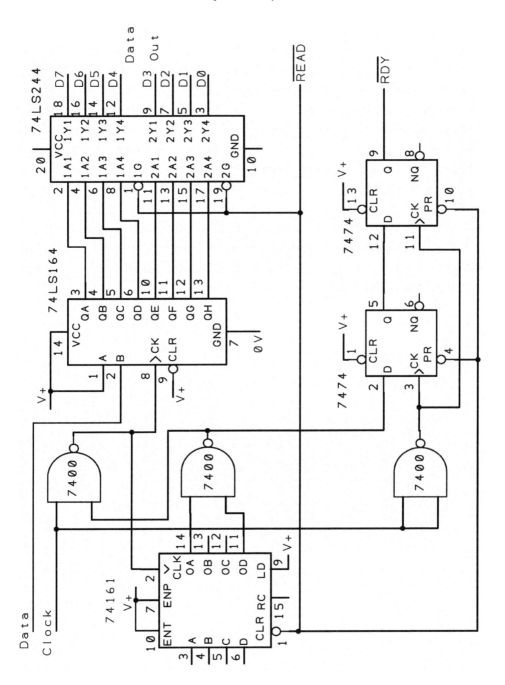

Figure 10-6 PS2 Improved PS2 Interface Circuit

It is now time to add our first interrupt routine to our test code so that we can properly test the keyboard and also determine if there are any timing constraints which need to be considered when processing the key strokes. I will not go as far as creating a key stroke buffer at this time although we will need to add one when writing the operating system. For now we will create a simple software system which prepares the interrupt handler and responds to the PS2 interface so that we can read and process incoming keyboard key strokes.

Unfortunately before we can do this we need to add the actual interrupt handling mechanism for our computer and in the next chapter we will design a suitable Z80 mode 2 interrupt controller circuit for our project.

ॐ ☯ ॐ

Chapter 11 - Z80 Interrupts

Z80 Interrupts

When small computer systems first started to appear it fell on the emerging field of software engineering to make the best use of them and apply them to practical applications. These engineers soon began to encounter problems as system designs began to become more demanding and complex. Although these new devices offered almost unlimited scope for processing information and controlling machines there was an issue which became increasingly difficult to overcome. This problem was one of scheduling events within a system when more than a single task needed to be handled at the same time. The processors did not really handle these multiple tasks simultaneously but instead they jumped from one to the other at high speed to give the appearance of concurrent operation.

The difficulty in designing such systems was how to share the processing time available in such a way that the system provided the required responsiveness. This became even more of a design nightmare as system speeds increased and the processors were expected to deal with ever increasing work loads.

For example if a software module was performing a specific operation which may take some time to complete but another part of the system needed accurately timed software responses then how could both of these tasks be accomplished?

These timing constraints became even more of a problem to reconcile as more tasks were added to a design.

Interfacing and controlling hardware added to the problem because mechanical systems operate at vastly different speeds compared to a microprocessor.

Waiting until one task had completed before moving on to the next one would work for non critical applications but not for operations which required quick responses from the processor.

Take a keyboard handler for example and consider how frustrating and difficult it would be to use a computer which had random delays each time you pressed a key before it responded or a real time clock which 'ticked' at random speeds.

Luckily a solution was quickly found to this sticky problem and it is one that transformed the way microprocessors could be used and is one of the most powerful tools in any software design engineers' arsenal.

I am of course talking about the microprocessor *INTERRUPT*.

Interrupts are so important to the efficient operation of a computer system that modern microcontrollers usually have many levels of interrupts with programmable priorities. The interrupts offered by the Z80 are very basic compared to their modern counterparts but they were still an improvement on the Z80's predecessor and allowed the Z80 to be used in systems where multiple tasks needed to be handled at the same time and yet which may have tight time constraints.

I should point out here that multi tasking and time sharing within computer systems was around long before the Z80 but devices such as the Z80 made extremely good use of interrupts.

If you are not familiar with the concepts of microprocessor interrupts then I strongly advise spending some time investigating this topic as it is a fascinating aspect of processor operation and getting comfortable with interrupts as part of system design can really help you in designing well behaved software systems.

One of the biggest advances when microprocessors were introduced was the ability to jump from one part of the running code to another based on the outcome of a previous operation.

For example you can branch to a subroutine if a counter variable reaches a value of zero. Without this ability to branch to different addresses the processor would only be able to execute instructions in the order they were present in its memory and this would make them very restrictive.

The jumps and branches effectively allowed the microprocessors to make decisions and alter course accordingly.

The interrupt mechanism adds another level of operation to a microprocessor by allowing it to instantly (almost) stop what it is currently doing and go off to complete another task before resuming where it left off.

Earlier I gave the example of input from a keyboard causing problems if the processor did not respond quickly each time you press a key but by using interrupts the processor can stop what it is currently doing as soon as a key is pressed and it can do whatever it needs to with the incoming key data.

Once it has completed the key handling task it can go back to whatever it was doing before you pressed the key as if nothing had happened.

This means that there will be no noticeable delay when you press a key irrespective of the task currently being performed by the processor. This does of course assume that the system software has been programmed to handle the interrupt properly.

Early processors tended to have very rudimentary interrupt handling capability but as the importance of this processor feature was recognised the interrupt handling mechanism was greatly improved to provide multiple levels of interrupt. This allows one interrupt to interrupt another depending on which is more important. There are also specific hardware linked interrupts where different hardware devices can generate different interrupts which makes the task of system software development very much easier.

If you have developed any embedded systems then you are almost certainly very familiar with interrupts and appreciate how vital they are to system design and performance. You are also most likely familiar with the vast variety of interrupt systems and how some systems work better in some circumstances than others.

The Z80 interrupts were relatively simple but they did offer a much greater degree of flexibility than was typically available from its competitors of the time.

In fact the Z80 provides three different modes of interrupt operation and I will very briefly describe them here but if you want to know more about these then once again I would suggest consulting the Zilog Z80 user manual.

Interrupt Mode 0

In interrupt mode 0 the interrupting device must lower the '_INT' pin on the Z80 and put a valid instruction opcode onto the data bus. The Z80 will respond by executing this instruction and it will then continue to fetch and execute instructions from that point until the program code returns at the end of the interrupt handler. This is similar to the way a function call works except that the jump to the required code is created by the interrupt mechanism and the first instruction is provided by the device.

To explicitly enter this interrupt mode you must include the IM0 instruction early in your program code. Once you have selected this interrupt mode it is a bad idea to change it later in the code as this can lead to unstable system operation and the result will most likely be a system crash.

This is true for all three interrupt modes.

Interrupt Mode 1

In this mode the Z80 will complete the instruction it is currently processing and then branch to address 0038h if the '_INT' pin was lowered by an interrupting device.

The interrupt handling code entry point must be located at this address although this could of course simply be a jump to another address. Because this mode only has a single interrupt vector address it is up to the programmer to include any code required in order to determine which device triggered the interrupt if more than one device in the system is connected to the interrupt pin.

Execution of the interrupt handler will continue until a return from interrupt instruction is encountered at which time the Z80 will continue from the instruction immediately after the one it had completed when the interrupt was generated.

This mode of interrupt is relatively simple to set up although it can lead to inefficient handling of multiple interrupts due to the overhead required to determine the source of each interrupt.

For this reason it is not generally a good choice for systems which will generate many interrupts from different sources.

It is however a good choice for simple systems which only have a limited number of potential interrupts.

To explicitly enter this interrupt mode you must include the IM1 instruction early in your program code.

Interrupt Mode 2

This interrupt mode is the most complex of the three but also by far the most powerful and is the most frequently selected in modern systems where the large scale Z80 support chips I mentioned earlier are in use.

In this mode the device which generates the interrupt must put a vector address onto the Z80 data bus. The Z80 will use this vector as the lower 8 bits of an interrupt table lookup address and it will obtain the upper 8 bits of the required 16 bit address from its internal 'I' (Interrupt) register. It will then load the 16 bit value located at this address into the 'PC' register and this will cause the Z80 to branch to the appropriate interrupt handler.

Prior to jumping to the handler it will of course push the return address onto the stack so that program operation can continue once the interrupt handler has finished its task.

This multi-vector mechanism allows the programmer to setup an interrupt vector table and use the 'I' register to locate it in memory. Each device can then have its own interrupt handler which it can select when it generates the interrupt although it does have the added complication of requiring that the interrupting device must be able to provide the required lower 8 bits of the interrupt table lookup address.

For this reason this interrupt mode is most suited to the use of the large scale Z80 support devices which are able to automatically place a programmable vector onto the data bus when they want to trigger an interrupt. It is not particularly suitable for simple hardware designs although not especially difficult to implement using a few simple circuits.

To explicitly enter this interrupt mode you must include the IM2 instruction early in your program code.

For all three interrupt modes there are a few things which must be prepared before they can be used.

The first of these is required because in response to any interrupt the Z80 will automatically push some information onto the stack. It must do this so that it is able to successfully return from the interrupt and continue with what it was doing. Without saving its current 'PC' then it would have no idea where to go at the end of the interrupt handler and this is a situation which processors do not like at all.

It is up to the programmer to save any register(s) which may be altered during the interrupt although the Z80 does offer a very easy way to save and restore all registers using just a couple of instructions but I will come back to that in a later chapter.

Because the Z80, and possibly the programmer, will need to make use of the stack in order to handle interrupts then we will of course need to initialise the stack prior to any interrupt being generated.

This is simply a matter of deciding where the stack will reside in memory and loading the 'SP' register with the top of the stack memory address but bear in mind that this address will need to be available irrespective of the currently selected bank.

For example if your available memory ends at EFFF then you may want to set the 'SP' register to EFFF. The stack 'grows' down in memory as values are added so you must leave enough space below it for the maximum size your stack will use.

You then need to set the required interrupt mode using the appropriate instruction (IM0, IM1 or IM2).

The interrupt handlers, and possibly vector table if you are using mode 2, will need to be created and present at the appropriate memory addresses.

Finally interrupts must be enabled using the EI instruction.

The Z80 should then be able to process interrupts as they are triggered without any noticeable delays.

So an important decision we must now make is which interrupt mode our JMZ computer system will use.

After we have selected a particular interrupt mode it is not really practical to change this once the system has been started as this will almost certainly lead to erratic operation of the system.

Mode 0 is not really suitable for our application because it requires some additional hardware and does not really provide any advantage to us. In fact this mode is only present in the Z80 to make the processor backwardly compatible with its predecessor.

Mode 2 may be over complex for our system because this would also require that we add additional hardware in order that the various devices could place the required interrupt vector onto the data bus each time they wanted to generate an interrupt. While this works very well and is simple to implement in a system which is making use of the large scale Z80 support devices it would add some complexity to our discrete design. There is no doubt that being able to vector interrupts to specific handlers based on which device generated the interrupt would be useful but the added overhead in hardware design complexity makes this a far less attractive proposition.

On the other hand the mode 1 interrupt mechanism would only require a simple OR gate arrangement in hardware for multiple devices to be able to generate interrupts and we can easily have each device set a hardware control line to indicate that it is responsible for the request. The initial interrupt handler could then poll the various control lines in order to determine which handler to call.

This seems to be a good option for interrupt mode as it is the simplest to design although it does have a few draw backs.

Interrupt Mode Selection

I stated above that mode 2 interrupts were not really needed in a simple computer such as the one we are designing here but hopefully this computer will be the starting point for many more advanced machines as the design is expanded. I also stated that interrupts become increasingly important as systems become more complex and so it would possibly be a mistake to select either mode 0 or even mode 1 interrupts for our design because this would almost certainly create limitations or complications later as additions are made to the initial design.

I must also bear in mind that I am trying to demonstrate how to design a Z80 computer system and so trying to avoid commonly used techniques may make this book less useful or interesting.

I have therefore decided to select the mode 2 interrupt option and this will not only provide much more flexibility for our JMZ computer but it will also be interesting to design the circuits required in order to implement this type of interrupt handler.

This choice will add a few components to the design because we are not intending to use the large scale support devices which simplify the mode 2 interfacing but it is not as complicated to add support for this feature as it may sound.

As with all discrete logic designs the secret is to keep each circuit as simple as possible because this in turn tends to make other parts of the system less complex as well.

The description of the Z80 mode 2 interrupt mechanism may sound very complicated but the Z80 designers did a fantastic job in the way they implemented this feature and this makes our job much easier.

I will now recap on what functionality we must now add and then we will go on to design a discrete logic circuit which will provide our system with mode 2 interrupts.

Mode 2 Interrupt Sequence

For our computer we will be using the single '_INT ' input pin of the Z80 to request interrupt handling from the Z80. There are actually a few additional ways to generate interrupts when using a Z80 which make use of the _BUSRQ and _NMI inputs of the Z80 but we will not need to use them in our design.

These two additional options can be used to provide extra levels of interrupt control but the circuit we will design should allow us to generate interrupts and it will also include a hardware priority control mechanism to deal with situations where more than one device generates an interrupt at the same time.

In mode 2 interrupt operation when a device wishes to generate an interrupt it pulls the '_INT' pin of the Z80 low and this can occur asynchronously to the Z80 instruction execution.

Lowering the '_INT' pin does not therefore generate an immediate interrupt because the Z80 will complete processing the current instruction before it checks the state of the '_INT' pin.

It actually checks the level on this pin on the rising clock edge of the last clock 'T' cycle in the current instruction sequence.

The device wanting to interrupt the processor must now wait until the Z80 gives it permission to continue with the request before it does anything else.

Towards the end of the current instruction the Z80 will see that the '_INT' pin is low and when it finishes the instruction it will then perform a few checks before it authorises the interrupting device to continue with its interrupt request.

Firstly the Z80 checks that interrupts are enabled because we are using the '_INT' input which can be masked, or disabled, by the programmer using the DI instruction. It must be enabled with the EI instruction or the Z80 will simply ignore any interrupt requests.

Assuming that interrupts are enabled the Z80 will then check that a
_BUSRQ is not active and then it will check that the _NMI is not
active as both of these have a higher priority than the _INT
controlled interrupt.

As we will not be using either _BUSRQ or _NMI they will not be
active and so in our system the Z80 will continue as long as
interrupts are enabled.

The Z80 will then begin a special type of M1 cycle which is similar
to the instruction fetch M1 cycle except that the _IORQ line is taken
low instead of the _RD line.

Figure 11-1 shows the interrupt timing sequence.

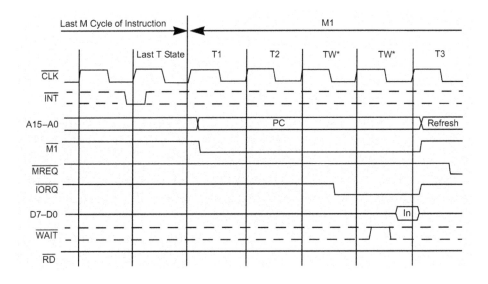

Figure 11-1 Interrupt Timing Sequence

We can use this special M1 cycle to inform the interrupting device
that it can now continue with its request and it will do so by placing
its interrupt vector onto the Z80 data bus.

It must do this before the _IORQ line goes high again because that is the point at which the Z80 reads the vector from the data bus. There is however plenty of time for the device to do this because the Z80 automatically inserts 2 wait states in the T2 phase of the interrupt specific M1 cycle (Shown as TW*).

Once the Z80 has read the 8 bit vector from the data bus it retrieves the 8 bit value currently stored in its internal 'I' register and it combines the two 8 bit values to create a single 16 bit lookup address which it can use to read the interrupt handler vector from the interrupt vector table.

It then pushes the current PC onto the stack so that it knows where to go when the interrupt handler returns.

The 16 bit lookup address is then used as the source address for reading a 16 bit interrupt handler vector address and the Z80 branches to this interrupt handler address by loading it into the PC register and it then begins executing code starting at that address.

It continues executing code until a return from interrupt instruction (RETI) is encountered at which point it pops the saved PC from the stack and code execution continues from the instruction immediately after the instruction during which the interrupt was originally flagged.

Note that it is up to the programmer to save any registers which may be modified by the interrupt handler and failure to do this will almost certainly result in a system crash.

The programmer must also re-enable interrupts using the EI instruction as the Z80 disables maskable interrupts in response to the interrupt request.

As you can see this is a very powerful mechanism which gives us a great deal of control over which interrupt handler is associated with each device and where in memory these can reside.

It also has the advantage in a system such as ours in that the interrupt table and all the interrupt handlers can be situated in the common RAM area rather than in the ROM.

This means that the interrupts can operate without needing to switch the memory bank which makes the system much more efficient.

So now we know what our circuit must be able to accomplish we need to actually design it and ensure that it can not only pass the required interrupt vectors to the Z80 but that it can also schedule interrupts which may occur at the same time based on an interrupt priority mechanism.

This may sound extremely complicated but it is surprisingly easy to design a discrete logic based circuit which is able to provide this complicated set of requirements, so lets get started.

Each device that needs to generate an interrupt will also be assigned an interrupt priority and as the system designers it is our responsibility to determine which priority each device is allocated. This is required so that the system knows how to handle situations where two or more interrupts happen at the same time.

Higher priority, or more time critical, interrupts will be processed first followed by the next lowest priority interrupt and so on until all pending interrupts have been serviced.

If interrupts occur faster than the Z80 is able to process them the system should generate a 1202 alarm. Not really that is just a bit of fun, in reality the system is likely to crash in such cases.

There is a very simple way to create a circuit which will provide multiple inputs and also assign each of these inputs incremental levels of priority. We will implement this using a priority encoder and the device I selected is the 74LS148 which has 8 inputs and assigns incrementally higher priorities to each of these inputs.

It also has a couple of additional features which will make our design less complex by avoiding the need to add separate logic.

The first of these features is an additional output which goes low whenever one of the inputs is driven low and we can use this output to directly drive the '_INT' pin of the Z80.

The second useful feature is that the 74LS148 encodes the inputs as a 3 bit binary output although this is not a combination of multiple inputs but is the value which represents the current highest priority input. This means that if two or more of the inputs are driven low at the same time then the output bits will be set to a value representing the active input which has the highest priority.

This device can therefore be used by up to 8 devices to generate priority based interrupts and also provide a different interrupt vector for each along with driving the Z80 interrupt input.

Figure 11-2 shows how we can arrange this circuit.

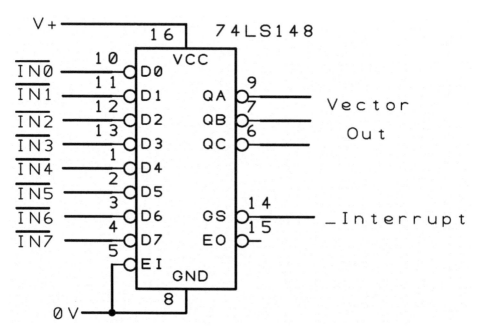

Figure 11-2 Priority Encoder

The interrupts from each device are connected to one of the _INx inputs and the resulting output vector then appears on the vector out pins while at the same time the _Interrupt output goes low.

Note that the inputs to this circuit are active low and the outputs use low level logic so we need to invert the outputs.

This circuit gives us a total of 8 interrupts and any unused inputs must be tied to V+ to ensure that the correct vector is produced.

The interrupt priority starts with _IN0 which has the lowest priority and _IN7 has the highest priority.

Unfortunately the 74LS148 does not have tri-state output pins so we cannot connect it directly to the Z80 data bus as this would create bus contention. In addition it only provides three output lines and we need to drive all 8 of the Z80 data bus lines when we output the interrupt vector although bit 0 will always be set to a '0'.

Bit 0 will always be set to '0' because the required vectors are 16 bits which requires two bytes for each so we must increment the applied vector addresses 2 addresses for each vector.

The first vector (in binary) will be 00000000

The second 00000010

The third 00000100

And so on.

If you look at the 74LS148 datasheet you will also notice that it has inverted outputs which ideally we would like to re-invert as this would make our addressing logic easier.

Once again there is a very simple solution to all three of these issues and we can deal with all of them with the addition of one more logic device.

In this case we will add a 74LS240 octal inverting buffer as this will allow us to control when the vector is allowed onto the data bus and it will also provide all 8 data lines if we tie the unused inputs to appropriate levels.

Finally it will invert the output from the priority encoder to give us the preferred logic levels to send to the Z80.

Figure 11-3 shows the interrupt circuit with this buffer added.

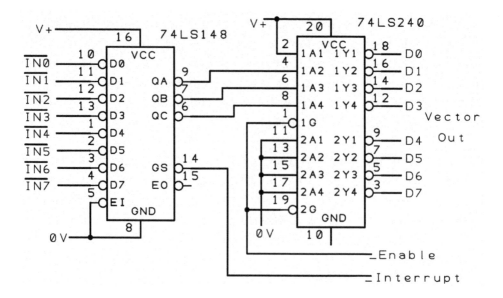

Figure 11-3 Interrupt Data Buffer

Now that we have the vector generation in place along with a buffer the last piece in this particular puzzle is a means to control the tri-state buffer so that it only outputs the interrupt vector onto the data bus when it is required by the Z80.

If you look at the timing diagram in Figure 11-1 you will see that the Z80 already provides us with most of what we need in order to accomplish this.

As I mentioned earlier the Z80 generates this special M1 cycle in response to the interrupt request and a unique feature of this cycle is that the _M1 and _IORQ lines are both low at the same time and this is the only time we see this combination. Also notice that the Z80 reads the interrupt vector at the end of the extended T2 phase of this cycle. We can therefore make use of the _M1 and _IORQ lines to control the interrupt vector buffer by only enabling this buffer if neither _M1 OR _IORQ is high.

A note here which may help anyone new to this sort of design.

In the previous sentence I wrote...
"if neither _M1 OR _IORQ is high"
This may sound like an odd way of stating this condition but when you are designing logic based circuits it is often easier to think in terms of the required logic rather than grammatically correct language. In this case it has given us the exact solution to our design requirement which is to add an 'OR' gate as is clearly indicated by the phrase " if neither _M1 *OR* _IORQ is high".

By adding this OR gate we have the entire circuit designed and this simple circuit will provide up to 8 priority controlled interrupt channels each of which will provide its own 8 bit vector and output these vectors onto the data bus at the required time.
You will have noticed in the schematic shown in Figure 11-3 that I have connected the three encoder outputs to data lines D1, D2 and D3 and not D0, D1 and D2 and also that D0 is always '0'.
This is because each full 16 bit interrupt vector actually occupies two address spaces and by connecting the encoder in this manner we increment by two addresses at a time and this will allow us to use the resulting 16 bit address directly to load the correct 16 bit interrupt vector from the interrupt table.
Also notice that the upper 4 bits of the vector applied to the data bus are set to give a value of 'F'. The inputs are connected to 0V but as the buffer inverts then we end up with a value of 1111.
Once again this is done to simplify our software task and system configuration.
We ideally want to place the interrupt vector table at the top of a block of memory and we define the memory block by loading the upper 8 bits of its address into the Z80 'I' register.
As we only wish to use a block of 8 interrupt vectors we can avoid wasted memory space by pushing the table up to the top of the memory block if we set the unused bits of the lower byte to 1's.

For example
I = EF00
Device vectors = F0, F2, F4, F6, F8, FA, FC, FE

When we combine these then the address for each 16 bit entry in the table becomes...
EFF0, EFF2, EFF4, EFF6, EFF8, EFFA, EFFC, EFFE

This makes very efficient use of the memory but if the vectors did not have the unused bits set the addresses would be...
EF00, EF02, EF04, EF06, EF08, EF0A, EF0C, EF0E
This would result in a small block of unused memory and although we could use it for other purposes it is always best to simplify things where possible. In this case we have minimised the memory space occupied by the interrupt vector table without the need to make any special provisions in our software design.
The full circuit for our interrupt handler is shown in Figure 11-4.

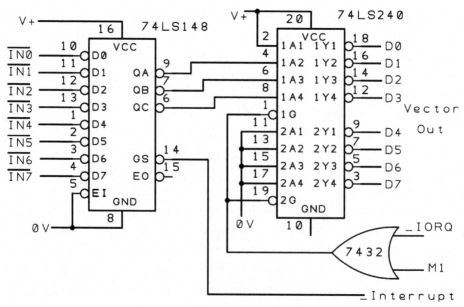

Figure 11-4 Interrupt Handler Circuit

We now have a mode 2 interrupt system which will make our system very flexible and also make writing the interrupt handlers much easier by allowing us to put both the vector table and the handlers themselves into common RAM and so avoid any bank switching problems.
It has only cost us a few additional logic devices and so it is well worth the extra effort.

Now that we have the interrupt system in place we can go ahead and write some software to test it and we will begin by writing a very simple handler for the keyboard.
We will however need to add some code to properly initialise the system so that it can process mode 2 interrupts.

Example Mode 2 Interrupt Table

Table 11-1 below shows an example of a Z80 mode 2 interrupt table. The values in this table are just random values which I made up for the sake of this explanation.

Interrupt	Device	Table	Table Value
7	0E	E00E / E00F	B234
6	0C	E00C / E00D	5678
5	0A	E00A / E00B	C123
4	08	E008 / E009	BA22
3	06	E006 / E007	A002
2	04	E004 / E005	A0FF
1	02	E002 / E003	D992
0	00	E000 / E001	CE00

Table 11-1 Example Z80 Mode 2 Interrupt Table

In this example we would need to load the Z80 'I' register with a value of E0h because as you can see this is the most significant byte of the table address which begins at E000h.

Any peripheral device connected to the interrupt control circuit would trigger the following sequence of events.

1) Device generates the interrupt by pulling line low
2) Z80 gives permission for device to continue with M1 cycle
3) Interrupting Device places vector onto data bus
4) Z80 reads this and combines it with the value in its I register
5) Z80 Pushes current program counter onto stack
6) Z80 loads vector address into PC causing a jump to handler
7) Handler does its thing, including removing cause of interrupt
8) Handler returns when it has finished
9) Z80 pops PC and continues from where it left off

For our first keyboard test program we will just read keyboard key strokes and echo the received data directly to the display.

We will need to connect together the CPU module, Video module, PS2 interface and Interrupt Controller circuits.

The data ready output of the PS2 interface can be connected directly to the _IN1 interrupt controller pin although we may need to move this later to change the keyboard interrupt priority.

We can then connect the read control line of the PS2 interface to the memory mapped _IOCE line from the memory map decoder circuit. This line will go low any time we try to read or write to the memory mapped IO block and although we will need to add some additional decoding later we can use this as it is for now.

All we then have to do in order to read in the key stroke data byte is to read from any address in the IO block range which begins at 2000h in bank 1. We will most likely move this to a simple IO port once we have determined that it works as it should so that we can read key strokes without needing to switch banks.

If you recall the action of reading the data byte will also reset the PS2 interface circuit so we do not need to do this explicitly in our handler and also the PS2 interface is immediately available to accept the next keystroke input from the keyboard while we are processing the current one.

This sort of overlapping data handling design will make maximum use of our hardware design which was after all designed to make life easier for our Z80.

Next we need to create a suitable test program to determine if all the parts we have designed so far will play well together.

The code will need to perform a bit of preparation work before the Z80 can process the interrupts but it will also demonstrate how some of our system initialisation code will need to be arranged.

The code will need to perform the following steps...

    1)   Jump over the initial data block.
    2)   Set interrupt mode 2
    3)   Initialise the stack (Top of RAM is F7FE)
    4)   Clear video RAM (F800 – FFFF)
    5)   Initialise the video RAM pointer to F800
    6)   Create the interrupt vector table
    7)   Enable interrupts
    8)   Loop indefinitely waiting for an interrupt

We will also need to create the actual interrupt handler and copy it to the correct address which we will include in the interrupt vector table entry for the _IN1 interrupt.

All we will do for now is to wait for an interrupt and then vector to the handler. The handler will read the key stroke byte from the PS2 interface and copy it to video RAM and then increment the video RAM pointer.

It will also need to clear the interrupt to prevent an infinite interrupt loop.

When the Z80 returns from the interrupt it will be back in the infinite wait loop and ready for the next interrupt, and hopefully the typed character will have appeared on the display.

We will use a memory location to store our video pointer as this is good programming practice and will avoid any issues which would be caused in an interrupt handler if we tried to use a register for this purpose.

This code will run within the test ROM but the actual interrupt table and handlers will need to be placed into common RAM.

Test Program 4

```
;---------------- SYSTEM EQUATES ----------------------
RAMTOP              EQU F7EFh   ;Top of RAM
INT_TABLE           EQU F7F0h   ;Vector Table (F7F0-F7FF)
STACK               EQU E7EFh   ;Stack
VIDEO_RAM           EQU F800h   ;Start of video RAM
NON_VOLATILE        EQU FED8h   ;Start of non volatile RAM
ASCII_TABLE         EQU 0500h   ;ASCII table (PS2 index)
KB_HANDLER          EQU 0800h   ;Keyboard INT handler

  JP START                      ;Jump to start of code

TEXT1 DB 'H','E','L','L','O' ;Text

START:
        DI
        IM    2                 ;Set interrupt mode 2
        LD    A,F7h             ;Load I register
        LD    I,A
        LD    HL,STACK          ;Initialise stack register
        LD    SP,HL
        LD    HL,KB_HANDLER     ;Initialise interrupt table
        LD    (INT_TABLE + 2),HL
        LD    HL,VIDEO_RAM      ;Clear video RAM
        LD    C,08h             ;Load Count = 1920
CVL0: LD    B,F0h               ;240 x 8
CVL1: LD    (HL),20h            ;Clear this byte
        INC   HL
        DJNZ  CVL1
```

260

```
        DEC   C
        JP    NZ,CVL0
        EI                          ;Enable interrupts
LOOP:
        NOP
        JP LOOP


;------------ ASCII CHARACTER LOOKUP TABLE --------------
;PS2 scan code to ASCII
        ORG 0500h
;ASCII_TABLE:
        DB 00h,00h,00h,00h,00h,00h,00h,00h
        DB 00h,00h,00h,00h,00h,0Bh,60h,00h
        DB 00h,00h,00h,00h,00h,71h,31h,00h
        DB 00h,00h,7Ah,73h,61h,77h,32h,00h
        DB 00h,63h,78h,64h,65h,34h,33h,00h
ONLY 4 Lines of 32 shown


;-------------- KEYBOARD INTERRUPT HANDLER --------------
;KB_HANDLER
;On entry A = PS2 scan code
        ORG 0800h
KEY_INT_HANDLER:

        PUSH  HL
        PUSH  BC
        LD    B,20h                 ;Temporary Delay
LPP:    DJNZ  LPP

        IN    A,(1)                 ;Read Scan code from PS2

        LD    L,A                   ;Look up ASCII character
        LD    H,0
        LD    DE,ASCII_TABLE
        ADD   HL,DE
        LD    A,(HL)
        LD    HL,(VIDEO_PTR)        ;Load VIDEO_PTR
        LD    (HL),A                ;Save current char to video
        INC   HL                    ;Increment pointer
        LD    (VIDEO_PTR),HL        ;Save pointer to RAM
        POP   BC
        POP   HL
        EI
        RETI
```

If you compile this code and program a ROM it can be used to test the PS2 interface and the interrupt control system although it is of course far from being complete.

If everything is working correctly then each time you press a key you should see three characters appear on the screen.

These are the key down character followed by the special key up character and finally the key character again.

Design Flaw or Feature

One of the tricky aspects in designing vintage electronics and especially a project like this where we are intentionally avoiding the use of large scale devices in favour of discrete logic is in minimising component count.

It is always important to fully understand how each circuit will operate when it is in the system and not just a stand alone module and a very good example of this is the PS2 interface which we designed in the previous chapter.

When I designed this circuit it originally began life as a more complex circuit but I was able to simplify it and remove a few components due to the way I intended to use it in this design. As this topic is so important in vintage electronics design I decided to add this short section in order to explain my thinking for this part of the design although I apply a similar thought process to all aspects of design work.

In figure 10-5 shown in the previous chapter we see the schematic for the PS2 interface circuit and its task is to take incoming serial data from the keyboard and convert it into parallel 8 bit data which the Z80 can make use of.

It also generates an interrupt signal which is fed into the interrupt control circuit which we designed in this chapter.

It does however have what could be considered a serious flaw if you try to use it without proper consideration.

For anyone interested you may want to stop reading here and look closely at the circuit in Figure 10-5 along with the test program 4 listing to see if you can figure out the problem before proceeding.

The Problem

The problem is a subtle but important timing issue caused by the big difference in operation speed between the PS2 keyboard and the Z80 system.

When a key is pressed on the keyboard it begins sending an 11 bit serial data stream to the PS2 interface but it does this at a fairly low clock frequency. This clock frequency varies between different keyboards as it is generally derived from simple RC oscillators within the keyboard.

In general the clock frequency is between 5kHz and 25Khz and this equates to a clock period which is between 40uS and 200uS.

This is of course very slow compared to the Z80 execution speed of around 1 instruction every 4 uS (although this also varies).

Our PS2 interface circuit generates the interrupt signal output immediately after the 9th bit of the 11 bit data packet has been received and it ignores the remaining parity and stop bits.

Where the problem arises is in the rapid response of the Z80 to the interrupt and depending on what operations the keyboard interrupt handler needs to complete it may well read the PS2 data port before the last bit of the serial stream has arrived and you no doubt recall that this will reset the interface and enable it to resume counting clock pulses.

The reason this causes a problem becomes clear when you examine the signals which control the PS2 interface circuit.

Figure 11-5 shows how these signals look.

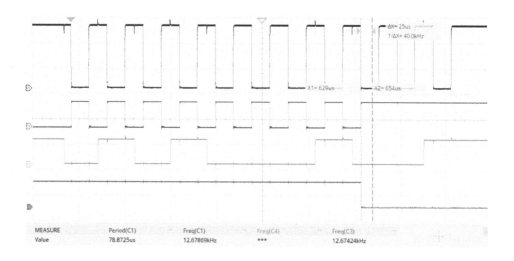

Figure 11-5 PS2 Interface Signal Overlap

In this diagram the top trace is the PS2 clock signal, the second trace is the gated clock signal and trace three is the PS2 data line. The bottom trace is the data ready signal and this goes low as soon as the last data bit has been clocked into the shift register.

As this occurs before the end of the 11 bit data stream then the PS2 interface circuit will become active before the last clock cycle and further clock cycles in this packet will then increment the PS2 interface counter.

The result will be that the counter value does not begin at zero for the next keyboard data packet and so the data shifted into the shift register when the counter next reaches a value of 9 will be incorrect. This error will accumulate as each packet is received

In Figure 11-6 the first vertical cursor line is placed at the point where the interface generates the interrupt and the second cursor line is position approximately where the Z80 reads the data port and re-enables the interface in the keyboard interrupt handler.

As you can see this is well before the final PS2 clock cycle and this would create a serious system fault.

264

Figure 11-6 shows the actual interrupt line on the bottom trace and you can see how quickly the interrupt resets the interface and how this happens well before the completion of the PS2 data packet.

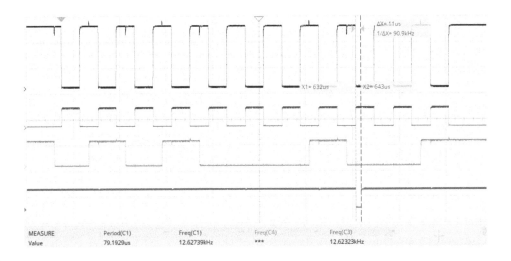

Figure 11-6 PS2 Interface Interrupt Error

In this case there are actually two additional clock cycles which occur after the PS2 interface circuit has been re-enabled with the effect of clocking the interface counter to a value of 2 prior to the end of this data packet.

Things are however not as bad as they seem and this is such a common issue in this type of design that I designed the circuit specifically with this in mind.

If you look back at the test program you will notice that the interrupt handler has the following lines close to its start.

```
        LD B,20h              ;Temporary Delay
LPP:    DJNZ LPP
```

These lines of code will be removed once the complete interrupt handler has been finished but they currently push the PS2 data 'IN' instruction within the interrupt handler forward a number of clock cycles to the position it will occupy once the handler is fully functional. This extends its execution time from the 16uS shown in Figures 11-6 and 11-7 to around 190uS which is long enough to place the 'IN' instruction after the arrival of the final PS2 clock edge. This completely removes the problem and the circuit will function exactly as intended but to do this I actually started by writing the complete interrupt handler before I designed the interface circuit so that I fully understood the timing constraints.

I will show the complete interrupt handler in a later chapter.

The interrupt handler I have created does not carry out many operations and for the most part it simply reads the incoming data bytes from the PS2 interface and converts them into ASCII characters or flags them as commands. It then stores the received character in a buffer and also stores a flags byte which the main program can use to keep track of the keyboard status and the availability of any pending characters.

There is of course a potential problem if you wish to reduce the tasks which are performed by the interrupt handler and which would result in a shorter execution time. With the simple interface circuit shown the minimum duration for the interrupt to 'IN' instruction in the handler is around 190uS and although this is fairly short it would be very easy to create a handler which completes in less time than this.

To allow for the creation of shorter keyboard interrupt handlers by anyone wanting to write their own operating system I modified the PS2 interface circuit so that this period could be reduced to as little as 25 uS if required. It is up to you which version of the interface circuit you use and your choice may depend on the interrupt handler code you intend to write but I advice giving this some consideration prior to building your system.

Figure 10-6 in the previous chapter shows the revised PS2 interface circuit with the extended ready signal trigger point.

This circuit is based on a 74LS74 dual flip flop which is connected as a simple clock divider circuit.

Figure 11-7 shows the timing of the signals of the revised circuit.

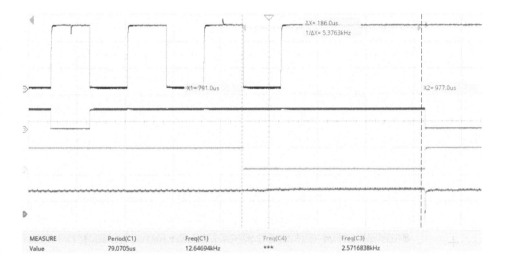

Figure 11-7 PS2 Interface Interrupt Error

The first flip flop is enabled once the 8 bit data byte has been received and the two flip flops then count two additional PS2 clock cycles before triggering the interrupt output.

The effect of this is to push the timing of the interrupt signal to half a clock cycle from the end of the data packet and this in turn means that the Z80 is free to read the PS2 data and re-enable the interrupts within approximately 25 uS of the interrupt being generated.

The top trace in this image shows the PS2 clock and the bottom trace shows the data _READ line which is also used to reset the interface circuit. The third trace down shows the data ready output signal produced by the interface.

As you can see the interrupt is reset well after the end of the last PS2 clock signal and so there is no danger that the interface counter will be inadvertently incremented.

In this image the interrupt period is around 190 uS but as you can see this time could be reduced significantly and still allow plenty of time for the interface to complete the current data packet before being reset.

Interrupt Control

Version 3 of the JMZ main CPU board has a number of jumpers which allow the general interrupt lines to be enabled. However the dedicated interrupts for the PS2 keyboard and RS232 interface are always enabled.

Although I will not be adding interrupt control to the main board in this book it would be a very useful addition to include firmware controlled interrupt enable and disable for each interrupt so that each level of interrupt could be disabled when not required.

This would only need 8 gates and an 8 bit register or latch which could be controlled through one of the OUT ports.

The hardware jumpers could then be removed and the Z80 would have total bit level control over each interrupt source.

Although I will not be including this addition to the version of the system I am showing in this book I thought you may be interested in seeing how simple such an addition would be.

What is required is the addition of a circuit which would allow the Z80 to individually enable or disable the individual interrupt lines.

Figure 11-8 shows the circuit for firmware control of the individual interrupts.

Note that the latch has inverting outputs.

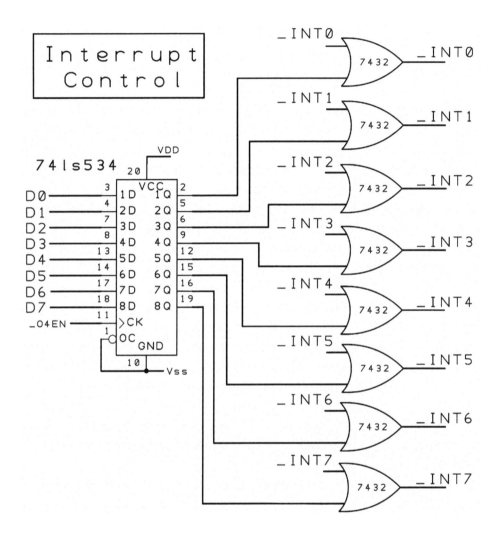

Figure 11-8 Interrupt Control Circuit

To control the individual interrupt lines all that would be needed is to write the required bit mask value to the latch. In the circuit shown I have connected the control latch to output port control bit 4 and so the required interrupt control bit mask can simply be written to output port 4.

For example the instruction

OUT (04),A

Would write the value in the Z80 A register to the interrupt control register and any bits set to '0' would be disabled and any bits set to '1' would be enabled.

This circuit would work well although it would require that the operating system software maintained a variable to keep track of which interrupts were set as there is no way to read the value which has been stored in the interrupt control latch.

This may not be a problem as it only requires a single 8 bit value to be stored somewhere in RAM and the programmer can then define bit masks for each interrupt which can be OR / AND with the current value in order to control the individual interrupt bits.

If you preferred then you could of course add a buffer which would allow the value in the latch to be read and this would remove the need to store the current interrupt enable status byte in RAM as its value could then be read directly from the system hardware.

Figure 11-9 shows a version of the interrupt control circuit which would allow the Z80 to read the current interrupt enable bit settings from the control buffer.

As you can see this circuit has a buffer which is controlled through one of the input ports. Reading from this port will allow the Z80 to determine the current settings of the hardware interrupt control bits.

Either the firmware or the hardware approach for keeping track of the interrupt control status will work although if the hardware version is implemented then the programmer has the choice.

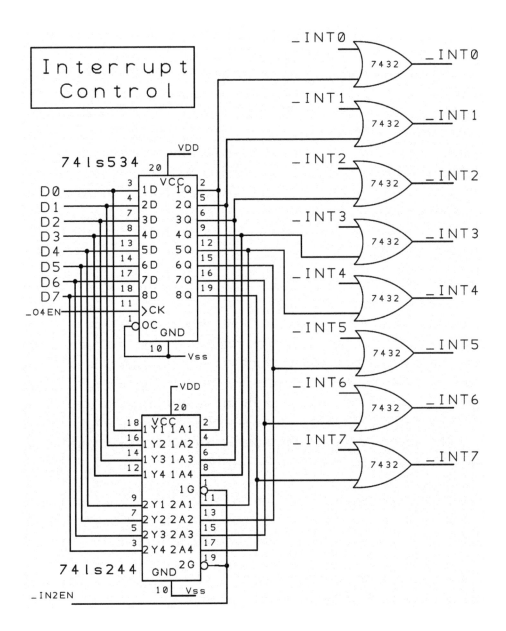

Figure 11-9 Interrupt Control Circuit with Read

If you do go ahead and add this circuit then be sure to properly initialise it in your boot ROM or the JMZ may fail to boot up.

Small additions such as this can greatly add to the flexibility and power of a computer system. I am avoiding adding them to the version of the system in this book simply because they are not required for the basic system to operate and would complicate the system explanations. I will however be adding features such as this to future versions of my system and I would recommend that you consider adding items such as this if you intend to build your own version of the JMZ.

A word of Caution

I feel that a word of caution is appropriate now that we have added hardware interrupts to our design.

Anyone that has ever spent some time working on vintage computer systems has no doubt come to realise that seemingly small faults can cause the machines to exhibit some truly baffling behaviour. Often when finally tracked down the apparent fault may seem to have nothing to do with the failure and this can make working on old computer systems something of a challenge.

It is of course also one of the characteristics that make working on them so interesting.

The JMZ most certainly falls into this category of computer as it would be very easy to be fooled into thinking that your machine hardware is not working as it should when in reality you have a firmware error.

The interrupt hardware which we have added in this chapter makes the JMZ a potentially very powerful and flexible machine.

However there is a price to pay for this in the form of potentially erratic behaviour if you fail to program it correctly.

As long as you fully understand how the hardware operates then you should be able to easily avoid such issues and this is especially true if you are familiar with vintage computer systems.

The issue I am referring to is of course unhandled interrupts caused by either improper interrupt configuration or inappropriate firmware handling of the interrupts. It is also possible to completely forget to include a suitable entry in the interrupt vector table or failure to clear an interrupt that has been generated by the hardware.

By way of example let us consider the keyboard hardware interrupt.

When a key is pressed on the keyboard the JMZ will generate a hardware interrupt and may even set a bit in the global status register if it has been configured to do so.

The interrupt makes its way through the interrupt priority system and into the interrupt vector generation circuit before finally flagging the interrupt with the Z80.

The Z80 will respond by using the appropriate vector in the interrupt vector table to branch to the required interrupt handler routine.

That is all fine unless you forget to clear the interrupt or accidentally try to clear the wrong interrupt.

In this case the interrupt is cleared by simply reading the keyboard data input port but if this is not done then the Z80 will continually generate interrupts.

Worse still if the wrong vector is selected then the code may well branch off into a great firmware void causing the machine to crash.

The point here is that once you have configured the system to generate hardware interrupts then you must put in place a suitable vector table entry along with a matching handler located at the correct address.

This handler or some other mechanism must include suitable steps to ensure that the interrupt is cleared even if the resulting data is not required.

A very good option to avoid potential problems is to create a generic interrupt handler to intercept any unexpected interrupts.

Any entries in the vector table which are otherwise unused should be directed to this handler.

The handler itself can be very simple and could for example just print some text on the screen such as...

Error Unexpected Interrupt

This could easily save many hours of frustration in trying to figure out why your system appears to be failing.

I will go into much more detail in the next book which will cover the creation of a boot ROM and operating system.

We can now display characters on our computer monitor so the next part of our design challenge is to add some cursor control which we will look at in the next chapter.

Chapter 12 - Cursor Control

Throughout the development of this computer I have attempted to simplify the design wherever possible in order to minimise the complexity of the circuits we are putting together. This is especially important in a discrete logic design such as this because it is very easy to end up with incredibly convoluted and over complicated designs. As we continue to add more functionality to our computer system you will hopefully see how this approach plays an increasingly important role in our project by making each addition easy to implement.

A very good example of this is in the cursor control system we will now be designing because I included much of the cursor control function within the circuits we have already created.

Some of you may have been wondering why I have selected a character ROM which is twice the capacity it needs to be to in order to store the entire character set.

As I described earlier the characters are stored in the character ROM as a series of bitmaps and each of these bitmaps requires 8 bytes. There are 256 characters in the entire character set although we only use the first 128 in our system.

8 x 256 x 8 = 16384 or 16k

If you decide to use the cursor generation circuits I have shown so far you can use a 16k EPROM but later in this chapter I will show the circuit I used in the final design of this system and this requires the use of a 32k EPROM although 16k will work for 128 characters.

Hardware or Software Cursor

There are two general methods for creating a cursor display and control mechanism in a system such as the one we are designing here.

The first method is to design a series of counters which will keep track of the current cursor position and as the screen display counters are used to create the video output they are compared to the cursor position control registers. If the current display output counters match the current cursor position counters then the cursor is generated for that character position.

This approach requires a fair amount of additional circuitry although it minimises the amount of work the computer system needs to do in software in order to produce and maintain the cursor display.

The second method for cursor control is to have the computer system output the cursor from software by keeping track of the current cursor position and modifying the character displayed at that position to indicate the cursor location.

Both of the above methods require that the computer maintains a pointer to the current cursor position so that it knows where to display the next character which is the normal purpose of a cursor.

The method I selected for this design is the second although it includes some additional hardware features which will minimise the work required by the computer in order to create the cursor.

You may recall when we were designing the video system way back in chapter 5 that I included a feature in the video circuit memory control which would allow us to use the most significant bit of the video memory to store the current cursor location.

We can now make use of that in order to allow us a very simple but effective means of generating the display cursor.

The video system uses bit 7 of each character value to indicate if the character is at the cursor location or more specifically if this character is displayed inverse. If bit 7 is set then this character is at the cursor position and all other characters should have bit 7 clear.

The video circuit uses bit 7 of the character to invert the video output which flips the video from white on black to black on white or vice versa depending on the state of the video invert control input. This causes a cursor to be displayed in whichever position we choose and all we need to do is to ensure that we set bit 7 of the correct character.

There is a complication in this approach although it is one which we have already mostly dealt with in the design of the video circuits.

When we move the cursor around the screen we will be doing this in one of two basic ways. The first is when we enter a new character on the keyboard and it is displayed on the screen. This action should cause the cursor to advance across the screen one character position or down to the beginning of the next line if we have reached the last character on the current line.

For this to work all we need to do is advance the cursor to the next character position as each character is entered.

The second way in which the cursor will be moved is through the use of the cursor keys in which case the cursor can be moved to any character position on the screen irrespective of which character is currently displayed there.

This means that we must be able to read the current character value when we move the cursor so that we can update bit 7 of that character without actually modifying the character value itself.

Naturally this requires that we add appropriate circuits to our video system so that the Z80 can read from the video RAM as well as write to it.

From a design perspective this is a very good feature to have anyway because if a programmer wishes to create their own programs and need to be able to read character values from any screen position then the only way to do this if the video RAM cannot be read is to maintain a separate video buffer but this is fairly cumbersome and wasteful in terms of memory and processor overhead.

With this in mind it is almost certain that I would have added the video RAM read circuitry even if we did not need it for the cursor control and so it could be argued that this is a 'free' addition as far as the cursor display is concerned.

So we already have the required circuits in the video system which allow the video SRAM and associated circuits to be put into both write and read modes. However there is still one piece of this puzzle missing which we will now resolve with the addition of just a few logic gates. We have already been writing to the video SRAM in order to display characters on the screen and we have previously designed the memory mapping circuits required to control the location of the video SRAM within the system memory map.

The way in which we were controlling the memory write cycle to the video SRAM was through the use of the _VRAMCE output from the memory mapping circuit. Unfortunately we must now change this arrangement because that control line goes low for both read and write operations to the video Ram and so we must now allow these two functions to be separated.

Luckily this is very easy to accomplish because as I stated at the beginning of this chapter we have been designing each circuit in our design in such a way that they simplify later additions.

If you go back and look at the video circuits then you will see that we have a _WR input which is active low and we also have a RD input which is active high.

All we need to do in order to control read and write operations to the video RAM is to ensure that these two lines are driven to the correct states during memory read and write cycles to the SRAM.

The circuit in Figure 12-1 shows the circuit we can use to perform this task.

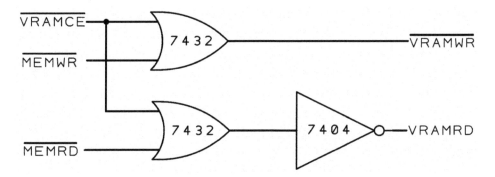

Figure 12-1 Video Ram Read – Write Control Circuit

This circuit is very simple and provides a logic low level on the _VRAMWR output when the Z80 executes a write instruction to the video RAM and a high logic level output when the Z80 wishes to read from the video RAM.

An alternative form of this circuit is shown in Figure 12-2 and this is the version I used in the final design. I used the version in Figure 12-1 for the breadboard version as it saved adding an additional device to the overcrowded board.

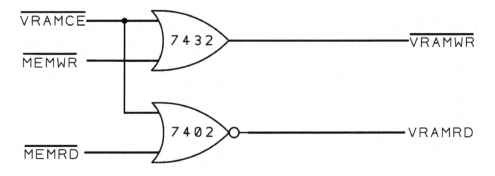

Figure 12-2 Video Ram Read – Write Control Circuit – V2

This circuit provides identical functionality as the one shown in Figure 12-1 but uses fewer gates and of course the required gates were already available on the Z80 CPU board.

This circuit is the only addition we need to make to the design in order to implement cursor control although we will of course still need to keep track of the cursor location in our software system.

Creating the cursor now simply requires us to read the character at the current cursor location and set the cursor control bit and then write the character back to the video RAM. To delete the cursor we perform the reverse operation and clear the cursor control bit. The video circuits will then take care of the actual cursor display.

In addition simply writing a normal character to the current cursor location will effectively delete the existing cursor and the software can then simply set the cursor bit when it writes the new character.

A better Cursor Control Design

As I stated at the beginning of this book my intention is to take the reader through the process of designing a system such as this rather than simply describe a finished design.

Part of the development process involves improving circuits were required or adding intended elements to the design when it is appropriate.

The cursor control system is a good example of this because the circuits I have shown so far have been intended to allow easy testing of the system blocks which we have designed so far.

You may wish to continue using the previous cursor design but I will now show the intended design for the final system.

I mentioned earlier that the entire character set could be stored in a single 16k EPROM and yet I have been using a 32k device for all the testing so far. The reasons for this will now hopefully become clear.

While the cursor control system I have shown works well it requires a few extra steps in the system code to make it function properly and it has a characteristic which I do not really like.

If you look closely at the cursor it generates then you will notice that it spans the entire 8 pixel character space and this causes it to start at the last column of the previous character bitmap on the screen and end at the first column of the character bitmap which follows the current character position. I do not think this looks very nice as the character is not always centred in the cursor and as we are designing the system from scratch we can easily deal with such issues to make the display more to our liking.

There are a number of ways in which we could tidy up the cursor display to make it look better such as inserting a latch in the cursor invert circuit which is clocked by the character column counter.

Unfortunately this would require the addition of a couple of additional IC's and while that is not a particular problem I had always intended to use a slightly different method for the cursor handling circuits. Our design so far has been very useful in allowing us to properly test the system but the circuit we will use in the final design is shown in figure 12-3.

The circuit shown in Figure 12-3 is probably familiar and is almost identical to the character ROM circuit I showed previously.

The only real difference is that all 8 data bits are now connected from the character ROM data pins to the shift register inputs.

We will still be using bit 7 of the character data stored in the video RAM to indicate the current cursor location and we will do this in exactly the same way as we did previously and this is also why we used the previous circuits to test the design.

The difference now is that we actually store the inverted character bitmaps in the second half of the character ROM and bit 7 of the character data from the SRAM is used to select either the normal character or the inverse character by controlling bit 10 of the EPROM address.

The bitmaps stored in the second half of the character ROM do of course need to be inverted and they also need to be shifted 'left' one bit to place them in the centre of the cursor when it is displayed.

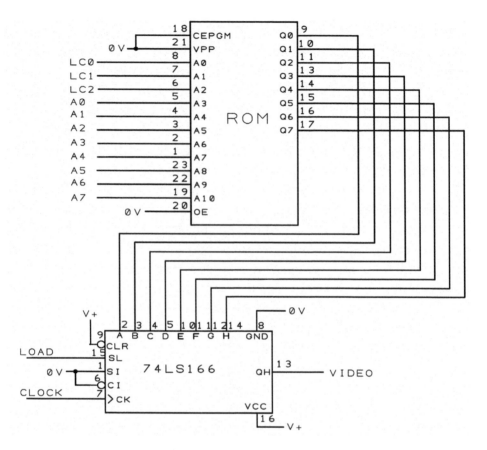

Figure 12-3 Revised Cursor Generation Circuit

An added advantage is that we can now support a far wider range of characters sets because we are not limited to a 5x 7 bitmap although we are still limited to a maximum of 8x8 pixels per bitmap because of the number of counter bits we are using.

This arrangement provides a much more pleasing display because the cursor has a small space at its left and right edges so it looks a lot clearer.

We can also now remove the additional gates from the cursor inverse circuit because it is no longer needed although we will still retain the blank and screen invert functions.

Figure 12-4 shows the revised inverting circuit and you will notice that it no longer needs to handle the cursor display.

The only real disadvantage in this design is that we need to use a 32k EPROM instead of a 16k device but the improvement in the display makes this worth while.

You may prefer to retain the previous circuit but I will use this new version from this point.

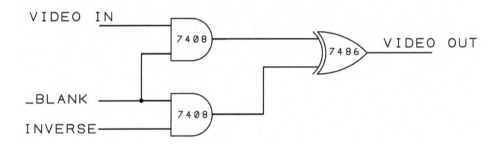

Figure 12-4 Revised Inverting Circuit

This circuit now simply blanks the video output when the _BLANK input is low and allows the entire display to be displayed as black on white or white on black.

I much prefer the appearance of the cursor with this arrangement as it looks much clearer and more professional.

As I mentioned earlier you can still use a 16k ROM if your system will only use 7 bits to select each character.

I actually designed the final main board layout in such a way that either a 16k or 32k ROM could be used without needing to make any modifications. You could even use a 32k ROM to provide two complete character sets and switch between them as required.

At this stage in the project the collection of smaller boards and bread boards was getting somewhat messy and so I decided to design a single circuit board to bring them all together.

This will make the next steps in our project much easier as we will have what amounts to a fully functional computer system without the rats nest of jumper wires.

The new board is shown in the Prototypes chapter.

Once I had built and tested this board we had all the basic elements for our Z80 computer system and so it was time to start adding the peripheral circuits and I decided to begin by adding an RS232 interface which we will look at in the next chapter.

ℰℋℭ

Chapter 13 - RS232 Interface

Our Z80 computer system design is progressing nicely and all the core features required are now in place so we will continue by incorporating an RS232 serial interface.

Unlike many simple single board Z80 computers we do not need to use the serial port as the only means of communicating with our machine as we have a fully functional video display and keyboard. It will however allow us to connect our system to the outside world and it should also be an interesting addition to this computer.

When I was initially considering the approach I was going to take for the system serial port I was very tempted to select a UART integrated circuit because these were actually available as far back as 1971 in the form of the WD1402A.

This device incorporates much of the circuitry required to implement an RS232 communication channel with very little effort. While it is very basic compared to later types of UART it still included many of the features we find in modern versions of large scale serial chips.

While the 1402A meets the design concepts I laid down for this project in terms of vintage availability of technology it does not really allow us to see the inner workings of a serial communication circuit so was perhaps not the ideal choice.

After a great deal of thought I finally decided against using such a device in favour of a much less capable but discrete logic design.

The circuit we will develop will offer far less functionality and flexibility than a large scale UART but it will allow us to design our own version and the reader is then free to develop this further if they wish to add more of the features found in the large scale equivalents. The circuit we will be designing will however use very similar, if greatly simplified, techniques for sampling the incoming serial data and converting it to a parallel form that the Z80 can use and similar methods for serialising and transmitting the serial data to a target system.

Before we begin our design it would be useful to have a closer look at the RS232 communication protocol so that we know what we are aiming for and to identify any key features that may help us.

There are many on line resources which give lots of information relating to this protocol so I will not bore you with all the details but I will cover the important points which we need to know in order to develop our own interface.

The RS232 Protocol

In an earlier chapter we developed a serial communication interface for allowing connection of a PS2 keyboard to our computer system. Although RS232 is also a serial communication protocol which sends information in data bit frames which are somewhat similar to the PS2 protocol the two differ in a very important way.

Unlike PS2 the RS232 protocol is a single wire system and it does not include a clock line to define the position of each bit in a data frame. The RS232 protocol actually defines more than a single line but I am specifically referring to the data transfer line.

This makes the protocol more efficient in terms of interconnection cables but it has the disadvantage that the bit timing needs to be recovered at the receiving end of the link and the data must be transmitted at much more specific frequencies than can be used for clocked protocols such as PS2.

Let us begin by having a look at a typical RS232 data frame or data packet. This is shown in Figure 13-1.

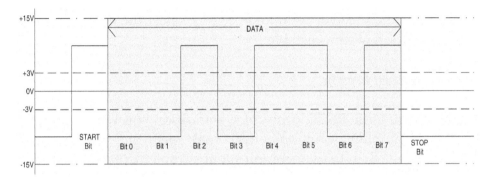

Figure 13-1 RS232 Protocol Signal Diagram

As you can see the general appearance of the data stream is very similar to the PS2 data frame packets we looked at in an earlier chapter. The big difference is of course the lack of a transmitting clock signal which was used in the PS2 interface to synchronise the point at which the receiver could sample the incoming data.

Without a clock signal the receiver must effectively recover the clock in order to determine the correct point at which to sample the data so that it can correctly determine if a bit is a '0' or a '1'.

The specification for the RS232 protocol gives a required accuracy of +/- 4% for the maximum timing error of the transmitted data bits although it must be remembered that there will also be timing accuracy errors at the receiving end which may add to the degree of uncertainty for the correct sample point.

In addition to the actual timing precision for the transmitting and receiving ends of the serial link there is also the added problems caused by lack of a common clock signal. This means that the receiving device has no prior knowledge of the exact time at which a transmitted data bit starts and ends.

In an attempt to minimise the potential errors the usual approach is to over sample the incoming signal so that the potential timing errors can be reduced. Typically the sample clock period is at least 16 times shorter than the expected bit period and this has the effect of allowing the receiver to more precisely select the correct sample timing position within each bit.

A Brief History Lesson

If you examine the RS232 protocol specification you will find that it contains a number of options which may seem to serve no useful purpose other than to over complicate the implementation a system which intends to make use of it.

To understand why these 'complications' exist and to also aid in designing a suitable circuit to handle RS232 communications you only need to look back at what this protocol was originally used for. RS232 was introduced at a time when most serial communication was carried out using mechanical devices such as teleprinters or teletypes. These machines were generally complex mechanical devices which operated at relatively high speeds, for a mechanical machine, and so certain operational controls were introduced.

For example at the beginning of each data frame the machines may have had to engage a large solenoid in order to begin decoding the incoming data. This mechanical operation took a relatively long time and to allow sufficient time for the machine to prepare itself for the following data bits the data packet began with at least one start bit. The purpose of this start bit was to allow the machine time to get its mechanism ready to decode the data. As a data frame could be variable in length there were also stop bits which allowed the machines to correctly identify the end of a data packet and complete the mechanical cycle. Different machines had slightly different requirements for the number of bits required by their mechanisms in order that they could operate as they should.

The result of all this was that we ended up with some aspects of the protocol which we do not really need in the electronic equivalents of teletypes and so we can generally simply ignore them.

The actual size of data being transmitted also varied and again this led to the RS232 protocol specifying different length data fields.

Once again it is up to us which of these features we wish to incorporate into our serial communication module but it is very unlikely we will need all of them. Modern UART devices have many options for handling the required protocol configuration but this was mostly to allow a single device to be configured for use in many different types of equipment. It is rare for system designers or operators to need to switch between more than a few different configurations for a specific machine.

The most common setting which requires changing by the operator is the rate of data transfer which is referred to as the BAUD rate.

Because we are designing the serial data circuit for a specific computer we can simply select whichever protocol format we think will best meet our purpose.

For the JMZ I decided to implement an RS232 with fixed packet length but with selectable BAUD rates between 2400 and 38400 as this should meet the requirements for most applications.

The packet format I decided on was 1 start bit, 8 data bits, no parity and 1 stop bit (1-8-N-1).

Designing an RS232 Receiver

Before we begin designing our RS232 system we will make a list of the things it needs to do and we will also start by designing the receiver as this is the most complex part of the system.

Once we have designed a working serial communications receiver which can be integrated into our computer design we will go on to develop a transmitting module so that we can implement two way communications although remember that we will not be using this as the primary form of interaction with our machine.

The RS232 receiving circuit must provide the following functions.

1) Identify the start of a new data frame
2) Select an appropriate sample point based on BAUD rate
3) Allow BAUD rate selection
4) Identify and correctly sample each data bit
5) Stop the data capture at the end of the data packet
6) Signal the receipt of a data packet
7) Provide an optional hardware handshake signal
8) Buffer the received data so that it can be read by the Z80
9) Shift the signal levels from RS232 to TTL
10) Allow the receiver module to be reset for the next data

This may sound like a very complex circuit will be required but as ever with a bit of thought we can implement a fully functional serial receiver module using a surprisingly simple circuit.

As I mentioned earlier in this chapter it is often a good idea to think about what a protocol was originally designed for when trying to implement a circuit to take advantage of it.

In this case we know that each frame of an RS232 data stream will begin with a 'Start' bit and in our design they will end with one 'Stop' bit. We can make use of this to help us simplify our hardware design.

One interesting feature of the RS232 protocol is that the data bits are inverted and again this has historical origins but if we think of the packet bits as if they were not inverted then each packet frame begins with a rising edge and a high start bit.

RS232 was designed to send data over relatively long cables and to make the data transfer more reliable the data is sent using a symmetrical voltage swing relative to 0V. The actual amplitude of this signal can vary a great deal and it will of course also be affected by the length of the interconnecting cable. In general the signal level will be somewhere in the range of +/- 3V to +/- 15V as shown in Figure 13-1.

RS232 is NRZ

An important aspect to remember when dealing with RS232 is that it is 'None Return to Zero' or NRZ which basically means that although each bit has a defined position within a data frame there is no guarantee that it will have a leading or a trailing edge.

For example the data packet for an uppercase ASCII character 'K' is shown in Figure 13-1.

You can see that the signal level does not change between bits 4 and 5 and this means that we cannot use an edge detection circuit in an RS232 receiver because we are not guaranteed that any edges will be present in the received data stream.

We must implement our circuit as an over sampling data detection circuit which starts and stops at the correct points during each received data frame.

As with most serial communication hardware designs we will build our circuit around a shift register and as we want to capture 8 bits I selected the 74LS164 device.

We will use this to store incoming data bits by latching data bits into it at the correct time within each packet bit.

To know when to sample the data we will need a counter to divide a suitable clock source to provide an accurate timing signal which can be synchronised with the incoming asynchronous data stream.

We already have several clock sources available from our Z80 main clock divider and I decided to use the 625 KHz clock as the starting point for our receiver circuit.

The reason I selected this clock is because it is the slowest of our available clock sources and so it will require the lowest number of clock divider stages to bring it down to a suitable frequency.

It should be noted here that our 10.0 MHz main clock is not an ideal frequency source for use in an RS232 system because it does not divide to an exact BAUD rate frequency.

For example the closest we can get to 9600 BAUD is 9765.625 Hz which is what we get if we divide 625 KHz by 64, bearing in mind that we can most easily implement division by 2 ratio's.

This is however well within the RS232 specification as it results in an error of 1.7% although it also allows for an over sampling rate of 64 which further reduces the error.

The error during a specific data packet will accumulate as each data bit arrives and so the error will increase by the end of the data packet although it will still be well within acceptable limits.

If we put together the shift register and the counter we get the circuit shown in Figure 13-2.

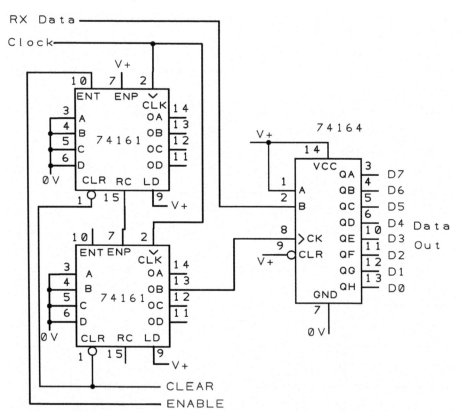

Figure 13-2 An RS232 RX Counter and Shift Register

I have implemented an 8 bit binary counter to give us the required division ratio of 2 to 256 as this will allow us to select a BAUD rate of between 2400 and 38400. It also provides automatic over sampling selection based on the selected BAUD rate.

The over sampling rates for each BAUD rate are indicated in the table below.

BAUD RATE	OVER SAMPLING FREQUENCY RATIO
2400	256
4800	128
9600	64
19200	32
38400	16

The circuit shown in Figure 13-2 can clock data bits into the shift register but we now need to add a means by which it can accurately determine when to start this process and how to ensure it shifts each bit at the correct time. It will also need to know when to stop shifting data so that it does not simply shift the captured data back out again before the Z80 has had an opportunity to read it.

In addition also need to shift the signals levels of the incoming data from the RS232 line voltages to TTL.

To change the voltage levels we will use a MAX232 dual line receiver / driver for both the transmitter and receiver circuits.

Starting the counter at the correct time is very simple because we can make use of the fact that the packet will always start with the rising edge of the start bit. All we need to do is add a flip flop which can be reset and which will then enable the counter as soon as the first rising edge of the data packet is detected.

A slight complication is that we must ensure that the first rising edge of the clock which is driving the shift register occurs half way through the first bit in the data frame but that subsequent clock edges occur at full bit intervals.

Again we can arrange for this very easily by taking advantage of the polarity of the output signal of the counters. The first rising edge for each counter output will occur half way through the first full counter cycle and each rising edge after that will occur at full cycle intervals and this exactly meets our requirement. Figure 13-3 shows the circuit with the level shifter and the start flip flop added.

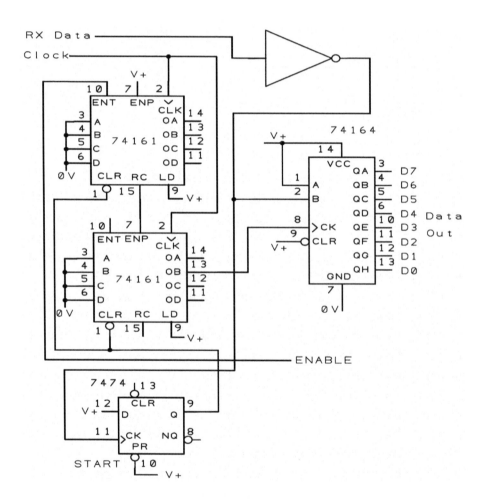

Figure 13-3 RS232 RX Packet Start Timing

The start flip flop is reset during a buffer read operation which we will look at shortly and this also holds the counter reset line low. When the first rising edge of the next data packet is received the flip flop clocks the value on its data input to the Q output. The data input is connected to V+ and so when the clear input to the counters goes high the counters can then start counting.

With the circuit shown the counters would continue to clock data into the shift register until the clock is stopped which would result in the required data passing completely through the shift register and being lost before the Z80 was able to read it.

We therefore need to add a second flip flop to stop the counters after the 9th rising edge has been received. That will result in the start bit and the 8 data bits being clocked into the shift register and as long as the counters are stopped at the correct time the required 8 bits will be available at the data outputs of the shift register.

If you connect a scope to the clock pin of the shift register and the incoming data then you will see that the data bits are being clocked into the shift register very close to half way through each bit period. In other words we are sampling the bits at the correct time and the large over sampling ratio ensures that we do not drift too far from this optimum position as the data packet is processed.

To stop the counters at the correct time we can connect a flip flop so that it is reset during a data read operation and we can then take advantage of the way the RS232 data packet is configured.

We know that the first bit of every packet is the start bit and we also know that this bit will always be high.

If we clear the shift register as part of the data read operation then we can be sure that initially all the bits within it will be set to '0'.

We can then monitor output bit 7 of the shift register and when it goes high we know that the start bit has reached that bit. Or in other words we have clocked the start bit along with 7 of the 8 data bits into the shift register.

Figure 13-4 shows the circuit with the second, Stop, flip flop added.

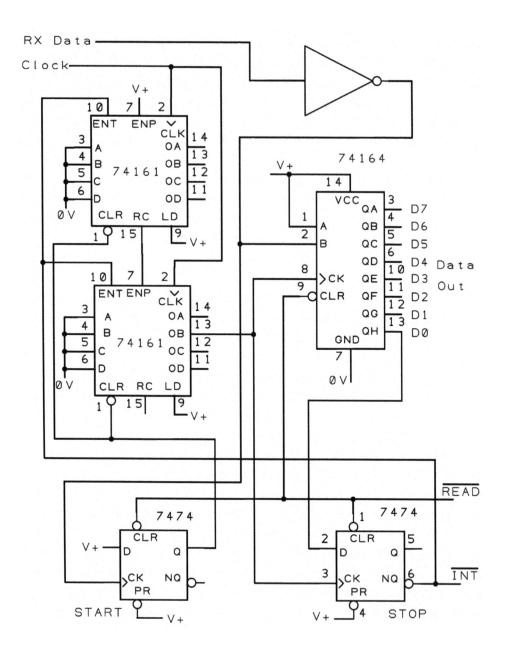

Figure 13-4 RS232 RX Packet Stop Timing

We can then connect bit 7 bit of the shift register to the data input of the flip flop and clock it using the shift clock.

This will have the effect of clocking a '0' to the Q output of the flip flop until bit 7 of the shift register goes high. On the following clock cycle, which will be clock cycle 9, the Q output of this flip flop will go high and the _Q output will go low. We can therefore use the _Q output to control the enable pin of the counters and as long as we reset it into the correct state during a data read operation then it will stop the counters after bit 9 of the data packet has been received. This gives us the exact behaviour we require as the counters will start as soon as the rising edge of the packet start bit is detected and each bit will be sampled and shifted into the shift register close to the centre of each bit time period. The counters will be stopped after the last data bit has been shifted into the shift register and no more data packets will be allowed until the Z80 has read the data.

Notice that the circuit also now generates an interrupt signal in a very similar way to the PS2 interface which we developed earlier and so we can connect this circuit directly to an appropriate interrupt input with a suitable priority to let the Z80 know that serial data is available.

If required we can also use the output of the stop flip flop as a hardware handshake output to stop the remote device from sending any more data until the Z80 reads the current data which will reset the circuit (and clear the handshake output).

The last thing we need to add is a buffer and latch so that we can connect the output of the shift register to the Z80 data bus.

We cannot connect it directly because the shift register does not have tri-state output pins and so this would cause bus contention.

We also need to latch the data to allow the Z80 sufficient time to read the data when it lowers the _READ line because this causes the shift register contents to be cleared.

A simple 8 bit latch is all we need although there is just one small complication we need to deal with to make it work correctly.

Figure 13-5 shows the circuit with a buffer and latch added.

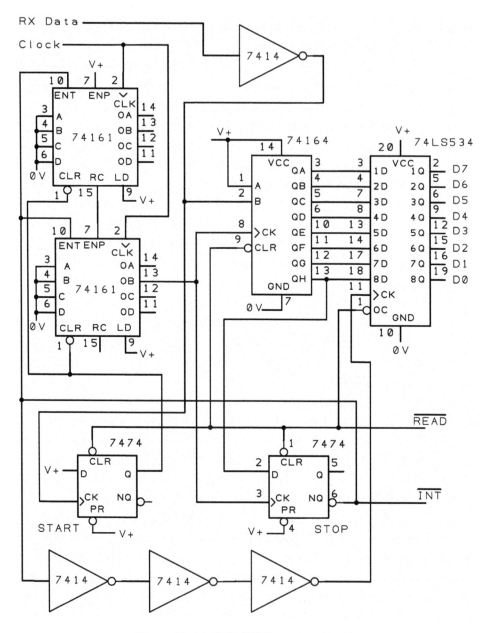

Figure 13-5 RS232 RX Complete Circuit

This is the prototype circuit for the receive section of our RS232 serial communication module but we will simplify it a little shortly.

The complication I mentioned is due to the presence of the inverter in the data input line which results in the data which is latched into the shift register being inverted.

This inverted is required to ensure that the timing of the start and stop flip flops occurs at the correct time relative to the clocking of the incoming data stream.

We could of course add another inverter to correct the polarity of the data bits but we also require particular data polarity with regards to the start bit to correctly clock the 'stop' flip flop.

A simpler way is to simply use a data output latch which automatically inverts the data.

You will notice that I have selected a 74LS534 latch for the output buffer as this does exactly what we require.

It accepts 8 bits of incoming data and it is edge triggered allowing us to transfer the data from the output of the shift register into the latch on the rising edge of its clock input.

This latch also has inverted data outputs and so the inverted data present on its input pins has the correct polarity on its output pins.

This totally avoids the need for any additional inverters or gates to handle the inverted data input.

Also note that the order of the data bits is reversed because the data appears in the shift register with bit 0 at the 'H' output.

You will notice in the schematic shown in Figure 13-5 that I have included a string of three inverters between the stop (_INT) signal line and the clock input of the output data latch.

These inverters are required to prevent a race condition occurring between the clocking of the last data bit into the shift register and the latching of the shift register data into the output buffer.

Without the delay which these inverters introduce the 9th shift clock would cause the stop flip flop output to change state at the same time as the same clock pulse is applied to the shift register clock input.

The shift register takes around 30nS to propagate the data following a clock edge and so we need to ensure the data is not latched until the shift register has had time to complete its final shift.

The three inverters add a 35ns delay from the clock signal to the latching of the data. There is around a 10nS propagation delay introduced by the 7474 flip flop and when combined we end up with a 45nS delay which is ideal.

Note that I selected a 74LS14 for this purpose rather than the more typical 74LS04 specifically because the 74LS04 devices have a propagation delay of only around 5nS compared to the 15nS of the 74LS14. In this application the 74LS14 is of course preferable as it provides the longer delay which is the only reason it is there at all.

Another point to consider in the overall design of this circuit is that it effectively stops very early in the final data stream bit period and immediately informs that Z80 through the interrupt line that data is available. This allows for very efficient handling of the incoming data packets because the Z80 can actually start processing the current data packet before it has even fully completed.

The end result of this is that the RS232 circuit we have implemented can be used at up to 100% of the maximum theoretical throughput for any give BAUD rate.

The received data is available at the output of the 74LS534 latch and can be read by the Z80 as soon as the stop flip flop is triggered.

The output of the latch can be connected directly to the Z80 data bus as it has tri-state outputs and it will be controlled from our I/O mapped decoder circuit.

The Z80 will therefore be able to access the data by using a simple IN instruction at the appropriate port.

The _INT output of the circuit will be connected to the interrupt controller circuit and this will generate an interrupt in the Z80 whenever a serial data packet has arrived.

As with the PS2 interface the read operation will also reset the interface so that it is ready for the next data packet.

BAUD Rate Setting

The BAUD rate can be changed by connecting the shift register clock to the appropriate output of the counter. In the circuit shown in Figure 13-5 it is connected to bit 5 of the counter and this will result in a BAUD rate of 9600. Moving this connection to other outputs of the counter will change the BAUD rate so that any value from 2400 to 38400 can be selected.
There are two methods for making the BAUD rate selection.

Hardware BAUD Rate Selection

This is the simplest method as it only requires that we include a jumper header on our circuit board to allow the required counter output to be selected.

Software BAUD Rate Selection

If we wish to allow the Z80 to change the BAUD rate in software then we will need to add a couple of additional components to the circuit.
The first is an 8 to 1 data selector IC which would be connected between the counter outputs and the shift register clock input. A device such as the 74LS151 would be ideal for this.
We would also need a latch so that the Z80 could control which clock is selected. This latch would be connected to another of the I/O mapped ports and so the Z80 could select the required BAUD rate by writing the appropriate value to the IO port.

This would add a lot of functionality to the circuit and it would start to operate much more like a modern UART.
There are many ways in which this circuit could be developed to provide much more functionality but hopefully you can see how starting with a simple design can allow many design options.

Supporting Vintage Equipment

As I have developed each module in our system I have attempted to keep the circuits and explanations as simple as possible and so I have omitted a lot of the complexities which were commonly encountered in the design of vintage computer systems.

They frequently needed to support specific types of hardware or meet the needs of custom designs. I have purposefully not included such features because they would only serve to complicate our system without adding anything to the end result.

However it is entirely up to you if you decide to add additional functionality to your project and I have specifically tried to describe the design process in such a way that it breaks the overall design down into much more manageable chunks.

This in turn should make it far easier to change the design of individual modules to meet more specific or demanding applications.

The RS232 module is a good example of this because different systems may have very different requirements to my own.

If you wish to support odd BAUD rates which cannot be achieved by simply dividing the master clock by factors of 2 then you can easily modify the circuit shown in Figure 13-5 to meet your requirement.

You may recall way back when we designed the video output system that I designed counter circuits with odd division ratios through the use of gates on their outputs which were used to reload them at specific intervals. Using this method you can create counters to generate any BAUD rate you need.

In the circuit shown in Figure 13-5 the counters I used included preload inputs which can be used to construct counters with any count you may require. Because I only intend to use BAUD rates which can be achieved by simply dividing the master clock by factors of 2 I connected all the load inputs to 0V.

If you will not need to support odd BAUD rates then it is possible to simplify this circuit and reduce the component count.
I have included a revised version which uses a counter without the preload feature and this is shown in Figure 13-6.

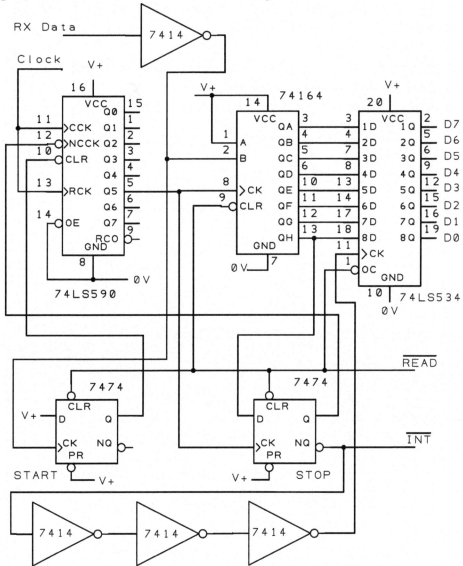

Figure 13-6 Simplified RS232 RX Complete Circuit

The circuit shown in Figure 13-6 operates in an identical manner to the previous circuit except that it uses a single 8 bit counter which does not have the load input pins.

It is up to personal preference which version of the circuit you build but bear in mind that the simplified version does not support odd BAUD rates.

Both versions of the circuit provide very good immunity to noise and provide very reliable serial decoding.

Figure 13-7 shows the data, clock and interrupt output signals from the RS232 receiver circuit.

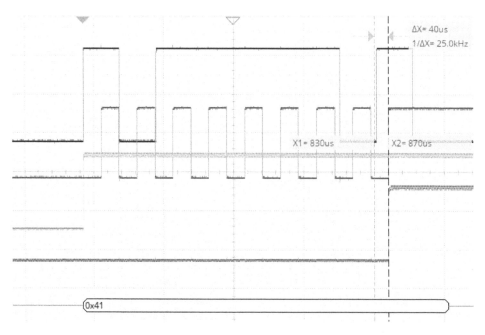

Figure 13-7 Signals from the RS232 Receiver Circuit

As you can see the sample timing (rising edge of the clock) is very close to the centre of each bit period and so the data capture is very reliable across a wide range of BAUD rates.

Notice that the rising edge of the last clock edge is slightly early and this is because our master clock is not running at an ideal frequency. The operation of the circuit is still well within acceptable limits for an RS232 communications device and extensive testing has not revealed any problems.

Hardware Handshaking

It would also be possible to implement hardware handshaking without adding any additional components. In this case we would simply connect an output of the stop flip flop to one of the line driver channels which we will add in the next section and then connect this to the appropriate RS232 handshake line.

This would allow the circuit to provide hardware data flow control if this is required and of course XON/XOFF handshaking control is also available if required.

As you can see it is very easy to add a great deal of functionality to the system once the basic circuit has been implemented as long as it has been designed in a way which gives stable operation.

We can now receive RS232 data and so the next item to add to the design is a serial transmitter module to allow our Z80 to send serial data.

RS232 Transmitter Module

Sending serial data is a bit less complex than receiving it because we do not need to concern ourselves with synchronising the data as long as we transmit it at the correct rate. We do however need to design the circuit so that it can be connected to our Z80 system in such a way that data can be sent efficiently without requiring a lot of effort from the processor.

For this circuit I again decided to use a shift register but instead of a serial in and parallel out type (SIPO) as we used in the receiver circuit we will select a parallel in to serial out (PISO).

This is of course because we need to load it with parallel data from the Z80 and convert it to a serial data stream.

There are a few to choose from so I selected one which would allow us to develop a very simple but effective circuit and would require very few additional devices.

The device I chose was the 74LS165 and the reason for selecting this device will hopefully become apparent as the circuit takes shape.

As with the receiver module we will also require a clock generator to provide suitable clock frequencies. The actual clock frequencies you require will depend on what you intend to use your machine for although if you wish you could include as a many options as you feel are appropriate. This will of course affect the specific design of your clock divider circuit, especially if you need to generate BAUD rates which are not evenly divisible by 2.

The same applies as for the receiver clock divider and you can produce any frequency you need through the use of gates and reloading of the counter.

For my design I do not require these odd BAUD rates and so as with the receiver circuit I decided to use the simpler device which does not have the counter load function and so once again I selected the 74LS590 8 bit binary counter.

Figure 13-8 shows the basic starting point for our circuit design.

As with the receiver circuit the final design allows the selection of different BAUD rates through the use of jumpers between the outputs of the counter and the input to the clock buffer.

See the full schematics in appendix B for more information on this.

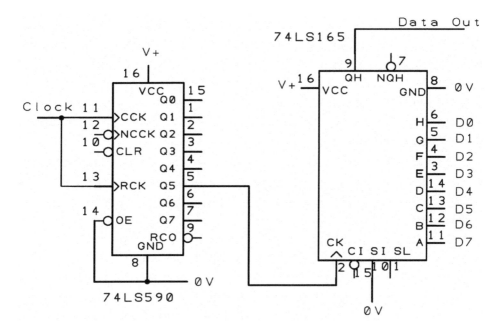

Figure 13-8 Initial RS232 Transmitter Circuit

Of course this circuit will not do anything but you can see some important features including the order of the data bits which like the receiver are reversed because the shift register shifts the data out from 'A' towards 'H'.

There will be no need to add a data buffer in this circuit because the data pins on the shift register are all inputs and so we can simply connect them to the Z80 data bus.

Unfortunately we cannot use the 74LS165 to shift out all the required data because it is only an 8 bit register and we will need to shift out at least 9 data bits. The entire data packet actually comprises 10 bits in total which are the start bit followed by 8 data bits (in reverse order) and finally a stop bit.

However the stop bit can be implied and so we only need to provide a dummy clock cycle for bit 10.

We do however need to extend the shift register to 9 bits and luckily this is very simple to do. Internally a shift register is usually made up from a series of latches which are daisy chained so that on each clock cycle data is passed through them in sequence.

If you wanted to explicitly add the stop bit then you can add a second flip flop at the other end of the shift register utilising its serial data input pin.

This pin can be used to clock new data into the shift register on each clock cycle and so if a flip flop is connected to this pin and its output is initialised to a suitable value then it can be used to provide the required data bit.

If the data bit will always be the same then you can make things even easier by just connecting the serial data input pin to V+ or 0V and then the tenth bit to be shifted out of the register will be whatever level you select for the serial input.

As long as the shift register clocks the data bits at the correct time and then stops shifting once all the required bits have been sent then the data output stream will be exactly as required.

In the same way you can add extra stop bits and even parity bits by simply adding extra flip flops which are setup prior to shifting.

To add our 9th bit we can therefore simply add an additional latch in the form of a 74LS74 flip flop as shown in Figure 13-9.

The additional flip flop is now able to provide the start bit and the subsequent bits will be passed through it in turn during each clock cycle. As with the receiver circuit the master clock input is derived from the main Z80 CPU clock divider and once again we are using the 625 KHz clock output.

Notice that we also have complimentary data outputs so we can select whichever best suits our output drivers. Additionally we can invert the polarity of the start and stop bits if we wish by connecting the serial input to the appropriate level and swapping the _CLR and _PR inputs of the start flip flop.

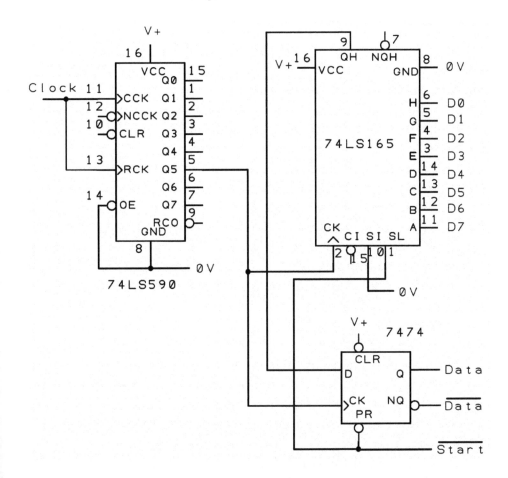

Figure 13-9 Extra bit for the RS232 Transmitter Circuit

The _Start input is used to load the data into the shift register and it is also responsible for resetting the circuit and triggering the beginning of transmission of the serial data.

This _Start signal can be taken from one of the spare IO port latch outputs which are already available in our system.

We are not finished with the design yet because the Z80 will need to know when the transmitter circuit has finished sending its data and can be loaded with the next data byte and so we will add this next.

I also wanted to make the circuit as flexible as possible so that it could be easily modified to add extra features if required such as a parity bit or an additional stop bit.

To allow for this I designed the control logic for this circuit in such a way that it could be adapted for alternative configurations with the minimal of effort.

The main function of the control logic for the RS232 transmitter is to determine when to stop transmitting data. In older systems the data shifting was effectively left enabled because it was provided by a mechanical system which was driven by a motor. To prevent the need to keep stopping and starting the motor the 'shifting' continued but as the last 'stop' bit was effectively at the idle level then no additional data was actually transferred. Data transfer for the next packet only began when the start bit was sent and this was then followed by the data bits.

We could of course duplicate this behaviour but in modern digital systems this approach can lead to noise issues because data can easily be inadvertently shifted and this can create ghost data packets. It is also not required when using electronic devices because they can be stopped and started instantly without any delay induced problems.

I therefore designed the control logic so that a latch is set when the _Start pulse is applied and this also loads a second counter.

This counter is loaded with a value which allows it to control the number of bits which are shifted out of the transmitter when a serial transmission is triggered.

Figure 13-10 shows the completed RS232 transmitter circuit.

Notice that I have inverted the start and stop bits to suit the line driver I will be using which I will explain shortly.

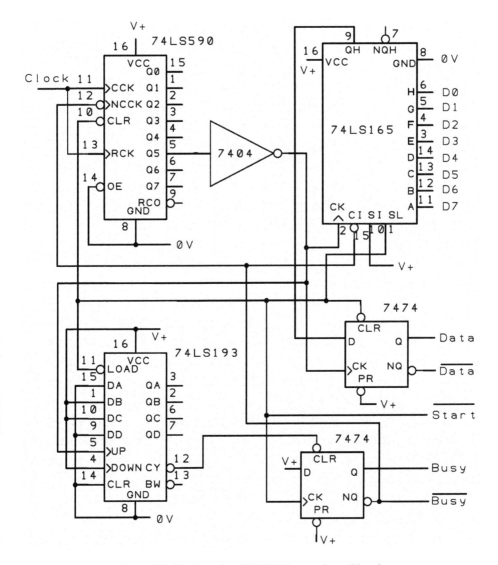

Figure 13-10 Complete RS232 Transmitter Circuit

In this design a value of 6 is loaded into the 74LS193 counter when the _Start pulse is received. This counter is clocked by the same clock that drives the shift register and so it is incremented as each serial data bit is shifted out.

315

The _Start pulse also causes a second flip flop to be set and the output of this flip flop is used to enable the clock divider and the shift register.

The shift counter will increment at each clock pulse and when the required number of pulses has been transmitted the carry out pin of this counter will reset the enable flip flop which will then disable the clock divider and the shift register. The bit counter is clocked from the output of the clock divider and so when the divider is disabled this also stops the bit counter as well. The circuit is therefore put into a stopped condition while it waits for the next _Start pulse to arrive and this makes it totally immune to spurious transmissions.

Notice that the serial input of the shift register is connected to +5V.

The enable flip flop outputs also provide the Busy/_Busy signals which can be used by the Z80 to generate an interrupt at the end of a transmission or can be simply polled by the Z80 in order that it can determine if the transmitter is available for the next data byte.

Operating the transmitter circuit in a tight interrupt handler loop can provide a very efficient way to transmit serial data while using very little Z80 processor time.

If you want to add additional features such as parity or stop bits then you can do this very easily by feeding the additional bits into the input of the shift register and changing the value which is loaded into the bit counter. For example if you want to send an additional bit then you can change the value loaded from 6 to 5 and this would add an extra bit to the transmit cycle.

Alternatively if you only wanted to send 7 data bits then you could change the counter load value to 7 and ensure that the most significant bit of the data byte is always a '0'. In this way the circuit would send a total of 9 bits comprised of the start bit, 7 data bits and the stop bit (stored in bit 7 of the data byte).

It is worth noting here that I designed this circuit with efficiency in mind and you may have difficulties if you try to test it outside of the Z80 system.

I wanted the RS232 data transfer to have the absolute minimal overhead in terms of processor time and so the transmit start bit begins as soon as the _Start pulse falling edge is received by the circuit. This is propagated to the transmit output and so to the remote device. The _Start pulse timing is actually part of the _Start bit duration and so must be kept short if the module is to work correctly. When driven from the Z80 this pulse is around 1uS in length which enables the circuit to operate with zero wasted time and so the serial link throughput is maximised.

If you wish to test this circuit on its own then be sure to drive it with a start pulse which is short compared to the bit period of the selected BAUD rate.

There are many options which can be easily added to this design.

One last issue we must deal with while we are working on the RS232 module is the serial line output voltage levels.

If you look at the diagram shown in Figure 13-1 then you can see that the voltage levels for an RS232 data link are anything between +/- 3V and +/- 15V and not the 0V to 5V used by the TTL circuits.

This applies to both the incoming receiver signal and the out going transmitter signals.

In the circuits shown for the receiver earlier in this chapter I used an MC1489 serial line receiver to convert the incoming RS232 data into suitable TTL levels so that we could apply them to the logic device inputs without causing any damage.

While this works very well and does not require any additional power supplies things are not quite as simple for the transmitter because we need to generate output signals which are within the acceptable RS232 range.

In most vintage equipment this was achieved through the use of multiple power supplies and suitable line drivers such as the MC1488. However for us to do the same would require adding +12V and -12V power supply rails to our system and while this is not difficult it is not an ideal solution as I wanted to design our system to use a single 5V power supply.

We could design a simple charge pump power inverter circuit in order to generate the +/- supply rails but there is an easier solution and although it is not strictly in keeping with my vintage 'feel' philosophy I decided to go with it because it will result in a reasonable overall solution but you can change this in your own design if you wish.

My solution was to use the MAX232 device which is a combined line receiver / transmitter and it also has an in built charge pump circuit which allows it to generate output signals of around +/- 8V which fully meets the RS232 specification.

I discuss this in more detail later in this chapter.

This completes the design of our RS232 module and it has only required us to add 10 logic devices to the computer.

The design allows the Z80 to receive and send RS232 data using either polling of interrupt handlers at relatively high BAUD rates while absorbing very little in the way of our precious Z80 resources. We will connect the receiver and transmitter circuits to the Z80 through a few of the spare IO ports and so we can access the serial port from any memory bank.

RS232 Port Further Development

The circuits I have presented in this chapter are very efficient and can be used up to very high RS232 data rates but they will also allow you to develop them further should you need to or if you just want to experiment.

I have tested this design using BAUD rates from 75 up to 460800 without any issues but it is up to you to take this further if you wish to.

It would be relatively simple to add a parity bit and additional stop bit settings or even software controlled BAUD rate selection as I indicated earlier. As with all such designs it is really up to you how far you want to take the development.

Systems Design

So far in this book I have described the development of a number of circuits required to construct a discrete logic computer system. There is however one topic which I have so far purposefully avoided because it is beyond the scope of this book but no discussion about the design of a system would be complete without at least mentioning *Systems Design*.

While systems design considerations apply to most aspects of a project such as the JMZ I have left it until now to cover because the RS232 circuits are a very good example of why systems design can be so important and I will use these circuits as an example.

If you search the internet for RS232 receiver and transmitter circuits you will find many example circuits ranging from very simple to very complex. It is actually very easy to put together small, stand alone circuits for different applications and RS232 interface circuits are no exception.

Things do however start to get much more complicated when these circuits are brought together in order to construct a complete system. Circuits which may appear to work perfectly on their own can often fail to operate as expected when they are linked to other modules or they are over complicated which makes the final system more cumbersome than it needs to be.

When I designed the circuits I have presented in this chapter I did so from a systems design perspective rather than trying to design general purpose modules.

To keep the circuits as simple as possible and to make the explanations as straight forward as I could they were designed specifically with our Z80 system in mind and may well require modifications if you wish to use them in other ways. This is really the basis of systems design where an element of a system is designed to work as efficiently within a specific system based on the manner in which it will be utilised within that system.

Some of you may have already wondered about certain aspects of the circuits I have shown so I will now give a brief explanation of the transmitter circuit systems design approach which I took to make the circuit work as effectively with the Z80 as possible.

You may have already realised that there is a very important aspect in the design of this circuit which I have not yet mentioned and that is synchronisation of the master clock with the control logic of the transmitter circuit.

To help explain the issue we must deal with I connected the circuit to a signal generator and fed it with a 625 KHz clock signal and also a series of 'start' pulses to simulate the operation of the circuit within our Z80 system.

The circuit is intended to be loaded and started by the Z80 with a simple 'OUT' instruction which will load the required data byte into the shift register and also trigger the start of transmission.

An important point to consider here is that the start pulse will be relatively short at around 500nS and may occur at any time.

I set the scope to have a display persistence of one second so that you could see the issue I am attempting to describe and the trace I obtained is shown in Figure 13-11.

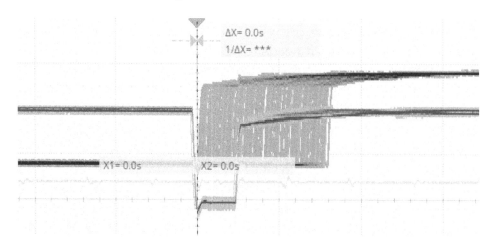

Figure 13-11 RS232 Transmitter Clock Jitter

In this image the negative going pulse is the 'start' pulse and the second trace is the output of the clock divider which is used to drive the shift register.

The start pulse shown here is 500 nS in duration and you can clearly see that the clock rising edges range in timing from a few nS after the start pulse falling edge to almost 1uS after the start pulse rising edge. This gives rise to errors in the transmitted data stream as shown in Figure 13-12.

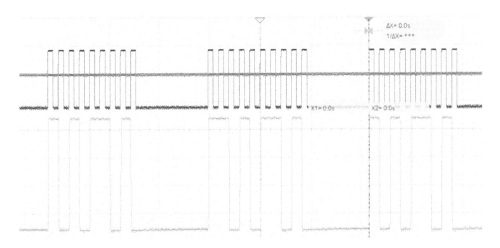

Figure 13-12 RS232 Transmitter Clock Jitter Errors

During this test the data byte was always the same but as you can clearly see in this image the data which is transmitted contains errors because the data in the lower trace, which is the output of the serial line driver is not always the same.

The second data packet of the three is not the same as the first and last data packets so clearly there is an error.

The reason for this is very simple and was fully expected in the circuit design but it is a problem which does not exist from a systems design perspective for reasons I will now explain.

As I stated earlier it is very easy to design a circuit which only needs to operate in isolation but when you begin systems design and need to develop circuits which operate reliably within a complex machine then things start to get a little more complex.

There are a number of ways to resolve the issue we are seeing but first we will take a closer look at what is causing it in Figure 13-13.

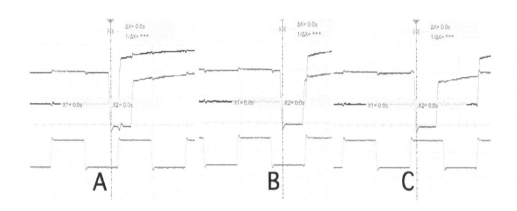

Figure 13-13 RS232 Transmitter Asynchronous Clock

In this image I am showing three separate single shot traces which show the start pulse and the relative timing of the shift clock rising edge. The bottom trace shows the incoming 625 KHz clock and hopefully the cause of the apparent jitter is obvious. It is caused by the lack of synchronisation between the main clock and the start pulse. This means that the start pulse falling edge can occur anywhere in the main clock cycle period and as the shift clock begins on the first rising edge after the start pulse falling edge then we see jitter in the shift clock which is equal to the period of the main clock. This in turn causes the start bit of the data packet to be incorrect where the first rising edge of the shift clock occurs after the rising edge of the start pulse as is happening in cycles B and C in the above image.

The cause of this is that the 74LS590 divider is a dual step counter / divider and it contains an 8 bit binary counter along with an 8 bit register. However the counter and register have separate clock inputs and if both of these clock signals are tied together then the output of the register will always be one clock cycle behind the counter. This does not matter for the actual clock divider function we are using it for but where we get a problem is during the clear part of the cycle.

When the clear input is driven low this will clear the internal counter but it does not clear the register and as this register is used to drive the output pins the outputs of the device remain in the state they were in prior to the reset.

This does not cause a problem if the register clock receives a positive going edge while the reset input is low because this will cause the reset (00000000) value in the counter to be clocked into the register and so onto the output pins.

This is the case in image 'A' in Figure 13-13 and in this instance the output of the circuit would be correct as the counter output would begin from 00000000 after the end of the reset rising edge.

On the other hand if the rising edge of the register clock occurs after the rising edge of the clear (_Start) pulse then the next clock edge will cause the counter value (00000000) to be clocked into the register after the reset has been released and this will in turn cause the output pin of the counter to change state after the reset input has gone high. Because the reset line also controls the start bit latch then the effect is to shift the bits in the shift register and start latch forward. The result is that the start bit will have a length which is equal to the time between the rising edge of the reset pulse and the first rising edge of the master clock as in cases 'B' and 'C' in Figure 13-13 and in the case of 'B' the start bit is only around 30 nS in duration and for 'C' it is around 900 nS but in both cases this is much less than the expected 104uS which is what we require.

The general effect is for the system to behave as if the start bit is missing from the data packet and so the remote device will not be able to properly decode the received data.

The solution to this if the circuit was intended for general purpose use is to simply add a latch to the start pulse control line which is gated by the main clock.

Figure 13-14 shows a suitable circuit for this.

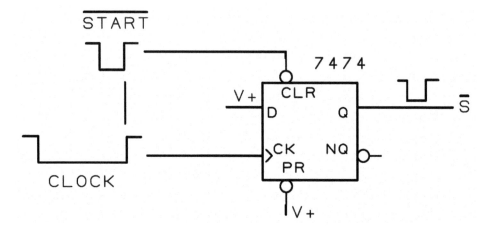

Figure 13-14 Clock Synchronisation Circuit

This circuit is set by the incoming _Start pulse and reset by the rising edge of the main clock so that the transmitter circuit always begins at the same point relative to the main clock phase.

While a circuit like this may be used to resolve the issue for general purpose application of our RS232 transmitter design we do not actually need to make any changes to our circuit because in our system design the problem does not exist.

In addition this solution will not work in all cases because it relies on the relative timing of the divider device counter and register clock inputs.

When I initially designed this circuit I selected a different type of divider device which did not have an internal register and so does not create this problem but after considering the systems design application I selected the 74LS590 as it resulted in a simpler circuit.

As I mentioned above this is an aspect of systems design which can be used when designing circuits such as this in order to simplify a design and also make it more efficient.

To understand why this problem does not arise in our actual Z80 system we need to go back to the basic timing of the Z80 IO write cycle. If you examine this cycle you will see that it is comprised of a number of 'T' cycles and each of these cycles has the same duration as our main RS232 clock cycle because the Z80 processor is running at 2.5 MHz and our RS232 clock is generated by dividing that clock by 4 to give 625 KHz but it is of course synchronised with the Z80 clock because they are derived from the same master clock. This means that the clock edges as seen by our circuit are always in response to the same part of the Z80 IO cycle and this in turn means that the two events are very closely linked without the apparent jitter that we see when using an external clock source.

If needed we can even change the relative positions of the clock edges relative to the start pulse by adding an inverter at the input of the RS232 divider so that it is clocked on an alternate 'T' cycle clock edge.

Although this circuit works very well when connected to our Z80 design I made a further systems design decision because as with all the other circuits I have shown I wanted to make the system as robust as possible. Anyone wanting to build a version of the JMZ system may want to increase the Z80 clock speed to increase the power of the system. As with the design of the DRAM system which I described in an earlier chapter I always like to give the circuits as much headroom as possible and in this case the fact that we were designing the entire system presented a very easy way to further improve the operation of the RS232 transmitter and would not require any additional components.

The circuit shown in Figure 13-15 can be used with a _Start pulse as short as 115nS. This is an example of systems design.

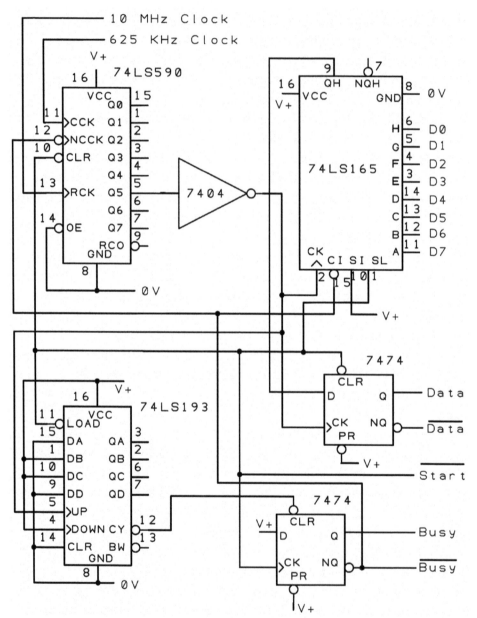

Figure 13-15 Modified RS232 Transmitter Circuit

As I described above the problem is caused by the possibility that the rising edge of the master clock feeding the divider register clock may occur after the rising edge of the _Start pulse. The start pulse is around 500nS so a simple way to avoid possible overlap is to drive the register clock input from the system 10 MHz clock. This will guarantee that several clock edges will occur during the _Start pulse period and this will in turn ensure that the output pins of the divider are cleared before the end of the pulse.

When we connect the transmitter circuit I have shown to our Z80 system the output is consistent and reliable as shown below in Figure 13-16.

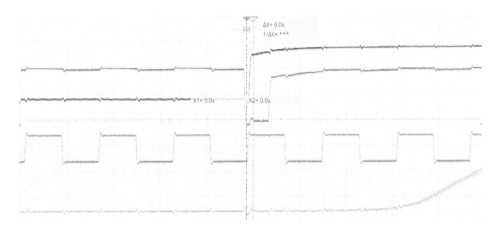

Figure 13-16 RS232 Output Signal

As you can see the relative timing of the start pulse and the shift clock are exactly as we require and this is consistent irrespective of the rate at which we transmit RS232 data because this relative timing is controlled by the phases of the IO cycle.

This circuit will work very well at much higher speeds that we will be using in our computer design.

I just mentioned RS232 data rates and it is worth noting here that I have been trying to make the point throughout this book that the main reason for designing this computer using discrete circuits is so that I could more easily explain the inner workings of the various circuits. It is easy to assume that designing systems in this way may result in them being inefficient and slow compared to the equivalent LSI devices which are available.

However this need not always be the case and very much like writing embedded code in lower level assembly language instead of a higher level language a well designed discrete circuit may well out perform a large scale integrated based system. Circuits such as the ones I have shown here have very little overhead and require very little in the way of processor resources. In fact these circuits can allow the Z80 to maximise the throughput of a duplex serial link while only requiring around 1% of the processor resources.

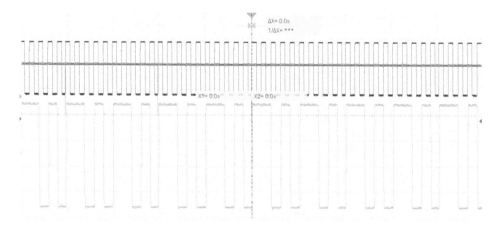

Figure 13-17 RS232 Streaming Output Signal

Figure 13-17 shows a serial data stream running at 100% utilisation while requiring very little Z80 overhead.

The RS232 circuits I have shown allow full duplex operation for our Z80 system and can be used in either polled or interrupt driven modes. They also are very easy to write code for in either mode and can give the Z80 just as much if not more serial link performance than can be obtained through the use of large scale devices and we have also, hopefully, had a lot of fun designing them.

That is not to say LSI devices have no place and in fact I would almost certainly use them in a commercial product unless ultimate performance was my goal but there is absolutely no reason why you *Must* use them.

You can also tailor your system to meet your specific requirements by connecting the various modules in a manner that is most suitable for your application.

For example the RS232 modules shown in this chapter can be used by connecting them to interrupt inputs and then you can write suitable handlers so that they provide the required functionality.

Global Status Port

If you use interrupts then you automatically benefit from port arbitration as the signal generated by the ready output is only generated once per cycle and so the ports cannot be inadvertently operated. Alternatively you may want more control over the ports in which case you can poll the ready outputs of each module to ensure that the module is not busy prior to using it. You could also write a suitable software routine using a data buffer to ensure that the modules are operated in an appropriate manner. The choice is entirely yours and it really comes down to personal choice and application. If you decide to poll the ready outputs of the modules then you will of course need some way to allow the Z80 to read the status of these signals.

Once again I will take a systems approach to this rather than treating it as a universal design issue for each module.

In other words instead of having a separate status byte for each of the computer modules I will show a simple way to combine multiple module status signals into a single byte and this will help to simplify the system hardware and the system software.

However if you prefer you could simply add a similar solution to each individual hardware module which you then add to your system although they could operate in an identical manner.

As I will be adding a single circuit to provide a single *Global* status byte for all the hardware modules in my system I will refer to this as the 'System Status Port'.

I am sure by now you know how we can go about adding this to our computer design but I will include it here for completeness and to avoid any confusion.

Figure 13-18 shows the circuit for the system status port.

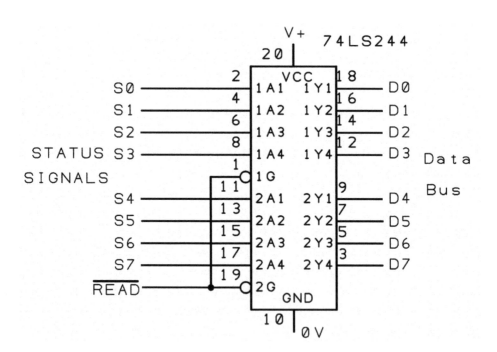

Figure 13-18 System Status Port Circuit

This circuit is very simple and if needed you can duplicate it to allow for more status bits as required.

The status signal outputs from each hardware module in the system are connected to the 'STATUS SIGNALS' input of the 74LS244 buffer. The output of this buffer is connected directly to the Z80 data bus and the _READ control input is connected to one of the IO port IN channels.

All the Z80 needs to do in order to read the status of the various modules is to execute an IN instruction for whichever port you have connected the _READ line to.

The Z80 can then determine the status of all the hardware modules by testing the state of each bit.

Before ending this chapter we will have a look at a simple test program which will allow us to properly test the RS232 module.

I will connect the receiver circuit to an IN port and an interrupt input and the transmitter circuit to an OUT port.

I will add a single interrupt handler and we should then be able to send and receive RS232 data in a very efficient way directly from our Z80 system.

All the receive handler will do is to send any incoming characters directly to the video RAM and they should then appear on the screen and it will also echo the character back out of the RS232 port.

Test Program 5

```
;------------------- SYSTEM EQUATES --------------------
RAMTOP        EQU F7EFh              ;Top of RAM
INT_TABLE     EQU F7F0h              ;Vector Table (F7F0-F7FF)
STACK         EQU E7EFh              ;Stack
VIDEO_RAM     EQU F800h              ;Start of video RAM
NON_VOLATILE  EQU FED8h              ;Start of non volatile RAM
ASCII_TABLEL  EQU 0500h              ;ASCII table (PS2 index)
ASCII_TABLEH  EQU (ASCII_TABLEL + 128)  ;ASCII table index
KB_HANDLER    EQU 0800h              ;Keyboard INT handler
RX_HANDLER    EQU 0900h              ;RS232 Receive INT handler
```

```
;------------------- SYSTEM VARIABLES -------------------
VIDEO_PTR       EQU 9000h        ;Video Pointer variable
VIDEO_FLAGS     EQU 9002h        ;Video State Flags
KEYBOARD_FLAGSEQU 9004h          ;PS2 Interface Flags
CHAR_AV_FLAG    EQU BIT0         ;1 = Character available
RELEASE_FLAG    EQU BIT1         ;1 = Key Down
SHIFT_FLAG      EQU BIT2         ;1 = Shift
KEY_BUFFER      EQU 9006h        ;Latest Keyboard Character


JP START                        ;Jump to start of code

TEXT1 DB 'WELCOME TO THE JMZ PROJECT',00h

START:
    DI
    IM   2                      ;Set interrupt mode 2
    LD   A,F7h                  ;Load I register
    LD   I,A
    LD   HL,STACK               ;Initialise stack register
    LD   SP,HL
    LD   HL,KB_HANDLER          ;Initialise interrupt table
    LD   (INT_TABLE + 2),HL     ;Keyboard handler address
    LD   HL,RX_HANDLER
    LD   (INT_TABLE + 6),HL     ;RS232    Receive    handler
address

    EI                         ;Enable interrupts

LOOP:                          ;Loop for ever
    NOP
    JP LOOP


;---------- RS232 Receive INTERRUPT HANDLER ------------
;RS232_RX_HANDLER
;On entry RX buffer contains received character
    ORG 0900h
RX_INT_HANDLER:
    PUSH AF
    PUSH HL

    IN   A,(06h)               ;Read character from RS232 port
    OUT  (06h),A               ;Send character to RS232 (ECHO)
```

```
LD   HL,(VIDEO_PTR)    ;Load VIDEO_PTR into HL
LD   (HL),A            ;Save the new
INC  HL                ;Increment pointer

LD   C,(HL)            ;Get char at the new position
LD   A,0b10000000      ;Set Cursor bit in new char
OR   C
LD   (HL),A            ;Save character and cursor

LD  (VIDEO_PTR),HL     ;Save screen pointer to RAM

POP  HL
POP  AF
EI
RETI
```

The MAX232

I stated earlier in this chapter that I used a MAX232 line driver device for the RS232 transmitter and receiver circuits.

While this device was not available when the Z80 was initially released I decided to use it in the JMZ for a couple of reasons.

Firstly it contains a charge pump to generate the differential voltages required by the RS232 line drivers and while it would have been possible to design a very simple charge pump circuit and use a more vintage line driver I decide against this.

A typical computer of the period we are aiming at would have actually used at least three separate power supply rails.

A +5V rail for the logic

+/- 12V rails for the RS232 and other hardware devices.

Because I wanted to avoid the need for multiple power supply rails I decided to use the MAX232 as the general circuit configuration would then be much more typical of a vintage design but without the need for the additional supply rails.

You can therefore view the RS232 line driver arrangement in the JMZ as very typical for a vintage machine but without the extra power requirements.

Our computer can now communicate with the outside world using a serial port but it is often useful to be able to send and receive data in parallel form using simple data ports.

In the next chapter we will add a few simple 8 bit ports to the system which will add this capability.

ᘒ ᔑᙓ

Chapter 14 - Input Output Ports

In this chapter we will add a few simple data ports which will allow our computer to send data and receive data in 8 bit parallel format.

This is a surprisingly simple feature to add and I was originally intending to incorporate this into an earlier chapter but as you may want to expand it to add more complex data ports I decided to describe this in a separate chapter.

I have already explained the basics of how to add input ports in the previous chapter when we added the system status port because this is just an input port and we will use exactly the same method to add more ports except that instead of them being connected to internal module status signals they will take data from an external connector and send data to an external connector.

The only real decisions you need to make for a simple data port is if it needs to latch the data and what port to map it to.

For our input ports we will not latch the data so each time the Z80 reads the data it will be reading the data present on the port input pins at the time of the read.

I decided to use latches for the output ports because the external devices which may be connected will most likely be working asynchronously to our Z80 and therefore it simplifies the system operation if data sent to the output ports is latched.

The data on these output ports will then only change when the Z80 writes new data to them.

Figure 14-1 shows the IN and OUT port circuits.

337

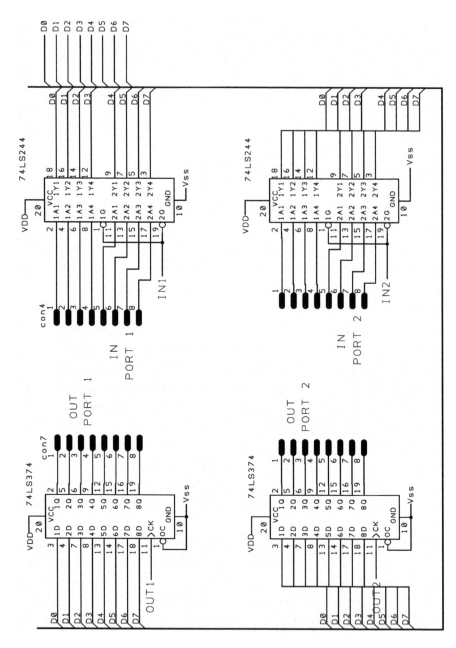

Figure 14-1 Input and Output Port Circuit

As far as port mapping is concerned I decided to keep things as simple as possible and so the two input ports will use IN ports 1 and 2 and the two OUT ports will also use ports 1 and 2.

The ports are accessed by simply executing an IN instruction for an input port or an OUT instruction for an output port.

For example
OUT (2),A

This instruction will write the value in the A register to output port 2 where it will be latched into the port buffer and remain until the Z80 writes a new value.

IN A,(1)

This instruction will read the data value currently present on input port 1 data input pins and save the value to register A.

It would of course be very simple to add additional ports and assign them to a spare IN or OUT port number from the port decoders.

Our computer now has a display and the means to communicate with the outside world but it still needs the ability to start itself up and allow users to interact with it.

The addition of the ports shown in this chapter will allow many different types of hardware to be attached and controlled from our Z80 computer.

This can take the form of simple serial or parallel data control or complex hardware controllers such as floppy drives or even hard drives. Many computers designed in the early days of the Z80 used this exact method to expand the functionality of the systems and incorporate all the required hardware.

You could also attached devices such as a PIA to a port and extend the input and output capabilities in that manner.

In the next chapter we will discuss the design steps which would be required in order to turn the current design into a complete computer system.

At this stage in the project I decided to incorporate the RS232 and IO ports into a new main board design. I also added some additional features such as the universal status port which would allow easier development of both ROM code and system software code.

If you have been keeping count then this will of course result in version 3 of the JMZ main board and this is the final design I will be covering in this book.

This version of the board is also the version which will form the basis for development of a much more complete operating system although I will be covering that in a future book.

For now I will limit the discussion over the next few chapters to a simple overview of the basics required to turn the current JMZ hardware design into a complete computer system.

ℒ ℐ ℰ

Chapter 15 - Monitor Program

When I originally began planning this book I was intending to include several chapters on the development of a monitor ROM and operating system which could be used to produce an operational computer system. However it became clear during the development of this project through questions and feedback that it would be far better to give a complete and thorough explanation along with a demonstration of the entire process of developing a boot loader and BIOS ROM with a fully functional operating system for this type of computer system.

I have therefore decided to only show very limited firmware and software snippets in this book and I hope to be producing a follow up book which will be dedicated to the full ROM and operating system development process.

I would also encourage anyone building their own version of this system to write their own software system in order to get the maximum value from their project.

Writing a complete operating system from scratch is a major undertaking but is also an enormous amount of fun which will provide the best possible way to learn the inner workings of a system such a the one we have developed in this book.

As I have mentioned in the previous chapters I designed this computer system in such a way that the software could be configured to suit different applications including the use of complex bank switching systems and hardware interrupt driven sub systems.

In the next few chapters I will limit the explanations to a greatly simplified approach to developing an operating system.

I do however include a listing for version 1.0 of the JMZ monitor program in appendix F and I will explain how to use this monitor later in this chapter.

The hardware circuits I have included in this design will allow the inclusion of many different types of hardware by making use of the In/Out ports and interrupt system.

At the start of this project I made it clear that wherever possible I would avoid the use of large scale integrated circuits and during the project I did receive a lot of 'constructive advice' which recommended that I use large scale devices for the various circuits.

I have not done so because this project was intended to be as discrete as possible for a number of reasons.

Firstly I though it would be more interesting to design discrete circuits rather than simply drop in a number of large scale devices. Not only would a discrete approach make explanations on how the circuits work easier to follow but would also give far more flexibility in the design. This approach also allows far more scope for experimentation to those who want to modify or further develop this design.

There are of course disadvantages to a discrete design such as cost and component count but as this is not intended as a commercial product then this is immaterial.

Performance is also a limitation although I have shown that many of the discrete circuits I have designed for this computer can easily keep pace with more modern large scale integrated designs.

The main penalty will come when adding devices such as floppy disk drives or hard drives as you will be limited to the bandwidth of the In/Out ports. I do not consider this to be an important limitation as the entire purpose of my approach was to expose the inner workings of a Z80 based computer system rather than produce a performance optimised machine.

It is however worth bearing in mind that the design approach I have taken in making each circuit modular instead of interdependent means that if you really wanted to you could replace each of the circuits I have described here with an equivalent large scale device.

For reasons I have already explained that is not something I will be covering here but it would make interesting projects to see how the large scale equivalents compare to the discrete circuit designs.

So with all that said I will now give a brief over view of how I will be going about developing an operating system for the JMZ computer.

Monitor Program Basics

The complexity of a monitor ROM for a system will depend entirely on the functionality it is expected to provide. This may sound obvious but there are a number of different things to consider when planning the development of the ROM firmware.

Before we continue I wish to clarify the difference between what I am considering firmware and what I am considering to be software. In reality some of this software is technically firmware but it may be easier to think of different blocks of code as either firmware or software depending on their function rather than where they are stored.

Normally any code stored in a system ROM is considered to be firmware but to keep explanations as clear as possible I will be referring to blocks of code as either firmware or software depending on where they are executed from.

In the case of our Z80 system the ROM will contain both firmware and software (although as stated above it is technically all firmware).

Any code which is executed directly from the ROM I will refer to as firmware and any code which resides and is executed from RAM I will refer to as software.

When the computer is booted it is common practice for operating systems such as CP/M to copy blocks of code from the system ROM into system RAM and execute it from RAM and not the ROM. This is done to make the system operation more efficient and to minimise the complexity of the bank switching circuits.

If the computer had to switch memory banks every time it wanted to access code from the ROM then this would be very inefficient when code is trying to access both ROM and RAM.

By copying the code to common RAM the code can be executed after switching banks and this of course makes life very much easier.

We do not really want to map the ROM into a common RAM address space so it is generally better to simply copy the required code from the ROM to common RAM during the boot process and then the code is available to the Z80 from any bank.

Naturally this is only an advantage in multi-bank machines which need to access code which is not entirely loaded into RAM when it is to be executed.

For example your system may only use the ROM as a boot loader or monitor program and then hand control to the loaded or entered program code.

A lot of the firmware and software design decisions will come down to how you designed the hardware and it has hopefully become clear throughout this book that I designed the circuits in this computer in such a way that they would place minimal load onto the Z80 processor so giving you plenty of scope for software development.

If we take the display and DRAM circuits as examples then it can be noted that both can operate autonomously and do not need Z80 processor cycles except when they are being modified.

The hardware interrupt system also allows efficient interrupt driven processes to be created with minimal processor overheads.

The hardware design also allows a great deal of flexibility depending on your system requirements such as the display system allowing hardware controlled display RAM refresh to minimise screen artefacts if the display you intend to use requires it.

Clearly we need to start our ROM code design by deciding what functions we require it to provide and what software code, if any, will be required by the operating system.

For those of you that wish to run operating systems such as CP/M you will most likely want to include a boot loader that will copy some BIOS routines into common RAM and then copy CP/M itself from your mass storage into a suitable RAM location before it hands control to CP/M.

You may also want a firmware or software monitor program to allow program code to be entered directly into RAM or for test and fault finding purposes.

These decisions are what make a project such as this so much fun because the possibilities are almost endless although it can seem very daunting for the very same reasons if this is new to you.

If you are not familiar with writing such system code then my advice is to start with something simple to get a code framework up and running and then add to it.

For example you could start with the JMZ monitor program and modify it for your own purposes.

For those of you familiar with CP/M then you will most likely only need to modify it to suit the particular address assignments and limitations of this system.

For my system I decided to initially test it by trying to get CP/M to run on it although I intend to develop a new operating system and boot ROM of my own.

It is beyond the scope of this book to cover this in any detail although the next book in this series will cover this development step by step.

The first phase in developing my ROM is to make a list of the functions I want it to provide.

1) Boot loader (Copy the operating system from MS into RAM)
2) Monitor program for basic code entry and memory checks
3) BIOS functions to provide common In/Out functions

The easiest way to get this up and running is to begin with the monitor program and then add some stub (non functional) software functions which will be copied into RAM to act as the BIOS.
Each can be fleshed out and tested as the code develops.

Examples of this type of code would be functions such as character input and output for the display or reading and writing mass storage.
Once the monitor program and BIOS code is up and running it will be time to begin work on the operating system.
A major decision to make in the design of the operating system if it uses BIOS function calls is how the Z80 can 'find' the functions.
Systems such as CP/M use a simple function lookup mechanism which is very common in this type of computer and is the method I will employ in my own system.
This can be as simple as loading a Z80 register or RAM address with a function index and then jumping to a specific address. The function indexed is then branched to although you do need to ensure that the system returns properly and also saves and restores any system resources that it uses which are not intended to be altered.
You can get as inventive as you want with this but remember to keep the mechanism efficient as some operations can require many thousands of BIOS function calls and you do not want your system grinding along too slowly.

Although it is theoretically possible to develop the software operating system and BIOS entirely within a PC based development system I would recommend against this.

Hardware systems do not always respond exactly as expected and so I would suggest fully testing each step of the development before moving on to the next as this is more likely to pick up on any system design issues.

For anyone who wishes to build their own version of the JMZ presented in this book I decided to include the following section which describes how to use the monitor program which I developed for this computer.

There is also a listing of this monitor source code in appendix F although this does not include the BIOS or boot loader.

I will cover these in a later book which will detail development of the operating system.

Monitor Program Operation

I do not cover the mass storage circuits in this book but bear in mind that the system will eventually include a floppy drive system (not covered in this book) and so I designed the monitor program in such a way that it can be called as a separate program.

During system boot up the JMZ initially looks for a floppy drive controller and if it finds one it checks to see if a boot disk is present.

If not then it calls the monitor program which is what we will now take a look at. As with all such systems this will no doubt develop over time so bear in mind that the information presented here relates to version 1.0 of the monitor program.

You may wish to use this program as a starting point for your own system or you may want to ignore it completely and write your own version from scratch.

The following descriptions assume that you have fitted a Rom to the JMZ system ROM socket which has been programmed with the monitor code.

After powering on the JMZ you will see the welcome screen and pressing any key will show the following monitor program prompt.

JMZ Z80 Monitor V1.0
H – Help

>

Any time the '>' prompt is displayed the monitor is waiting for you to enter something from the keyboard.

When the above is displayed it is waiting for a command input or you can enter 'H' to display the help screen which will list all the available options. All monitor commands are uppercase letters.

Figure 15-1 shows the help screen which has the following options.

C - Clear Screen
D - Dump RAM
D - Dump RAM with ASCII
+ Print next memory block
- Print previous memory block
E - Edit memory
F - Fill memory Range
G – Run from address
K – Call address
L – Load file
M – Copy memory block
O – Port output
P – Print registers
R – Reset monitor
Z – Load file fast
S – Send RAM to RS232

To use any option simply enter the character shown such as 'C' to clear the screen. You do not need to press the 'Enter' key as each command is executed as soon as you press the character key.

I will now explain the purpose of each of these functions.

Note that numbers should be entered as either 4 digit hexadecimal number from 0000 to FFFF or as 2 digit hexadecimal 00 to FF.

Figure 15-1 JMZ Running the Monitor

C - Clear Screen

Perhaps unsurprisingly this option simply clears the monitor screen and then displays the monitor prompt (>).

D - Dump RAM

Selecting this option allows a block of 100 hex bytes of memory to be displayed on the screen. After selecting this option you will be asked to enter the starting address for the memory block you wish to examine.

Note that the memory block can be system RAM, ROM or video RAM or a combination of these.

A - Dump RAM with ASCII

This works in an identical way to command 'D' except that it includes the ASCII characters in the display.

+ Print next memory block

This option is used when the memory dump option has already been selected and it will cause the next 100 hex bytes of memory to be displayed. Each time this option is selected the memory block following the previously shown block will be displayed.

- Print previous memory block

This option is used when the memory dump option has already been selected and it will cause the previous 100 hex bytes of memory to be displayed. Each time this option is selected the memory block prior to the previously shown block will be displayed.

E - Edit Memory

This option will allow you to directly edit memory locations although this function will of course not work for ROM addresses.

After selecting this option you will be asked for the memory address you wish to start editing.

Once you have entered a memory address the current address and data value at that address will be displayed followed by the monitor prompt as in the following example.

```
9100:    00>
```

You can now enter a new data value for that address.
Enter a two digit hexadecimal number.
The value you enter will be saved to the displayed address and the next address and data value will be displayed as in the following example. This example assumes that an address of 9100 and a data value of 78 were entered.

```
9100:    00> 78
9101:    C3>
```

You can continue entering new data values or you can enter a non hex digit to terminate the edit function.

F- Fill memory
You can use this option to fill a block of RAM memory with a single data value.
When you select this option you will be asked for the starting address. After entering the starting memory address you will be asked for an ending address and then finally a data value which will be used for the fill.

```
Start address (HEX):   9100
End address (HEX):   9300
Data value (one byte): 34

>
```

After entering the data value the requested memory block will be filled with the data value and once complete the monitor prompt will be displayed.

In the above example an address range of 9100 to 9300 was entered and a data value of 34 was used.

This operation is very fast and will fill the memory block without any noticeable delay.

G - Run from address

This option allows you to force the Z80 to branch to a new address.

After selecting this option you will be asked for a target address and once entered the Z80 will jump to that address and begin executing instruction from that location.

Note that unless there is valid program code at the target memory address then the computer will almost certainly crash.

K - Call address

This option is similar to the 'Run from address' function except that it expects the called code to 'RETURN' (RET).

Once the called code issues a 'RET' instruction the Z80 will branch back to the start of the monitor code block as its address was pushed onto the stack before the call.

This will result in the monitor header being displayed and the monitor will be ready for the next command.

Note that unless there is valid program code at the target memory address then the computer will almost certainly crash.

L - Load file

This option allows a binary file to be uploaded through the RS232 serial communication port.

When you select this option you will be asked for a start address where the file will be saved.

After you have entered the start address you will then see the text 'Waiting for file' appear on the screen.

The required file can now be sent to the JMZ through the RS232 port from a remote machine.

Once the transfer has started the text 'Receiving file' will be displayed and the data will begin appearing on the screen.

Once the transfer of the file has finished the text 'Download complete' will be displayed followed by the monitor prompt.

The file contents will now be stored in memory starting at the memory address you entered.

If the file contained valid program data then you can use one of the monitor run commands to execute the code.

Note that it can take several minutes to transfer a large file using this option.

IMPORTANT

The sending terminal must include a 3mS delays after each character is sent to allow the JMZ time to update the display if a scroll is required.

Z - Load file fast

This option is very similar to the 'Load file' option described above except that it does not display the incoming data on the screen.

It is therefore much faster and does not require the delay following each transmitted character.

This will result in a much faster file transfer and this can be very useful when transferring large files.

You can use this function to assist in the testing of new programs or the loading of system test code.

For example if you are developing BIOS or BDOS code for an operating system then instead of creating a boot disk every time you wish to test your code you can simply send it directly to the intended memory block.

This can save a huge amount of time when testing new software.

M - Copy memory block

This option allows a block of memory to be transferred from one location to another.

After selecting this option you will be asked for the starting address of the memory block you wish to copy from (source).

You will then be asked for an end address of the memory block and then a target address for the copy (destination).

Once the target address has been entered the copy will take place and when complete the monitor prompt will be displayed.

```
Start address (HEX):   9100
End address (HEX):   9200
Destination address (HEX): 9500

>
```

O - Port output

Using this option you can send a data value out of a Z80 port.

Once the function is selected you will be prompted for the port number and data value.

The port and data should be entered as two 2 digit hexadecimal numbers.

Once you have entered the two values the data value will be written to the supplied port number and the monitor prompt will be displayed.

```
Port & Data   34 56

>
```

This function can be used to switch memory banks although you must be sure to load a copy of the monitor into common RAM and run it from there before switching banks or the computer will crash.

Note that if you intend to run the monitor from an address other than 0000h then the monitor should be recompiled to run from the target RAM address.

For example if you wish to load the monitor into the memory block starting at address 9100 then you should change the 'Base_Origin' equate in the source code to 9100 and then recompile the code.

If you fail to do this then the first jump instruction at the beginning of the monitor will attempt to jump to the ROM based monitor.

P - Print registers
Selecting this option will cause the current Z80 register values to be displayed.

R - Reset monitor
This option causes the monitor program to reset but it does not reset the Z80 or clear any RAM.

As you can see the monitor includes all the basic options which allow manual manipulation of the computer memory space. This can be very useful for both initial testing and future experimentation or development.

In order to properly configure the operating system or write effective BIOS routines we need to know how to access each piece of the hardware system. Although I have stated how each hardware circuit can be addressed in the appropriate chapter table 15-1 on the next page summarises the hardware access for this system.

You can use this table to determine how to access the various parts of the JMZ computer system.

S - Send RAM to RS232

Using this command allows the contents of a selected block of RAM to be sent to a remote terminal through the RS232 port.

When you select this option you will be asked for a start address and an end address.

Once these have been entered the contents of the selected RAM block will be transmitted to the remote terminal.

When the data is being sent the text

'Sending data'

Will appear on the screen and once the transmission is complete

'Data send complete'

Will be displayed followed by the monitor prompt.

JMZ Hardware Map Table

Table 15-1

Device	Address (Hex)	Bank	Instruction
Bank 0 Select	Port 0 (out)	x	OUT (0)A (A=0)
Bank 1 Select	Port 0 (out)	x	OUT (0)A (A=1)
RAM	0000h – F7FF	0	Read / Write
ROM	0000h – 3FFFh	1	Read
Mapped IO	4000h – 7FFFh	1	Read / Write
Common RAM	E000h – F7FF	x	Read / Write
Video RAM	9800h – 9F80h	x	Read / Write
PS2 Keyboard	Port 3 (in)	x	IN A,(3)
RS232 TX	Port 6 (out)	x	OUT (6)A
RS232 RX	Port 6 (in)	x	IN A(6)
Input port 1	Port 1	x	IN A,(1)
Input port 2	Port 1	x	IN A,(2)
Output port 1	Port 2	x	OUT (1),A
Output port 2	Port 2	x	OUT (2),A
Global Status Byte	Port 0 (in)	x	IN A,(0)

Chapter 16 - Mass Storage

I will not be describing mass storage in detail in this book as it will be covered in the next book which deals with the development of the JMZ operating system and boot ROM.

However it has hopefully become clear that there are many options for how to go about attaching some type of mass storage device to this computer.

The method you choose will mostly depend on the type of storage you will be using but you have the choice of either a serial storage device making use of the RS232 ports or custom serial port or by making use of one or more of the 8 bit In/out ports which can be used as polled ports or used within a hardware interrupt design.

If you want to create a dedicated interface then you could of course make use of a device such as one of the floppy disk drive controller chips and drive this through a couple of the Z80 In/Out ports.

It is even possible to control a floppy drive directly from the ports although this will most likely result in floppy disks that can only be read from your machine due to variations in data rates which would be created without the use of a closed loop control system.

Controlling a device such as a floppy drive directly is not difficult although it does require some time critical code loops and this is one of the many reasons I designed most of the circuits in this computer to be as autonomous as possible without them placing a burden on the Z80. This allows very simple interface routines to be used as the routine would have almost dedicated access to the Z80.

Of course if you want to build a system which can read and write disks that will be readable in other systems or have been written in other systems then you would need to use a dedicated interface circuit. It is perfectly possible to design a suitable circuit using discrete IC's but I will not be showing that in this book.

As an experiment I did attach a 5.25 inch floppy drive to my JMZ through a couple of In/Out ports and wrote a few very simple BIOS routines which allowed me to read and write a floppy disk.

This was very limited in its operation although it could easily be developed further.

I used the version 3 JMZ system to do this as it needed the ports which were added to this design.

Figure 16-1 shows this arrangement although I did not use this beyond simple testing and for the final version I used a FDD controller.

While this is not in keeping with the discrete design philosophy which has been instrumental in the design of the JMZ I wanted to focus on the computer design rather than the ancillary circuits. If you prefer then you could use similar techniques which I have discussed throughout this book to replace the FDD controller with a discrete circuit design.

You could even create a totally new disk format specifically for the JMZ although you should be aware of the limitations this would create.

Floppy disk formats are generally not complicated but because there are so many variations it is easy to think of floppy drives as somewhat mystical.

In reality it is simply a case of extracting a suitable clock from the data on the disk and then using some form of data detector or slicer in order to read the data.

In fact one of the most important features of floppy drive controllers is to be able to detect the varying bit rate of data being read from a disk.

Without that you will not be able to swap disks from one machine or even from one drive to another.

There are some additional complications if you wish to use high density disks because you really need to incorporate some form of write pre compensation into your design otherwise your disk drive may struggle to reliably read the data.

Once you can decode the data the next step is to put in place appropriate interpretation for the disk track layout and header information. All of this is actually your choice as a designer although sticking to a standard format will allow you to read files which were written on another type of machine.

Essentially I would encourage experimentation rather than simply trying to copy machines which already exist.

The general idea with this project was to create a discrete Z80 core design which can be the basis for many additional development projects.

I have intentionally omitted elements which would normally be found in complete computer designs such as floppy drive controllers as this approach results in a much more flexible base on which to add additional capabilities.

Version 3 of the JMZ design contains almost all the elements which are required in order to add just about any more advanced features.

If you examine the designs of most Z80 machines designed when the Z80 was first available then you will see that they are built around a functional Z80 core which is coupled to a number of additional circuits. Once you have the basic system up and running with hardware interrupt control and suitable memory mapping along with a number of ports then adding any additional functionality becomes increasingly straight forward.

Although I will not be going into any detail regarding the floppy drive controller I decided to include an image of some initial testing I had carried out.

The JMZ is very easy to connect to external interface devices and the Z80 makes writing code to develop them very quick and easy.

I hope to include more detail on the actual interface and code in the next book but for now Figure 16-1 shows the JMZ connected to a floppy disk drive through a FDD controller and a couple of buffers.

Figure 16-1 Floppy Disk Drive

Our Z80 system is actually very fast considering its clock speed and could easily keep up with the floppy drive timing requirements. Interestingly it was also possible to write a few simple test routines to allow manual control of the floppy drive such as stepping the head motor.

This is yet another example of how a project like this can be used as a very good learning tool.

The interface shown here is in no way complete and it requires further development but even with such a simple circuit the reading and writing of data was reliable.

ᘒ ᖇ ᘚ

Chapter 17 - Software

As I stated in the previous two chapters I will not be covering the development of the operating system in this book as it will be included in the next but I also hope that many of you will wish to develop your own operating systems from scratch.

Software programs for the JMZ are expected to be loaded into the Bank 0 user RAM area although they can of course make use of the BIOS functions which are normally stored in the common RAM memory block.

It is fairly common for many programs to add addition 'BIOS' routines by loading additional blocks of code into these specific RAM areas in order that they are then available from all banks.

The JMZ can also be used to load a version of BASIC if required as long as the required BIOS functions are made available.

I began development of my system by loading a cut down version of CP/M and then wrote a very simple version of the space invaders program. This was only for basic test purposes and was not intended as a fully functional operating system but it did perform very well.

My main goal was to create a simple operating system that could be used to load and run software programs in such a way that anyone building one of these systems could experiment with their own software projects.

The first thing I wanted to fully test was the ability of the system to correctly load program data and execute those programs. I also wanted to create a very simple boot loader which I could use to load my operating system.

As I explained in chapter 16 I had not developed a suitable mass storage interface when I began working on this. While my aim is to add support for floppy disk drives in the future I did not want to have to deal with the creation of a new disk every time I wanted to test the system.

You may have noticed in several earlier chapters that I have put a lot of effort into designing a very robust RS232 interface and one of the reasons for doing this is that I intended to use it in the test boot loader in a similar way that the monitor program uses it to copy files from a remote machine into RAM.

The general idea was to initially load software in a similar way that you would on a machine such as the Altair 8800 through the serial port.

Once everything is starting to run as I want it to I will go on to incorporate a floppy drive system so that the JMZ can boot from floppy disk and also use floppy disks as a mass storage medium.

However the first step was to write a boot loader which would initialise the machine and then wait for an operating system image file to be sent to it through the serial port.

This operating system would be saved to a suitable location by the boot loader and then control handed to it so that the system could complete its start up.

Rather than beginning by writing an operating system from scratch I decided to put together a very rough and ready version of CP/M and the boot ROM would then initialise the system accordingly.

The boot loader would copy the BIOS and BDOS to the common RAM area and also setup the call vectors at the bottom of the main RAM so that calls to the BIOS would work.

Figure 17-1 shows the JMZ after booting into this version of CP/M.

Figure 17-1 JMZ booting into CP/M

I should stress here that this is in no way a fully functional version of CP/M as I simply wanted to test the JMZ boot up sequencing but it was very exciting the first time the CP/M start screen appeared on the JMZ screen.

The operating system would of course not work correctly as I had replaced many of the real CP/M programs with stub programs that simply wrote a name onto the screen but this did prove that the calls etc were working and that the command interpreter was up and running.

This will now form the basis for the creation of a complete JMZ operating system.

You may wish to configure a version of CP/M to run completely on the JMZ which would certainly be a lot of fun and something I will almost certainly be doing at some time in the future.

If you wish to write your own programs then I would recommend the use of a Z80 compiler as this will make the operation much easier and a lot more enjoyable.

That is as far as I intend to take the operating system development in this book. If you want to see more on this subject and how the full operating system will be designed then please watch out for the follow up book in which I will detail this process.

$\mathcal{L} \mathcal{K} \mathcal{E}$

Chapter 18 - Prototyping and Testing

As a professional systems developer I would typically design an entire system using one or more types of development tool. That may be a 3D CAD drawing system or a schematic capture and printed circuit board development environment or software design package or most commonly a combination of these.

These design tools do not lend themselves well to demonstrating or explaining design ideas and concepts and so when planning this book I decided to avoid showing such methods. This book is after all intended to show how development can be carried out using vintage components and methods. That is not to say that there were no such tools available to developers back in the 1970's and 80's but they were very limited compared to what is available today and somewhat ironically they also required very expensive computers to run them on.

If you have developed systems using modern high speed surface mount component then you already know that for the most part you need to design your circuits either on paper or in a CAD environment and then go straight to prototype printed circuit boards. This is definitely one area in which designing with vintage components lends itself more readily to the hobbyist.

Designing electronic systems with older component technologies was certainly more challenging due to the less predictable nature of their behaviour but it was, and still is, somewhat easier to assemble prototypes because in the initial states it could be carried out with very limited resources.

Things did get more involved as systems became more complex but as long as the projects were divided into sub assemblies and sub systems then it was often feasible to carry out the early prototype stages relatively quickly and easily.

While it would have been possible to design the entire system I am presenting in this book within a software development system and never go through the prototyping stage I wanted to show the steps which were typically carried out when developing vintage systems.

I therefore decided to design and build each sub system in such a way that they could be easily prototyped and tested and this would also make it much easier to describe the designs and concepts. It is also much more fun which is, after all, the entire point of undertaking this project in the first place.

I did use modern pcb CAD software to turn the circuit designs into actual printed circuit boards but I did first carry out all the design work the old fangled way using pencil, paper and my imagination.

Once I had a design on paper I used bread boards to assemble a prototype of the circuits which I could then test.

Back before modern bread boards were available this stage was carried out using something such as wire wrap prototyping boards but the principle is the same. Although I would say that wire wrap assemblies tended to be more reliable and better behaved than their bread board counterparts.

It is very quick and easy to build circuits onto one or more breadboards but this approach does have its drawbacks, especially when designing high speed circuits such as those in the JMZ.

Laying out circuits on a breadboard is not very efficient in terms of space and so the assemblies grow in size very rapidly and as they do they tend to become increasingly unreliable and problematic. Once you go beyond a certain complexity in a single bread board layout you will find that you begin to spend an increasing amount of time chasing apparent faults which often turn out to be caused by the bread boards themselves.

The types of issues that manifest themselves can be anything from simple poor connections to noise or timing errors due to the physical layout but the random nature of these faults can make them frustrating to deal with.

Unlike a printed circuit board you have very little control over things such as 'track' impedances or routing and this can create unpredictable results.

The best approach to minimise such problems is to try to design the system in smaller sub systems which can then be more easily prototyped and tested without too many of the above issues arising. It may also be possible to simply leave out some details of the circuit which are not really needed for initial testing as this will simplify the layout and make testing less problematic.

You do of course need to be very careful when taking this approach to ensure that you do not design something which works fine until the missing parts are added.

For the project I am describing in this book I began by deciding how I was going to sub divide the design into smaller blocks and then the order in which these blocks were to be developed.

It is worth taking some time at this stage of the project as good planning at the start can save a lot of time later and make the overall design less complicated and may also possibly result in a better final design.

Once I had my list of sub assemblies I started with the first, which in this case was the video display system, and I designed it on paper before assembling it onto bread boards.

I was then able to test the circuits and when I was happy that they were working as they should, according to my design, I translated the paper drawings into my pcb CAD system.

During testing I was able to make changes where required and so the prototype circuit boards could then be made and as each was only a small part of the final computer they were relatively small and easy to design.

Once I had assembled a prototype sub assembly board I was able to test it more extensively than was possible with the bread board versions and while they all worked there were a couple of cases where I went back to improve the design and then go back through the paper / bread board / pcb / test phases.

It is well known that a design is never complete and can always be improved upon so it is important not to get caught in a never ending loop at this phase of development or the project may never get completed although that may be exactly what to want.

As each sub assembly became available as a working board I could start to connect them together and because I had designed each as a complete sub system it was then very easy to begin more complex testing.

For example once I had the CPU board and video display board available I could connect them together and it was then possible to connect a ZAX in circuit emulator which I could then use to start writing more complex test programs and investigate the operation of the sub assemblies as a single system.

If you do not have an in circuit emulator then you can still carry out extensive testing by writing some test programs and running them from a ROM plugged into the CPU board. I always find this stage of a design very exiting and it is a huge amount of fun and also very satisfying to see a complex system beginning to come to life.

Naturally there are times when things do not go as planned but by working through problems and investigating any unintended behaviour it is normally fairly easy to located and correct any design issues, although sometimes it is not so simple.

One thing that I cannot over stress is what a fantastic learning tool and experience it can be to design a complete and complex electronic system such as the one in this project.

This type of design spans many aspects of electronic circuit operation and behaviour and the use of vintage components really brings the basics of system design into view.

For anyone interested in design it is also a huge amount of fun and once you have a working machine it can be the basis for almost unlimited experimentation in both electronics and firmware.
It is also a very good way to learn how to use more advanced test equipment such a logic analysers and in circuit emulators if you are lucky enough to have access to them.

I will now show each sub assembly from bread board to prototype circuit board and describe any issues which I encountered as the development progressed starting with the video display system.

Video System Prototype

Figure 18-1 shows the early video system built onto bread boards and while it may not be pretty it is functional.
Using this assembly I was able to determine that the various timers and counter values were correct and that they provided the required text output format.
In fact this is the second version of the bread board assembly because as I explained in an earlier chapter I decided to change the format from 80 x 24 characters to 64 x 30 characters and this required a number of changes to the various circuits on this assembly.
As I was putting this part of the system together I connected it to the CRT monitor which I had selected for this project and this allowed me to test each aspect of its design as I added them.
Initially I was simply checking that the division ratio and reload value for each counter was correct but once I had the decoding for the horizontal and vertical drive signals in place it was able to produce a good stable raster on the screen. I could then adjust the various settings on the monitor in order to centre and stabilise the raster. In this case the settings were the height, width, vertical hold, vertical linearity and the centring magnets.

At this stage in the design I connected a signal generator to the video input of the monitor and applied a pulse steam which was an exact multiple of the horizontal frequency. This allowed me to check that the system was generating properly synchronised and stable drive signals because the monitor displayed a series of vertical lines which changed in response to the applied pulse frequency and pulse width.

Had the display been unstable or erratic then this would have indicated that something was wrong but luckily everything looked good so far.

I then determined the format and style of character set I intended to use for my system and created a suitable ROM image.

I explained earlier how the bitmap images for the text characters are arranged in the ROM.

Figure 18-1 Video System Bread Board Prototype

Once I had added an SRAM and shift register the video system was able to generate a serial stream of video data which was perfectly synchronised with the display and so a stable screen full of garbage was generated. Things were looking promising.

The garbage was to be expected as so far there was no way to enter character data into the video RAM so this was actually a very good indication that the video system was working.

At this stage the bread board assembly had grown to the point where it was not really practical to add anything further to it so I turned the circuits developed into a printed circuit board design.

At the same time I added a few additional features which I had intentionally omitted from the bread board version for the reasons I explained above.

These features included address multiplexers and a bi-directional data buffer along with some video circuit control logic.

The purpose of these additions was to allow the writing of data into the video SRAM by the CPU which is of course needed if the system is to be able to write text to the screen.

The first prototype video circuit board is shown in Figure 18-2.

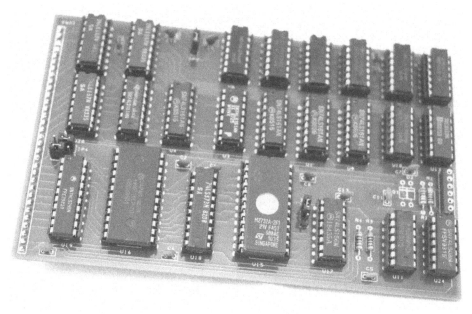

Figure 18-2 Video System Pcb Prototype

Once the prototype video driver board had been assembled I was able to carry out more extensive testing and I initially did this using a microcontroller to send data to the video RAM.

I appreciate that this is not the way it would have been done back in the day but I did this in order to make the development process a little more transparent to those who were following it.

Previously this step would have had to wait until the CPU prototype assembly was ready to use as a test platform.

It may be worth pointing out here that if you have access to a logic analyser which has a pattern generator then this can also be used for this type of testing.

The early testing revealed that the 80 x 24 character format was not ideal for me so I went back and changed the design to the final 64 x 30 format. I could then move on to the Z80 CPU system design.

Figure 18-3 shows the revised version of the video driver board.

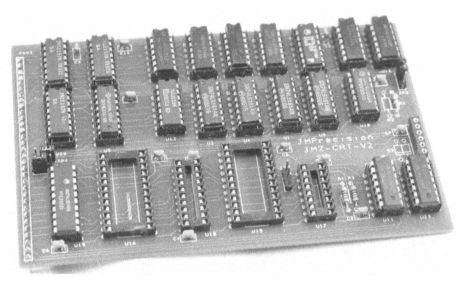

Figure 18-3 Version 2 Video System Pcb Prototype

CPU Prototype

Although this project was aimed at the design and development of a computer system I needed to begin the actual processor core system development on a smaller scale as this would allow me to design the required memory control and mapping circuits without resorting to large prototype boards.

In a commercial project I would design the entire system and then build a complete product prototype but I had decided to break the overall design into smaller blocks in order to allow more detailed explanations. By sub dividing the design into these smaller sections I could focus the descriptions and explanations on specific elements of the design without the need to constantly refer to the other parts of the design.

This approach also allows much more specific testing on each sub section of the overall design.

It is important to remember that in this book I tried as much as possible to describe the entire development process and this means that there were some inevitable changes in some of the circuits as things progressed.

I also attempted to avoid dropping design ideas into the early circuits until they were needed even though I was aware that they would eventually be required. Again this was to avoid the need to explain the function of circuit elements that played no real part in the early circuit designs.

Clearly it would have been much easier to skip some of these steps but that would have made the book less clear and most likely caused confusion.

Figure 18-4 shows a very early version of the CPU design built onto bread boards and you can clearly see how it quickly develops into a rats nest.

Figure 18-4 CPU System Bread Board Prototype 2

In the case of the processor I decided to include only the basic system control circuits such as memory mapping and DRAM control. These functions all need to work together in order to provide a reliable and functional computer system but other peripheral circuits such as input and output ports, keyboard etc can be easily handled as separate designs and added later.

I began this part of the development by simply building a bread board circuit which comprised of nothing more than the Z80 itself and to this I added the clock generator and reset circuits.

Once I was happy that the Z80 was resetting reliably and that the clock generator circuit was stable I added a ROM and then an SRAM. The SRAM was only for initial test purposes to allow me to check the operation of the processor.

I used this in place of the intended DRAM because the SRAM does not need the complex drive electronics which would need to be put in place before the DRAM can be used.

After writing some very simple test code to check that the CPU could access the ROM and RAM I then turned my attention to the DRAM control circuits.

By taking this step by step approach I was able to quickly build a prototype bread board version of the DRAM control circuit and once I was happy that this was working I turned the design into a prototype printed circuit board.

This board included additional features which were not in the bread board assembly for the same reasons as previously described and it also included a number of connectors which would allow this board to be used for development in the next stages of the overall computer design.

I was fairly careful in deciding which parts of the design to omit from the bread board testing phase in order to avoid any nasty surprises later on. Items such as buffers and multiplexers are relatively predictable and so I felt fairly comfortable only adding these at the printed circuit board phase of design.

Figure 18-5 shows the first Z80 CPU circuit board prototype.

Before moving on and adding more circuits to the computer design I spent some time writing test code for this board which allowed me to fully test its operation and determine that everything was in order and that the Z80 was able to access all RAM blocks and switch banks without any timing issues or bus contention.

It is well worth spending considerable effort at this stage of the development to ensure that everything is in order because any issues here will make further development increasingly difficult.

In particular I paid attention to the DRAM control timing and memory bank switching and mapping. These circuits are fairly complex but are fundamental to the overall system operation and performance.

Figure 18-5 First CPU System Pcb Prototype

DRAM Daughter Board

While I was working on the breadboard version of the CPU I needed to be able to install the system DRAM as this was an important part of the overall core system design.

A major consideration in the design of the DRAM control circuitry was the critical timing of each control signal and phase which is required to ensure reliable operation of such a system.

It would have been perfectly possible to use bread boards in order to construct the DRAM circuitry but as I have mentioned previously the use of breadboards in circuits where critical timing is required can be very problematic.

It is entirely possible that I could have wasted a lot of time tracking down faults which were only present because of the use of the breadboards or worse still the system may have worked perfectly on the breadboards but then failed to function correctly when the design was translated onto a circuit board.

In order to avoid this type of potential problem I designed a small daughter board onto which the DRAM could be installed in order to minimise the potential for ambiguous operation or meaningless testing. This board would not be used in the future main boards but it was very useful for the bread board phase of the project.

Figure 18-6 shows this daughter board.

Figure 18-6 DRAM Daughter Board

Second CPU Prototype

As the project continued to develop I designed more advanced CPU boards which included the newly designed circuits and allowed further development of the JMZ.

Figure 18-7 shows the second JMZ CPU board design.

This board was used while developing the RS232 and IO circuits along with the various interrupt logic configuration.

As each new board was built I fully tested all aspects of the design and I paid particular attention to the timing constraints for each element within the design. Over the years I have encountered many vintage computers where insufficient attention was given to the interaction of each part of a system and this frequently resulted in erratic operation under certain conditions or even total failure of the design once components began to age.

As I demonstrated in earlier chapters I have been designing each circuit in such a way that no timing race conditions or overlaps would occur. Had I encountered any such issues then I would of course have dealt with them by modifying the circuits before moving on to the next phase of the project.

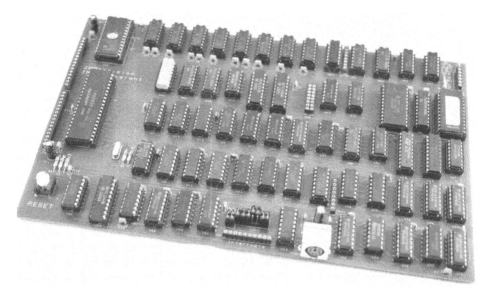

Figure 18-7 Second Version CPU System Pcb Prototype

Interrupt and PS2 Interface Prototype

The interrupt system I decided to implement was for the Z80 mode 2 operation and it was a very simple circuit which could easily be built onto a single bread board.

I designed the keyboard PS2 interface at the same time so that I could combine these two circuits at the bread board prototype phase and use them together to test the interrupt system. This also added support for keyboard input to the system and so I was finally able to interact with it which made further development much easier. The project was getting exciting.

Figure 18-8 shows the PS2 interface and mode 2 interrupt controller circuits built onto bread boards. The PS2 interface is on the board at the right and the interrupt controller is on the left.

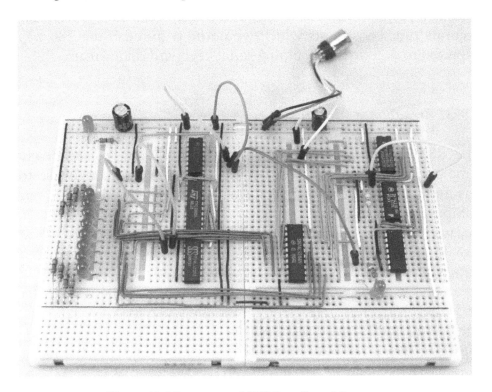

Figure 18-8 Interrupt and PS2 Breadboard Prototype

The row of LED's towards the left side was used to display the data bus output from these two circuits as both of these need to place data values onto the bus using tri-state buffers.

Using this prototype I was able to successfully test the operation of the keyboard interface and also us it to write and test some simple mode 2 interrupt code including an interrupt look up table and actual interrupt handlers.

Although these circuits are both very simple they were designed specifically to make the rest of the computer system design as easy as possible.

For example the interrupt controller circuit removes the need for individual devices to concern themselves with putting their vector onto the data bus as this circuit takes care of that task for them.

The PS2 interface reduces the number of interrupts required for each key pressed from 12 to just 1 and also removes the need for accurate time constraints which would be required if the Z80 was expected to decode the incoming serial keyboard data stream.

RS232 Breadboard Prototype

The RS232 serial communication interface circuit is a relatively simple circuit although it did require some though in order to ensure it could be used efficiently within the overall design of our computer.

Because RS232 is an asynchronous data stream there is no direct way to guarantee that the incoming data or indeed the transmitted data will be properly synchronised with the Z80 memory cycles.

In a very basic system it is possible to simply poll the transmitter and receiver circuits in order to determine when the next data byte can be sent and received respectively.

However this is not really feasible in a complex system due to the possible risk of data stream under run or over run.

To avoid such problems and also to make the system as flexible as possible the circuit I designed can be operated in a number of ways from a simple polling algorithm to complex hardware interrupt control. I initially built the circuit onto breadboards and used the version 2 JMZ main board to test this before finally adding the circuit to the JMZ version 3 design.

Figure 18-9 shows the RS232 circuit built onto breadboards.

Figure 18-9 Interrupt and PS2 Breadboard Prototype

In this image the transmitter circuit is on the left and the receiver is on the right. The breadboard on the right contains a clock divider and although it is not actually part of these circuits it was required for the initial testing.
In the final design the required clock signals are of course taken directly from the main system clock divider.

Final Computer Board Design

Although I will continue to develop my own version of this system I had to draw a line somewhere for the purposes of completing this project as far as this book is concerned.

Figure 18-10 shows version 3 of the JMZ CPU board design which includes all the features I describe in this book and which was used as the starting point for developing the operating system and software which I will describe in the next book.

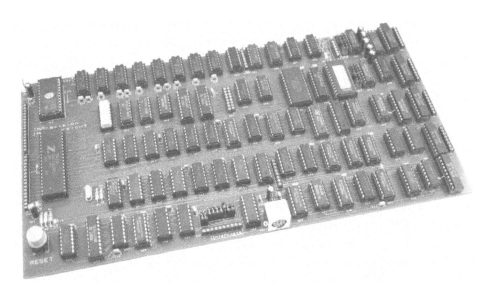

Figure 18-10 Third and Final JMZ CPU System Pcb Prototype

This version of the board adds more structured hardware interrupts along with the RS232 transmitter and receiver circuits. It also includes two eight bit input ports and two eight bit output ports.

Future JMZ Development

Although this is the last version of the JMZ which I will be presenting in this book it is by no means the final version of this system. I will be adding many more features to my design and that is what makes projects such as this so fascinating because they can provide an almost endless potential for experimentation and further development.

Appendix A – JMZ Z80 Computer Summary

The following table gives a summary of the JMZ Z80 Computer system (V3).

Processor	Z80
Processor Clock Speed	2.5MHz
Main RAM	64k DRAM (2k not available)
Video RAM	2k SRAM
Non Volatile RAM	128 bytes
ROM	8k
Memory Banks	2
Memory wait states	0
Keyboard Supported	PS2 – Character set 2
Serial Interface	RS232
Serial Baud Rate	2400, 4800, 9600, 19200, 38400
8 bit Input Ports	2
8 bit Output Ports	2
Display	CRT Monochrome
Video Output	Text 64 Columns x 30 Rows
Interrupts	Mode 2
Power Supply	Single +5V
Average current consumption	1100 mA
IC's used	80
Board dimensions (cm)	29cm x 15cm

Appendix B – JMZ Z80 Computer Schematics

The Following pages show the full schematic diagrams for the JMZ Version 3 Z80 computer main board.

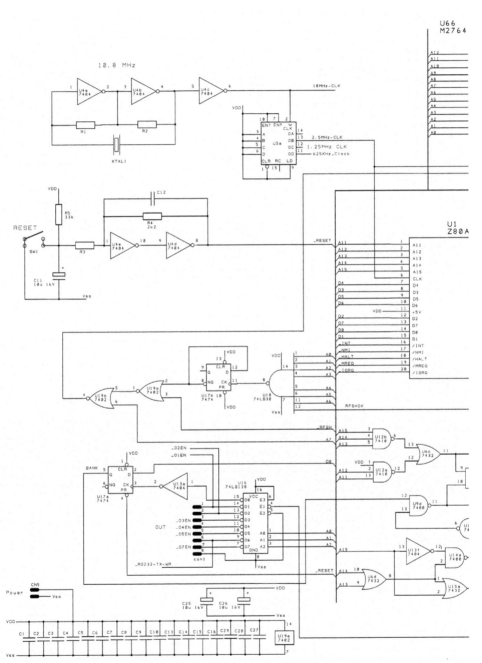

Figure 0-1 JMZ Schematics CPU-L

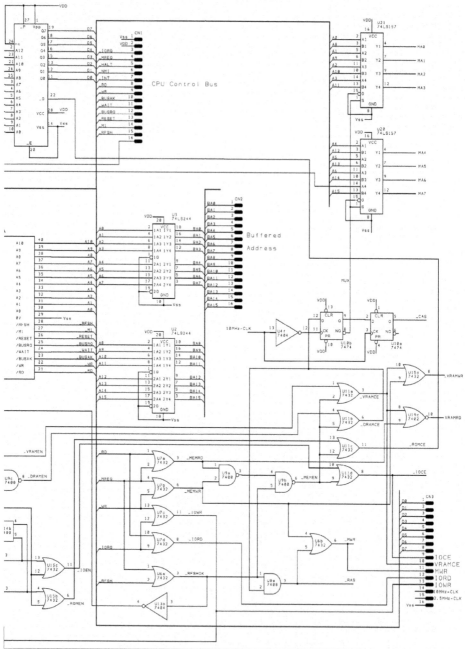

Figure 0-2 JMZ Schematics CPU-R

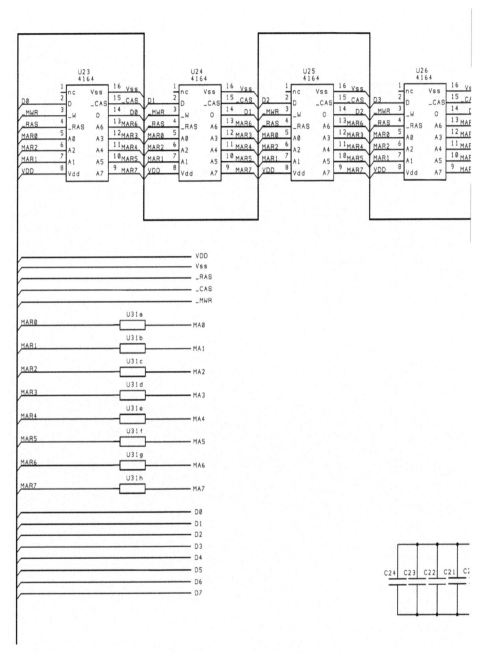

Figure 0-3 JMZ Schematics DRAM-L

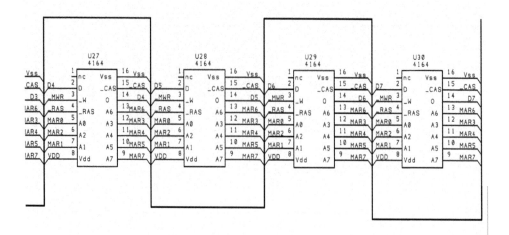

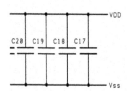

Figure 0-4 JMZ Schematics DRAM-R

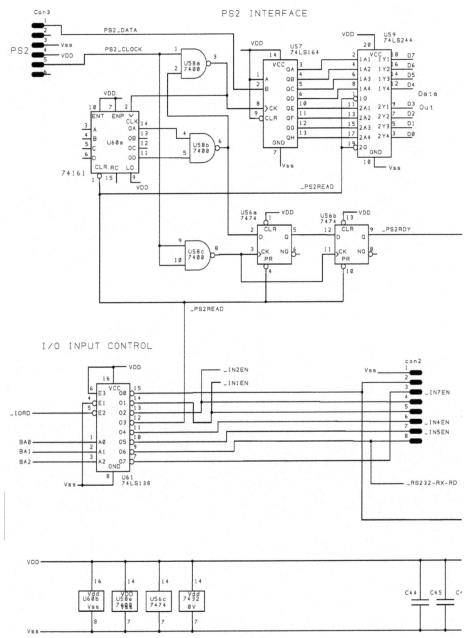

Figure 0-5 JMZ Schematics Interrupt-L

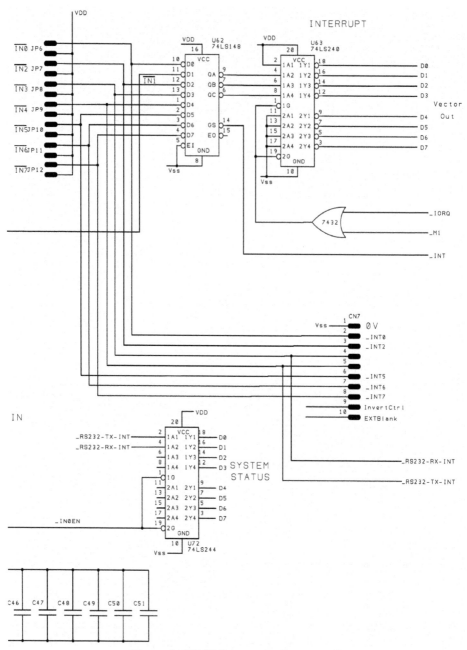

Figure 0-6 JMZ Schematics Interrupt-R

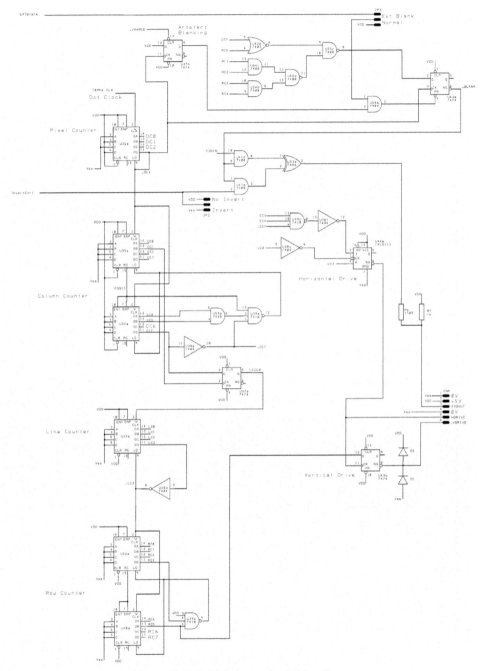

Figure 0-7 JMZ Schematics Video-L

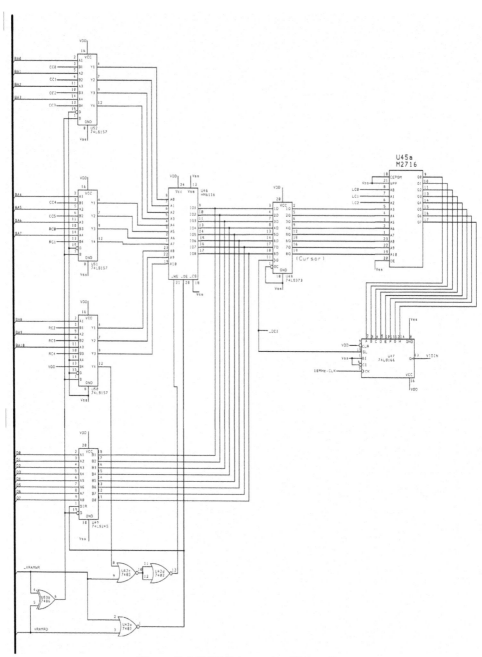

Figure 0-8 JMZ Schematics Video-R

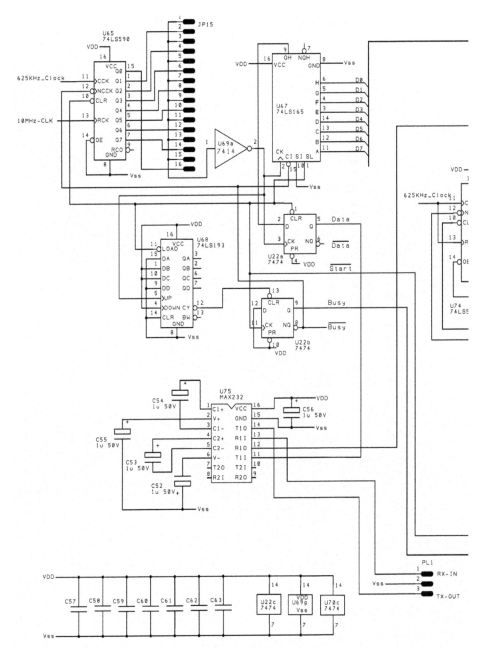

Figure 0-9 JMZ Schematics RS232-L

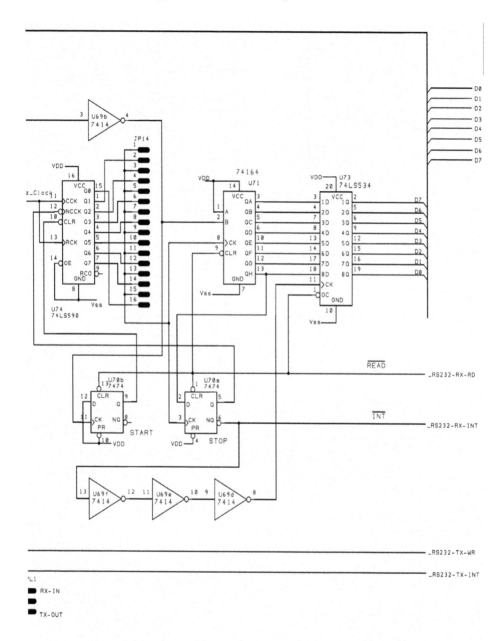

Figure 0-10 JMZ Schematics RS232-R

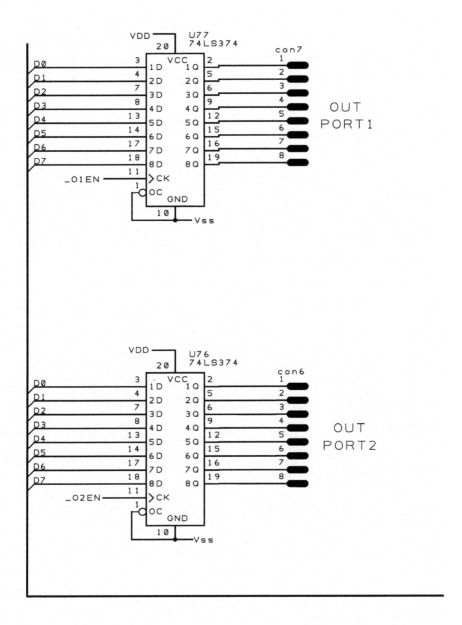

Figure 0-11 JMZ Schematics IO-L

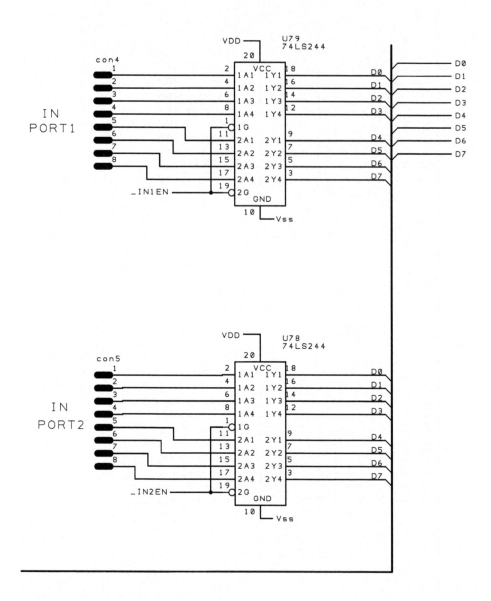

Figure 0-12 JMZ Schematics IO-R

Appendix B – JMZ Z80 Computer Schematics

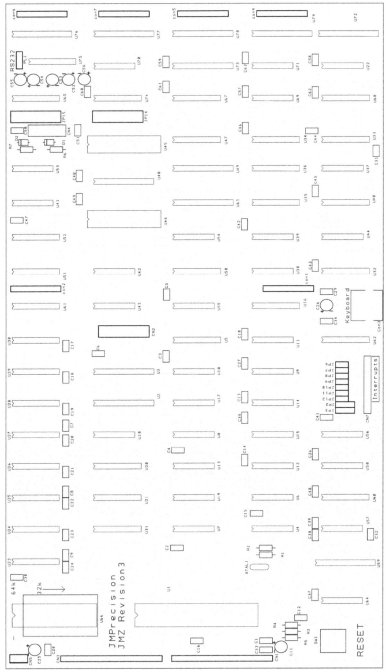

Figure 0-13 JMZ Version 3 pcb

407

Appendix C – JMZ Jumpers and Connectors

The Following pages show the purpose of the main board jumpers and connections.

This information relates to version 3 of the JMZ main pcb.

Be sure to check the orientation of each connector and the position of pin one for each connector as they are not all the same.

CN5	
1	+5V 2A
2	0V

CN3	
1	D0
2	D1
3	D2
4	D3
5	D4
6	D5
7	D6
8	D7
9	_IOCE
10	_VRAMCE
11	_MWR
12	_IORD
13	_IOWR
14	10.0MHz Clock
15	2.5MHz Clock
16	0V

CN1	
1	0V
2	+5V
3	_IORQ
4	_MREQ
5	_HALT
6	_NMI **
7	_INT
8	_RD
9	_WR
10	_BUSAK
11	_WAIT **
12	_BUSRQ **
13	_RESET
14	_M1
15	_RFSH
16	2.5MHz Clock

** If unused these inputs must be tied to +5V

CON2	
1	0V
2	_IN0EN
3	_IN7EN
4	_IN2EN
5	_IN1EN
6	_IN4EN
7	_IN5EN
8	_RS232-RX-RD

PL1	
1	RS232 RX-IN
2	0V
3	RS232 TX-OUT

CON1	
1	_O1EN
2	_O2EN
3	_O3EN
4	_O4EN
5	_O5EN
6	_RS232-TX-WR
7	_O7EN
8	0V

JP14 *	
1	RX 153600 BAUD – Not Used
2	RX 76800 BAUD – Not Used
3	RX 38400 BAUD
4	RX 19200 BAUD
5	RX 9600 BAUD
6	RX 4800 BAUD
7	RX 2400 BAUD
8	RX 307200 BAUD – Not Used

JP15 *	
1	TX 153600 BAUD – Not Used
2	TX 76800 BAUD – Not Used
3	TX 38400 BAUD
4	TX 19200 BAUD
5	TX 9600 BAUD
6	TX 4800 BAUD
7	TX 2400 BAUD
8	TX 307200 BAUD – Not Used

* ONLY FIT ONE JUMPER TO EACH BLOCK

CN4	
1	0V
2	+5V
3	VIDOUT
4	0V
5	HDRIVE
6	_VDRIVE

CON7 – PORT1 - OUT	
1	D0
2	D1
3	D2
4	D3
5	D4
6	D5
7	D6
8	D7

CON6 – PORT2 - OUT	
1	D0
2	D1
3	D2
4	D3
5	D4
6	D5
7	D6
8	D7

CON4 – PORT1 - IN	
1	D0
2	D1
3	D2
4	D3
5	D4
6	D5
7	D6
8	D7

CON5 – PORT2 - IN	
1	D0
2	D1
3	D2
4	D3
5	D4
6	D5
7	D6
8	D7

CON7 – INTERRUPTS	
1	0V
2	_INT0
3	_INT2
4	_RS232-RX-INT
5	_RS232-TX-INT
6	_INT5
7	_INT6
8	_INT7
9	InvertCtrl
10	EXTBlank

INTERRUPT JUMPERS	
JP6	Disable INT0
JP7	Disable INT2
JP8	Disable INT3
JP9	Disable INT4
JP10	Disable INT5
JP11	Disable INT6
JP12	Disable INT7

SELECT JUMPERS	
JP2 1-2	No Invert
JP2 2-3	Invert
JP3 1-2	Ext Blank
JP3 2-3	Normal Video

NOTE:

Improper connections or jumper configuration may prevent the JMZ computer system from booting correctly.

Appendix D – JMZ Port and Interrupt Assignments

The Following pages describe how the input and output ports and interrupts are assigned.

Input Port Assignments (IN A,(nn))	
IN Port 0	System Status Register
IN Port 1	Hardware Port 1 In
IN Port 2	Hardware Port 2 In
IN Port 3	PS2 Keyboard Data In
IN Port 4	General Purpose In
IN Port 5	General Purpose In
IN Port 6	RS232 Data In
IN Port 7	General Purpose In

Output Port Assignments (OUT (nn),A)	
OUT Port 0	Bank Select Port
OUT Port 1	Hardware Port 1 Out
OUT Port 2	Hardware Port 2 Out
OUT Port 3	General Purpose In
OUT Port 4	General Purpose In
OUT Port 5	General Purpose In
OUT Port 6	RS232 Data Out
OUT Port 7	General Purpose In

System Status Register bit Assignments (IN A,(00))	
Bit 0	RS232 TX
Bit 1	RS232 RX
Bit 2	Spare
Bit 3	Spare
Bit 4	Spare
Bit 5	Spare
Bit 6	Spare
Bit 7	Spare

Interrupt Assignments	
Interrupt 0	Spare
Interrupt 1	PS2 Keyboard Data Ready
Interrupt 2	Spare
Interrupt 3	RS232 RX
Interrupt 4	RS232 TX
Interrupt 5	Spare
Interrupt 6	Spare
Interrupt 7	Spare

The unused ports and interrupts can be connected to whatever hardware you wish. Bear in mind that the interrupts are priority based in sequential order.

Appendix E – JMZ Monitor Listing V1.0

```
;JMZ MONOTIR ROM V1.0
;--------------- GLOBAL STATUS BYTE EQUATES ----------------
GSF_RS_TX   EQU 0            ;RS232 TX Ready
GSF_RS_RX   EQU 1            ;RS232 RX Ready
GSF_2       EQU 2
GSF_3       EQU 3
GSF_4       EQU 4
GSF_5       EQU 5
GSF_6       EQU 6
GSF_7       EQU 7
;------------------ GENERAL FLAG EQUATES --------------------
GF0         EQU 0
GF1         EQU 1
GF2         EQU 2
GF3         EQU 3
GF4         EQU 4
GF5         EQU 5
GF6         EQU 6
GF7         EQU 7
;------------------------ KEYBOARD FLAG EQUATES ----------------------
CHAR_AV_FLAG    EQU 0            ;1 = Character available
RELEASE_FLAG    EQU 1            ;1 = Key Down
SHIFT_FLAG      EQU 2            ;1 = Shift
ADD_NL          EQU 3            ;Used to add NLCR
RX_CHAR_AV      EQU 4            ;1 = RS232 byte received
EOF             EQU 5            ;1 = End of RS232 file
DOWNLOADING     EQU 6            ;1 = File download in progress
FAST_FLAG       EQU 7            ;Used for fast file download
;------------------------ ERROR CODE EQUATES -----------------------
E_NONE      EQU 00h          ;No error
E_NOHEX     EQU 01h          ;Char not 0-9, A-F
E_PARAM     EQU 02h          ;Start greater than end
E_BUFSIZE   EQU 03h          ;Too long for buffer
E_HITYP     EQU 04h          ;Invalid record type
E_HICKSM    EQU 05h          ;Checksum error
E_HIEND     EQU 06h          ;End record found
E_GEN       EQU 07h          ;General error
;------------------------ SYSTEM EQUATES ----------------------
RAMTOP        EQU F7EFh          ;Top of RAM
INT_TABLE     EQU F7F0h          ;Vector Table (F7F0-F7FF)
STACK         EQU E7EFh          ;Stack
VIDEO_RAM     EQU F800h          ;Start of video RAM
VIDEO_RAM_TOP EQU FF79h          ;Top of video RAM
VIDEO_RAM_LEN EQU 0780h          ;Length of Video RAM
NON_VOLATILE  EQU FED8h          ;Start of non volatile RAM
ORG_BASE      EQU 0000h          ;Assembly base address
ASCII_TABLEL  EQU ORG_BASE + 0F00h ;ASCII table (PS2 index)
ASCII_TABLEH  EQU (ASCII_TABLEL + 128);ASCII table (PS2 index)
KB_HANDLER    EQU ORG_BASE + 0D00h ;Keyboard INT handler
RX_HANDLER    EQU ORG_BASE + 0E00h ;RS232 Receive INT handler
;TX_HANDLER   EQU ORG_BASE + 0A00h ;RS232 Transmit INT handler
```

```
HEXLINES            EQU 17                      ;Number of lines in memory dump
LCCHAR              EQU ' '
HCCHAR              EQU '~'
;----------------------- SYSTEM VARIABLES ---------------------------
ASCIIBUF            EQU 9000h                   ;Memory dump buffer (16 bytes)
ASCIIENDADD         EQU 9010h                   ;Dump end address
VIDEO_PTR           EQU 9012h                   ;Video Pointer variable
VIDEO_FLAGS         EQU 9014h                   ;Video State Flags
KEYBOARD_FLAGS      EQU 9016h                   ;PS2 Interface Flags
KEY_BUFFER          EQU 9018h                   ;Latest Keyboard Character
ERRCODE             EQU 901Ah                   ;Monitor error code buffer
DUMPADDR            EQU 901Ch                   ;Monitor Dump address
ADDRESS_BUFFER      EQU 901Eh                   ;Monitor buffer
FILE_PTR            EQU 902Ah                   ;File download address pointer
GEN_FLAGS1          EQU 902Bh                   ;General flags byte


ORG ORG_BASE
 JP START                                       ;Jump to start of code


;----------------------------- TEXT STRINGS -------------------------
TEXT1 DB 'WELCOME TO THE JMZ PROJECT',00h
TEXT2 DB 'DISCRETE Z80 COMPUTER',00h
TEXT3 DB 'VERSION 1.1',00h
TEXT4 DB 'Press any key',00h
TEXTM1 DB 'JMZ Z80 Monitor V1.0',00h
TEXTH DB 'H - Help',00h
TEXTC DB 'C - Clear screen',00h
TEXTD DB 'D - Dump RAM',00h
TEXTD DB 'A - Dump RAM with ASCII',00h
TEXTE DB 'E - Edit memory',00h
TEXTF DB 'F - Fill memory range',00h
TEXTG DB 'G - Run from address',00h
TEXTK DB 'K - Call address',00h
TEXTL DB 'L - Load file',00h
TEXTM DB 'M - Copy memory block',00h
TEXTO DB 'O - Port output',00h
TEXTP DB 'P - Print registers',00h
TEXTR DB 'R - Reset monitor',00h
TEXTZ DB 'Z - Load file fast',00h
TEXTPlus DB '+ Print next memory block',00h
TEXTMinus DB '- Print Previous memory block',00h
PORTData DB 'Port and Data ',00h
MONP DB '>',00h
MON_ERROR DB 'Error',00h
START_ADDRESS_PROMPT DB 'Start Address (HEX): ',00h
MEM_DUMP_HEADER DB '        0  1  2  3  4  5  6  7  8  9  A  B  C  D  E
F',00h
REG_HEADER DB ' HL   AF   BC   DE   IX   IY   SP   PC   IF',00h
WAIT_FILE DB 'Waiting for file',00h
RX_FILE DB 'Receiving file',00h
SENDING_DATA DB 'Sending data',00h
DATA_SENT DB 'Data send complete',00h
FILE_DONE DB 'Download complete',00h
FILL_DATA_PROMPT DB 'Data value (one byte): ',00h
END_ADDRESS_PROMPT DB 'End Address (HEX): ',00h
DESTINATION_PROMPT DB 'Destination Address: ',00h
```

```
START:
      DI
      IM    2                        ;Set interrupt mode 2
      LD    A,F7h                    ;Load I register
      LD    I,A
      LD    HL,STACK                 ;Initialise stack register
      LD    SP,HL
      LD    HL,KB_HANDLER            ;Initialise interrupt table
      LD    (INT_TABLE + 2),HL       ;Keyboard handler address
      LD    HL,RX_HANDLER
      LD    (INT_TABLE + 6),HL       ;RS232 Receive handler address
;     LD    HL,TX_HANDLER
;     LD    (INT_TABLE + 8),HL       ;RS232 Transmit handler address



              ;INITIALISE SYSTEM
      CALL  CLEAR_VIDEO              ;CLEAR VIDEO RAM

      IN    A,(3)                    ;Reset PS2 Interface
      IN    A,(6)                    ;Reset RS232 Interface

              ;INITIALISE VARIABLES
      LD    HL,VIDEO_FLAGS           ;Clear all flags
      LD    (HL),00h
      LD    HL,KEYBOARD_FLAGS
      LD    (HL),00h
      EI                             ;Enable interrupts

      CALL  WELCOME_SCR              ;WELCOME SCREEN
      LD    BC,TEXT1
      LD    HL,VIDEO_RAM + 0153h
      LD    (VIDEO_PTR),HL
      CALL  PRINT_STR
      LD    BC,TEXT2
      LD    HL,VIDEO_RAM + 03D5h
      LD    (VIDEO_PTR),HL
      CALL  PRINT_STR
      LD    BC,TEXT3
      LD    HL,VIDEO_RAM + 041Ah
      LD    (VIDEO_PTR),HL
      CALL  PRINT_STR
      LD    BC,TEXT4
      LD    HL,VIDEO_RAM + 0499h
      LD    (VIDEO_PTR),HL
      CALL  PRINT_STR

LD    HL,KEYBOARD_FLAGS
LOOPW1:
      BIT   CHAR_AV_FLAG,(HL)        ;Is the char ready flag set?
      JR    Z,LOOPW1                 ;No So wait
      LD    (HL),00h                 ;Clear kb flags

      CALL  CLEAR_VIDEO
```

```
;************************************************************************
;************************* ENTER MONITOR *****************************
MAIN
      IN    A,(6)                  ;Initialise RS232 RX
      CALL  CLEAR_VIDEO
      CALL  NEW_LINE
      CALL  PRINT_MON_HEADER       ;Print the monitor header
      CALL  NEW_LINE
      LD    A, 00h
      LD    (DUMPADDR),A
      LD    A, FFh
      LD    (DUMPADDR+1),A
      CALL  CLEAR_ERROR

;-------------------------- MONITOR LOOP ----------------------------
MONITOR_LOOP
      LD    BC,MONP                ;Print monitor prompt
      CALL  PRINT_STR
      CALL  GET_CHAR               ;Get input from user
      LD    A,(KEY_BUFFER)         ;Get character from buffer
      CALL  PRINT_CHAR             ;Print the character
      CALL  NEW_LINE               ;Print a new line
      CALL  COMMAND_PROCESSOR      ;Process Command
      CALL  NEW_LINE               ;Print a new line
      JR    MONITOR_LOOP

;------------------------- COMMAND PROCESSOR ------------------------
COMMAND_PROCESSOR:
      CALL  CLEAR_ERROR
      LD    A,(KEY_BUFFER)         ;Get character from buffer
      CP    'H'
      CALL  Z,DISPLAY_HELP
      CP    'C'
      CALL  Z,CLEAR_SCREEN
      CP    'D'
      CALL  Z,MEMORY_DUMP
      CP    'A'
      CALL  Z,MEMORY_DUMP_ASCII
      CP    'E'
      CALL  Z,EDIT_MEMORY
      CP    'F'
      CALL  Z,FILL_MEMORY
      CP    'G'
      CALL  Z,RUN_ADDRESS
      CP    'K'
      CALL  Z,CALL_ADDRESS
      CP    'L'
      CALL  Z,LOAD_FILE
      CP    'M'
      CALL  Z,MOVE_MEMORY
      CP    'O'
      CALL  Z,PORT_OUTPUT
      CP    'P'
      CALL  Z,PRINT_REGISTERS
      CP    'R'
      CALL  Z,RESET_MONITOR
```

```
        CP    'S'
        CALL  Z,SEND_RAM
        CP    '+'
        CALL  Z,NEXT_MEM_BLOCK
        CP    '-'
        CALL  Z,PREV_MEM_BLOCK
        CP    'Z'
        CALL  Z,LOAD_FILE_FAST
        CALL  ERROR_CHECK
        RET
ERROR_CHECK:
        LD    A,(ERRCODE)
        CP    E_NONE
        RET   Z
        LD    BC,MON_ERROR
        CALL  PRINT_STR
        LD    A, (ERRCODE)
        CALL  PRINT_HEX_BYTE
        CALL  NEW_LINE
CLEAR_ERROR:
        PUSH  AF
        LD    A,E_NONE
        LD    (ERRCODE),A
        POP   AF
        RET


;------------------------- PORT OUTPUT -------------------------------
PORT_OUTPUT:
        LD    BC,PORTData            ;Print Prompt
        CALL  PRINT_STR
        CALL  GET_HEX_BYTE
        LD    (ADDRESS_BUFFER),A     ;Store port number
        LD    A,(ERRCODE)
        CP    E_NONE
        RET   NZ
        LD    A,' '
        CALL  PRINT_CHAR
        CALL  GET_HEX_BYTE
        LD    (ADDRESS_BUFFER+1), A
        LD    A,(ERRCODE)
        CP    E_NONE
        RET   NZ
        LD    A,(ADDRESS_BUFFER)
        LD    C,A
        LD    A,(ADDRESS_BUFFER+1)
        OUT   (C), A
        RET


;------------------------- CALL ADDRESS -------------------------------
CALL_ADDRESS
        LD    BC,DESTINATION_PROMPT   ;Print Destination prompt
        CALL  PRINT_STR
        CALL  GET_HEX_WORD
        LD    A,(ERRCODE)
        CP    E_NONE
        RET   NZ
```

```
        LD      DE,MAIN                         ;Push Address of MAIN onto
        PUSH    DE                              ;Stack for return
        JP      (HL)
        RET


;----------------------- SEND RAM ----------------------------
;Send a block of RAM to RS232
SEND_RAM:
        LD      BC,START_ADDRESS_PROMPT         ;Start address prompt
        CALL    PRINT_STR
        CALL    GET_HEX_WORD                    ;Get block start address
        LD      A,(ERRCODE)
        CP      E_NONE
        RET     NZ
        LD      (ADDRESS_BUFFER),HL             ;Save start address
        CALL    NEW_LINE
        LD      BC,END_ADDRESS_PROMPT           ;End Address prompt
        CALL    PRINT_STR
        CALL    GET_HEX_WORD
        LD      A,(ERRCODE)
        CP      E_NONE
        RET     NZ
        LD      (ADDRESS_BUFFER+2),HL           ;Save end address
        CALL    NEW_LINE
        LD      BC,SENDING_DATA                 ;Sending data text
        CALL    PRINT_STR_NLCR
        LD      DE,(ADDRESS_BUFFER)             ;Start
        SBC     HL,DE                           ;End > Start ?
        JR      C,RS_ORDERR                     ;Yes so flag error
        LD      HL,(ADDRESS_BUFFER + 2)         ;Get end address
        EX      DE,HL
        LD      HL,(ADDRESS_BUFFER)             ;Get start address
        PUSH    HL
SEND_RS_DATA
        POP     HL
                        ;CHECK STATUS BYTE AND WAIT UNTIL RS232 IS READY
WAIT_TX_READY
        IN      A,(00h)                         ;Read the global status byte
        BIT     GSF_RS_TX,A                     ;Is the transmitter ready?
        JP      NZ,WAIT_TX_READY

        LD      B,04h                           ;Allow time for TX reset
TX_DELAY
        DJNZ    TX_DELAY

        LD      A,(HL)
        OUT     (06h),A                         ;Send character to RS232
        INC     HL                              ;Point to next address
        PUSH    HL                              ;Check if HL = END ADDRESS
        SBC     HL,DE
        JR      NZ,SEND_RS_DATA                 ;Not last byte so continue
        POP     HL

        LD      BC,DATA_SENT                    ;Data sent text
        CALL    PRINT_STR_NLCR
        RET
```

```
RS_ORDERR:                              ;Error so abort
      LD    A,E_PARAM
      LD    (ERRCODE),A
      RET


;----------------------- LOAD FILE FROM SERIAL -----------------------
LOAD_FILE_FAST                          ;Loads file without screen
      LD    HL,KEYBOARD_FLAGS
      SET   FAST_FLAG,(HL)              ;Set fast flag
      JP    START_FILE_DOWNLOAD
LOAD_FILE
      LD    HL,KEYBOARD_FLAGS
      RES   FAST_FLAG,(HL)              ;Clear fast flag
START_FILE_DOWNLOAD
      LD    BC,DESTINATION_PROMPT       ;Print Destination prompt
      CALL  PRINT_STR
      CALL  GET_HEX_WORD                ;Get start address into HL
      LD    (FILE_PTR),HL               ;Save destination address
      LD    A, (ERRCODE)
      CP    E_NONE
      RET   NZ
      CALL  NEW_LINE
      LD    HL,KEYBOARD_FLAGS           ;Clear flags
      RES   RX_CHAR_AV,(HL)
      RES   EOF,(HL)
      SET   DOWNLOADING,(HL)            ;Set downloading flag
      LD    BC,WAIT_FILE
      CALL  PRINT_STR_NLCR
      LD    HL,KEYBOARD_FLAGS           ;Wait for start of file
WAIT_FILE_START
      BIT   RX_CHAR_AV,(HL)             ;Has a byte been received ?
      JP    Z,WAIT_FILE_START
      LD    BC,RX_FILE
      CALL  PRINT_STR_NLCR
WAIT_FILE_END
      LD    HL,KEYBOARD_FLAGS           ;Wait for end of file
      BIT   RX_CHAR_AV,(HL)             ;Has a byte been received ?
      JP    Z,NO_BYTE                   ;No so continue
      RES   RX_CHAR_AV,(HL)             ;Yes so Clear char received flag
      LD    DE,0000h                    ;Load timer
      JP    WAIT_FILE_END
NO_BYTE
      DEC   DE
      LD    A,00h                       ;Has timer expired?
      OR    D
      JR    NZ,WAIT_FILE_END
      LD    A,00h
      OR    E
      JR    NZ,WAIT_FILE_END
FILE_COMPLETED
      RES   DOWNLOADING,(HL)            ;File completed so clear flag

      LD    BC,FILE_DONE
      CALL  PRINT_STR_NLCR
      RET
```

```
;---------------------------- PRINT REGISTERS ----------------------------
PRINT_REGISTERS
      LD    BC,REG_HEADER               ;Print header
      CALL  PRINT_STR_NLCR
      CALL  PRINT_HEX_WORD              ;HL already set
      LD    A,' '
      CALL  PRINT_CHAR
      PUSH  AF
      POP   HL
      CALL  PRINT_HEX_WORD
      LD    A,' '
      CALL  PRINT_CHAR
      PUSH  BC
      POP   HL
      CALL  PRINT_HEX_WORD
      LD    A,' '
      CALL  PRINT_CHAR
      PUSH  DE
      POP   HL
      CALL  PRINT_HEX_WORD
      LD    A,' '
      CALL  PRINT_CHAR
      PUSH  IX
      POP   HL
      CALL  PRINT_HEX_WORD
      LD    A,' '
      CALL  PRINT_CHAR
      PUSH  IY
      POP   HL
      CALL  PRINT_HEX_WORD
      LD    A,' '
      CALL  PRINT_CHAR
      LD    HL,0000h
      ADD   HL,SP
      CALL  PRINT_HEX_WORD
      LD    A,' '
      CALL  PRINT_CHAR
      CALL  GET_PC
      CALL  PRINT_HEX_WORD
      RET
GET_PC
      POP   HL
      JP    (HL)



;---------------------------- RUN FROM ADDRESS ----------------------------
RUN_ADDRESS
      LD    BC,DESTINATION_PROMPT ;Print Destination prompt
      CALL  PRINT_STR
      CALL  GET_HEX_WORD
      LD    A,(ERRCODE)
      CP    E_NONE
      RET   NZ
      JP    (HL)                        ;Jump to Address
```

```
;-------------------------- MOVE MEMORY BLOCK ------------------------
MOVE_MEMORY
        LD    BC,START_ADDRESS_PROMPT            ;Print prompt
        CALL  PRINT_STR
        CALL  GET_HEX_WORD
        LD    A,(ERRCODE)
        CP    E_NONE
        RET   NZ
        LD    (ADDRESS_BUFFER),HL
        CALL  NEW_LINE
        LD    BC,END_ADDRESS_PROMPT
        CALL  PRINT_STR
        CALL  GET_HEX_WORD
        LD    A,(ERRCODE)
        CP    E_NONE
        RET   NZ
        LD    (ADDRESS_BUFFER+2),HL
        CALL  NEW_LINE
        LD    BC,DESTINATION_PROMPT
        CALL  PRINT_STR
        CALL  GET_HEX_WORD
        LD    A,(ERRCODE)
        CP    E_NONE
        RET   NZ
        LD    (ADDRESS_BUFFER+4),HL
        CALL  NEW_LINE
        LD    HL,ADDRESS_BUFFER
        CALL  GETP                               ; Calculate block size
        JP    C,MERR
        LD    DE,(ADDRESS_BUFFER+4)
        SBC   HL,DE
        JR    NC,MVUP
MVDN:
        EX    DE,HL
        ADD   HL,BC
        DEC   HL
        EX    DE,HL
        LD    HL,(ADDRESS_BUFFER+2)
        LDDR
        inc   DE
        RET
MVUP:
        ADD   HL,DE
        LDIR                                     ;Move data
        DEC   DE
        RET
MERR:
        LD    A,E_PARAM
        LD    (ERRCODE),A
        RET;
GETP:
        LD    E,(HL)
        INC   HL
        LD    D,(HL)
        INC   HL
        LD    C,(HL)
```

```
        INC   HL
        LD    H,(HL)
        LD    L,C
        OR    A
        SBC   HL,DE
        LD    C,L
        LD    B,H
        INC   BC
        EX    DE,HL
        RET


;---------------------- RESET MONITOR -----------------------------
RESET_MONITOR
        LD    HL,VIDEO_RAM              ;Load VIDEO_PTR
        LD    (VIDEO_PTR),HL
        JP    MAIN                      ;Jump to MAIN

;--------------------- PREVIOUS MEMORY BLOCK ----------------------
PREV_MEM_BLOCK
        LD    HL,(DUMPADDR)
        DEC   H
        LD    (DUMPADDR),HL
        PUSH  HL
        LD    HL,GEN_FLAGS1
        BIT   GF0,(HL)
        POP   HL
        JP    Z,NOASCIIDUMP
        JP    DUMPBLOCKASCII
NOASCIIDUMP
        JP    DUMPBLOCK


;---------------------- NEXT MEMORY BLOCK -------------------------
NEXT_MEM_BLOCK
        LD    HL,(DUMPADDR)
        INC   H
        LD    (DUMPADDR),HL
        PUSH  HL
        LD    HL,GEN_FLAGS1
        BIT   GF0,(HL)
        POP   HL
        JP    Z,NOASCIIDUMPN
        JP    DUMPBLOCKASCII
NOASCIIDUMPN
        JP    DUMPBLOCK
;------------------------ CLEAR SCREEN ----------------------------
CLEAR_SCREEN
        CALL  CLEAR_VIDEO
        LD    A,FFh                     ;Invalidate Command
        RET

;--------------------- SAVE CHARACTER To BUFFER ------------------
CHAR_TO_BUFFER:
        CALL  TO_PRINTABLE
        LD    (DE),A
        INC   DE
        RET
```

```
;--------------------- MAKE ALL CHARACTERS PRINTABLE -------------------
TO_PRINTABLE:
        CP      LCCHAR
        JR      C,SWP
        CP      HCCHAR
        JR      NC,SWP
        RET
SWP:    LD      A,'.'
        RET


;------------------------- FILL MEMORY ----------------------------
FILL_MEMORY
        LD      BC, START_ADDRESS_PROMPT         ;Start Address prompt
        CALL    PRINT_STR
        CALL    GET_HEX_WORD
        LD      A,(ERRCODE)
        CP      E_NONE
        RET     NZ
        LD      (ADDRESS_BUFFER),HL              ;Start address
        CALL    NEW_LINE
        LD      BC,END_ADDRESS_PROMPT            ;End Address prompt
        CALL    PRINT_STR
        CALL    GET_HEX_WORD
        LD      (ADDRESS_BUFFER+2),HL            ;End Address
        LD      A,(ERRCODE)
        CP      E_NONE
        RET     NZ
        LD      DE,(ADDRESS_BUFFER)              ;Start
        SBC     HL,DE                            ;End > Start ?
        JR      C,F_ORDERR
        LD      HL,(ADDRESS_BUFFER+2)
        CALL    NEW_LINE
        LD      BC,FILL_DATA_PROMPT              ;Fill data prompt
        CALL    PRINT_STR
        CALL    GET_HEX_BYTE
        LD      (ADDRESS_BUFFER+4),A
        LD      A,(ERRCODE)
        CP      E_NONE
        RET     NZ
        CALL    NEW_LINE
        LD      DE,(ADDRESS_BUFFER)              ;Start
        LD      HL,(ADDRESS_BUFFER+2)            ;End
        SBC     HL,DE                            ;Length
        LD      B,H
        LD      C,L
        LD      A,(ADDRESS_BUFFER+4)             ;Fill byte
        LD      HL,(ADDRESS_BUFFER)              ;Source Address
        LD      (HL), A                          ;Seed the fill block
        LD      DE,(ADDRESS_BUFFER)              ;Destination address
        INC     DE
        LDIR
        RET
F_ORDERR:
        LD      A,E_PARAM
        LD      (ERRCODE),A
        RET
```

426

```
;------------------------- EDIT MEMORY ------------------------------
EDIT_MEMORY
      LD    BC,START_ADDRESS_PROMPT        ;Start Address prompt
      CALL  PRINT_STR_NLCR
      CALL  GET_HEX_WORD                   ;Get start address
      LD    A,(ERRCODE)
      CP    E_NONE
      RET   NZ
EDIT_LOOP:
      LD    A,':'
      CALL  PRINT_CHAR
      LD    A,' '
      CALL  PRINT_CHAR

      LD    A,(HL)                         ;Print existing value
      CALL  PRINT_HEX_BYTE

      LD    A,'>'
      CALL  PRINT_CHAR
      LD    A,' '
      CALL  PRINT_CHAR

      CALL  GET_HEX_BYTE
      LD    (ADDRESS_BUFFER+4), A
      LD    A,(ERRCODE)
      CP    E_NONE
      RET   NZ

      LD    A,(ADDRESS_BUFFER+4)
      LD    (HL),A                         ;Write new data value

      CALL  NEW_LINE
      INC   HL
      CALL  PRINT_HEX_WORD
      JR    EDIT_LOOP

;------------------- MEMORY DUMP WITH ASCII----------------------
;Dump 100h bytes of RAM AND INCLUDE ASCII CHARACTERS
;On Entry HL points to start address
MEMORY_DUMP_ASCII
      PUSH  HL
      LD    HL,GEN_FLAGS1
      SET   GF0,(HL)
      POP   HL
      LD    BC,START_ADDRESS_PROMPT     ;Start address Prompt
      CALL  PRINT_STR

      CALL  GET_HEX_WORD                ;HL points to start address
      LD    A,(ERRCODE)
      CP    E_NONE
      RET   NZ
      LD    (DUMPADDR),HL               ;Store Address to buffer
      CALL  NEW_LINE
      CALL  NEW_LINE

DUMPBLOCKASCII:
```

```
        CALL  PRINT_HEX_WORD              ;Print hex address
        CALL  NEW_LINE
        LD    BC,MEM_DUMP_HEADER + 5
        CALL  PRINT_STR_NLCR              ;Display dump header

        LD    C,HEXLINES                  ;Load C with line count
HEXDLINEASCII:
        LD    DE,ASCIIBUF
        LD    B,16                        ;Load B with byte count
        DEC   C                           ;Count this line
ASCBYTESASCII:
        LD    A,(HL)                      ;Load Acc with data byte (HL)
        CALL  PRINT_HEX_BYTE              ;Print hex data
        CALL  CHAR_TO_BUFFER              ;Store ASCII char
        LD    A,' '                       ;Print space
        CALL  PRINT_CHAR
        INC   HL                          ;Point to next address
        DJNZ  ASCBYTESASCII               ;Last byte   ?
        LD    A,00h
        LD    (ASCIIENDADD),A             ;Add string termination

        PUSH  HL
        PUSH  BC
        LD    BC,ASCIIBUF                 ;Point HL to ASCII buffer
        CALL  PRINT_STR                   ;Print buffer
        POP   BC
        POP   HL

        LD    B,C                         ;Last line ?
        DJNZ  HEXDLINEASCII               ;All 16 lines printed?
        LD    A,FFh                       ;Invalidate Command
        RET

;----------------------- MEMORY DUMP --------------------------
;Dump 100h bytes of RAM
;On Entry HL points to start address
MEMORY_DUMP
        PUSH  HL
        LD    HL,GEN_FLAGS1
        RES   GF0,(HL)
        POP   HL

        LD    BC,START_ADDRESS_PROMPT     ;Start address Prompt
        CALL  PRINT_STR

        CALL  GET_HEX_WORD                ;HL points to start address
        LD    A,(ERRCODE)
        CP    E_NONE
        RET   NZ
        LD    (DUMPADDR),HL               ;Store Address to buffer
        CALL  NEW_LINE
        CALL  NEW_LINE

DUMPBLOCK:
        LD    BC,MEM_DUMP_HEADER
        CALL  PRINT_STR_NLCR              ;Display dump header
```

```
        LD    C,HEXLINES                ;Load C with line count
HEXDLINE:
        LD    DE,ASCIIBUF
        LD    B,16                      ;Load B with byte count
        CALL  PRINT_HEX_WORD            ;Print hex address
        LD    A,' '                     ;Add space
        CALL  PRINT_CHAR
        DEC   C                         ;Count this line
ASCBYTES:
        LD    A,(HL)                    ;Load Acc with data byte (HL)
        CALL  PRINT_HEX_BYTE            ;Print hex data
        LD    A,' '                     ;Print space
        CALL  PRINT_CHAR
        INC   HL                        ;Point to next address
        DJNZ  ASCBYTES                  ;Last byte  ?
        LD    A,' '                     ;Print space
        CALL  PRINT_CHAR
        LD    B,C                       ;Last line ?
        CALL  NEW_LINE
        DJNZ  HEXDLINE                  ;All 16 lines printed?
        LD    A,FFh                     ;Invalidate Command
        RET

;------------------------- PRINT MONITOR HEADER -----------------------
PRINT_MON_HEADER
        LD    BC,TEXTM1
        CALL  PRINT_STR_NLCR
        LD    BC,TEXTH
        CALL  PRINT_STR_NLCR
        RET

;------------------------- HELP COMMAND -------------------------------
DISPLAY_HELP
        LD    BC,TEXTC                  ;Print all help strings
        CALL  PRINT_STR_NLCR
        LD    BC,TEXTD
        CALL  PRINT_STR_NLCR
        LD    BC,TEXTPlus
        CALL  PRINT_STR_NLCR
        LD    BC,TEXTMinus
        CALL  PRINT_STR_NLCR
        LD    BC,TEXTE
        CALL  PRINT_STR_NLCR
        LD    BC,TEXTF
        CALL  PRINT_STR_NLCR
        LD    BC,TEXTG
        CALL  PRINT_STR_NLCR
        LD    BC,TEXTK
        CALL  PRINT_STR_NLCR
        LD    BC,TEXTL
        CALL  PRINT_STR_NLCR
        LD    BC,TEXTM
        CALL  PRINT_STR_NLCR
        LD    BC,TEXTO
        CALL  PRINT_STR_NLCR
        LD    BC,TEXTP
```

```
        CALL  PRINT_STR_NLCR
        LD    BC,TEXTR
        CALL  PRINT_STR_NLCR
        LD    BC,TEXTZ
        CALL  PRINT_STR_NLCR
        LD    A,FFh                           ;Invalidate Command
        RET


;------------------------ GET HEX WORD ------------------------------
GET_HEX_WORD:
        CALL  GET_HEX_BYTE                    ;Get high byte
        PUSH  AF
        LD    A,(ERRCODE)
        CP    E_NONE
        JR    NZ,HEXW_ERR
        POP   AF
        LD    H,A
        CALL  GET_HEX_BYTE                    ;Get low byte
        PUSH  AF
        LD    A,(ERRCODE)
        CP    E_NONE
        JR    NZ,HEXW_ERR
        POP   AF
        LD    L,A
        RET
HEXW_ERR:
        POP   AF
        RET


;------------------------ GET HEX BYTE ------------------------------
GET_HEX_BYTE:
        CALL  GET_HEX_NIBBLE                  ;Get high nibble
        PUSH  DE
        PUSH  AF
        LD    A,(ERRCODE)
        CP    E_NONE
        JR    NZ,GHB_ERR
        POP   AF
        RLC   A                               ;Low nibble into high nibble
        RLC   A
        RLC   A
        RLC   A
        LD    D,A                             ;Save upper four nibble
        CALL  GET_HEX_NIBBLE                  ;Get lower nibble
        PUSH  AF
        LD    A,(ERRCODE)
        CP    E_NONE
        JR    NZ,GHB_ERR
        POP   AF
        OR    D                               ;Merge nibbles
        POP   DE
        RET
GHB_ERR:
        POP   AF
        POP   DE
        RET
```

```
;-------------------------- GET HEX NIBBLE ----------------------------
GET_HEX_NIBBLE:
      CALL  GET_CHAR
      LD    A,(KEY_BUFFER)

      CALL  CHAR_ISHEX                      ;Hex digit?
      JP    NC,NONHEXNIB                    ;Yes so continue
      CALL  PRINT_CHAR

      CP    '9' + 1                         ;Digit?
      JP    C,IS_DIGIT                      ;Yes so continue
      SUB   07h                             ;Adjust if A-F
IS_DIGIT:
      SUB   '0'                             ;Make 0->15
      AND   0Fh                             ;Strip off low 4 bits
      RET
NONHEXNIB:                                  ;Abort if not hex
      LD    A,E_NOHEX
      LD    (ERRCODE),A                     ;Error code
      RET




;-------------------------- IS CHAR HEX --------------------------------
CHAR_ISHEX:
                                            ;A = 0 to F ?
      CP    'F' + 1                         ;(Acc) >  F ?
      RET   NC                              ;No so continue
      CP    '0'                             ;A < 0 ?
      JP    NC,CNIB1                        ;No so continue
      CCF                                   ;Clear carry
      RET
CNIB1:
                                            ;A < '9' and > 'A'
      CP    '9' + 1                         ;A < '9' + 1 ?
      RET   C                               ;No so continue
      CP    'A'                             ;A > 'A' ?
      JP    NC,CNIB2                        ;No so continue
      CCF                                   ;Clear carry
      RET
CNIB2:
                                            ;A is 'A' to 'F'
      SCF                                   ;Hex so set carry flag
      RET


;----------------------- NIBBLE To CHARACTER --------------------------
NIBBLE_TO_CHAR
      AND   0Fh                             ;Only low nibble in byte
      ADD   A,'0'                           ;Adjust for char offset
      CP    '9' + 1                         ;Is the hex digit > 9 ?
      JR    C,NTOCHAR                       ;No so continue
      ADD   A,'A' - '0' - 0Ah               ;Adjust for A-F
NTOCHAR
      RET
```

```
;------------------------ PRINT HEX NIBBLE ---------------------------
PRINT_HEX_NIBBLE
      PUSH  AF
      CALL  NIBBLE_TO_CHAR
      CALL  PRINT_CHAR                ;Print the nibble
      POP   AF
      RET

;------------------------ PRINT HEX BYTE -----------------------------
PRINT_HEX_BYTE
      PUSH  AF                        ;Save registers
      PUSH  DE
      LD    D,A                       ;Save low nibble
      RRCA                            ;High nibble into low nibble
      RRCA
      RRCA
      RRCA
      CALL  PRINT_HEX_NIBBLE          ;Print high nibble
      LD    A,D                       ;Restore low nibble
      CALL  PRINT_HEX_NIBBLE          ;Print low nibble
      POP   DE
      POP   AF
      RET

;---------------------- PRINT HEX WORD -------------------------------
;Print the value in HL as a hex string
PRINT_HEX_WORD:
      PUSH  AF
      LD    A,H
      CALL  PRINT_HEX_BYTE            ;Print high byte
      LD    A,L
      CALL  PRINT_HEX_BYTE            ;Print low byte
      POP   AF
      RET

;-------------------------- GET_CHAR ---------------------------------
;Gets a character from the keyboard
;Character is in KEY_BUFFER
GET_CHAR
      PUSH  HL
      LD    HL,KEYBOARD_FLAGS

WAIT_FOR_CHAR:
      BIT   CHAR_AV_FLAG,(HL)         ;Is the char ready flag set?
      JR    Z,WAIT_FOR_CHAR           ;No So wait
      RES   CHAR_AV_FLAG,(HL)         ;Yes so Clear flag

      POP   HL
      RET

;-------------------------- NEW_LINE ---------------------------------
;Move to start of next line, scroll if required
NEW_LINE
      PUSH  HL
      PUSH  DE
      PUSH  AF
```

432

```
        LD      HL,(VIDEO_PTR)
        LD      DE,0040h
        ADD     HL,DE
        LD      A,FFh
        AND     H
        LD      H,A
        LD      A,C0h
        AND     L
        LD      L,A

        LD      A,H                         ;TEST FOR SCROLL
        CP      FFh
        JR      NZ,NOT_NL_SCROLL
        CALL    SCROLL_SCREEN
NOT_NL_SCROLL
        LD      (VIDEO_PTR),HL              ;Save video pointer

        POP     AF
        POP     DE
        POP     HL
        RET
;-------------------------- CLEAR VIDEO RAM --------------------------
CLEAR_VIDEO:
        PUSH    HL
        PUSH    BC
        LD      HL,VIDEO_RAM               ;Load VIDEO_PTR
        LD      (VIDEO_PTR),HL
        LD      C,08h                      ;Load Count = 1920
CVL0:   LD      B,F0h                      ;240 x 8
CVL1:   LD      (HL),20h                   ;Clear this byte
        INC     HL
        DJNZ    CVL1
        DEC     C
        JP      NZ,CVL0
        POP     BC
        POP     HL
        RET


;--------------------- PRINT STRING ON SCREEN ---------------------
;On Entry VIDEO_PTR points to video memory location
;BC points to the first character of the string
;Call PRINT_STR_NLCR if a NL CR is required after the string
PRINT_STR_NLCR
        PUSH    BC
        PUSH    HL
        PUSH    AF
        LD      HL,KEYBOARD_FLAGS          ;CRNL wanted so set flag
        SET     ADD_NL,(HL)
        JR      PRINT_LOOP
PRINT_STR
        PUSH    BC
        PUSH    HL
        PUSH    AF
PRINT_LOOP
        LD      A,(BC)
        OR      A
```

433

```
        JP    Z,STRING_DONE
        CALL  PRINT_CHAR
        INC   BC
        JP    PRINT_LOOP

STRING_DONE
        LD    HL,KEYBOARD_FLAGS          ;CRNL wanted?
        BIT   ADD_NL,(HL)
        JP    Z,END_OF_STRING
        CALL  NEW_LINE
        RES   ADD_NL,(HL)                ;Clear NL flag

END_OF_STRING
        POP   AF
        POP   HL
        POP   BC
        RET

;-------------------------- DRAW WELCOME SCREEN ----------------------
WELCOME_SCR
        LD    A,A0h
        LD    (VIDEO_RAM + 01D4h),A
        LD    (VIDEO_RAM + 01D5h),A
        LD    (VIDEO_RAM + 01D6h),A
        LD    (VIDEO_RAM + 01D7h),A
        LD    (VIDEO_RAM + 01D8h),A
        LD    (VIDEO_RAM + 01D9h),A
        LD    (VIDEO_RAM + 01DAh),A
        LD    (VIDEO_RAM + 01DCh),A
        LD    (VIDEO_RAM + 01E2h),A
        LD    (VIDEO_RAM + 01E4h),A
        LD    (VIDEO_RAM + 01E5h),A
        LD    (VIDEO_RAM + 01E6h),A
        LD    (VIDEO_RAM + 01E7h),A
        LD    (VIDEO_RAM + 01E8h),A
        LD    (VIDEO_RAM + 01E9h),A
        LD    (VIDEO_RAM + 01EAh),A
        LD    (VIDEO_RAM + 0217h),A
        LD    (VIDEO_RAM + 021Ch),A
        LD    (VIDEO_RAM + 021Dh),A
        LD    (VIDEO_RAM + 0221h),A
        LD    (VIDEO_RAM + 0222h),A
        LD    (VIDEO_RAM + 0229h),A
        LD    (VIDEO_RAM + 0257h),A
        LD    (VIDEO_RAM + 025Ch),A
        LD    (VIDEO_RAM + 025Eh),A
        LD    (VIDEO_RAM + 0260h),A
        LD    (VIDEO_RAM + 0262h),A
        LD    (VIDEO_RAM + 0268h),A
        LD    (VIDEO_RAM + 0297h),A
        LD    (VIDEO_RAM + 029Ch),A
        LD    (VIDEO_RAM + 029Fh),A
        LD    (VIDEO_RAM + 02A2h),A
        LD    (VIDEO_RAM + 02A7h),A
        LD    (VIDEO_RAM + 02D7h),A
        LD    (VIDEO_RAM + 02DCh),A
```

```
        LD      (VIDEO_RAM + 02E2h),A
        LD      (VIDEO_RAM + 02E6h),A
        LD      (VIDEO_RAM + 0314h),A
        LD      (VIDEO_RAM + 0317h),A
        LD      (VIDEO_RAM + 031Ch),A
        LD      (VIDEO_RAM + 0322h),A
        LD      (VIDEO_RAM + 0325h),A
        LD      (VIDEO_RAM + 0355h),A
        LD      (VIDEO_RAM + 0356h),A
        LD      (VIDEO_RAM + 035Ch),A
        LD      (VIDEO_RAM + 0362h),A
        LD      (VIDEO_RAM + 0364h),A
        LD      (VIDEO_RAM + 0365h),A
        LD      (VIDEO_RAM + 0366h),A
        LD      (VIDEO_RAM + 0367h),A
        LD      (VIDEO_RAM + 0368h),A
        LD      (VIDEO_RAM + 0369h),A
        LD      (VIDEO_RAM + 036Ah),A
        RET




;------------------------- PRINT_CHAR -----------------------------
;Send Char to screen - Scroll screen if required
;On Entry A contains character to display
;VIDEO_PTR points to video RAM location to put char
;On Exit VIDEO_PTR points to next location
PRINT_CHAR
        ;PUSH BC
        PUSH HL
        PUSH AF
        PUSH DE

        LD      HL,(VIDEO_PTR)          ;Load VIDEO_PTR into HL
        LD      (HL),A                  ;Save the new char(clears Cursor)

        INC     HL                      ;Increment pointer
        LD      A,H                     ;TEST FOR SCROLL
        CP      FFh
        JR      NZ,NOT_SCROLL
        CALL    SCROLL_SCREEN
NOT_SCROLL:

        ;LD     C,(HL)                  ;Get the character at the new position
        ;LD     A,0b10000000            ;Set Cursor bit in new character
        ;OR     C
        ;LD     (HL),A                  ;Save character and cursor

        LD      (VIDEO_PTR),HL          ;Save screen pointer to RAM

        POP     DE
        POP     AF
        POP     HL
        ;POP    BC
        RET
```

```
;-------------------- SCROLL SCREEN UP ONE LINE ----------------------
SCROLL_SCREEN
      PUSH DE
      PUSH BC
      PUSH HL

      LD    HL,VIDEO_RAM + 64          ;Move Video RAM up one line
      LD    DE,VIDEO_RAM
      LD    BC,VIDEO_RAM_LEN - 64
      LDIR

      POP   HL
      LD    DE,FFC0h                    ;Adjust video pointer
      ADD   HL,DE

      POP   BC
      POP   DE
      RET

;-------------------- KEYBOARD INTERRUPT HANDLER --------------------
;KB_HANDLER
;On entry A = PS2 scan code
;On exit KEY_BUFFER = character read from keyboard
      ORG ORG_BASE + 0D00h
KEY_INT_HANDLER:
      PUSH AF
      PUSH HL
      PUSH BC
      PUSH DE

      LD    B,10h
LPP:  DJNZ  LPP

      LD    HL,KEYBOARD_FLAGS   ;Get Keyboard flags into register B
      LD    B,(HL)

      IN    A,(3)               ;Read Scan code from PS2 interface

      CP    F0h                 ;Is the character the key release ?
      JR    NZ,NOT_KR           ;No so continue
      SET   RELEASE_FLAG,B      ;Yes so set release flag
      JP    SAVE_KB_FLAGS       ;And save flags before exit
NOT_KR:

                  ;CURSOR KEYS HANDLING
      CP    75h                 ;Cursor UP ?
      JR    Z,CURSOR_KEY
      CP    72h                 ;Cursor Down ?
      JR    Z,CURSOR_KEY
      CP    6Bh                 ;Cursor Left ?
      JR    Z,CURSOR_KEY
      CP    74h                 ;Cursor Right ?
      JR    NZ,NOT_CURSOR_KEY

CURSOR_KEY:
      BIT   RELEASE_FLAG,B      ;Is the release flag set (Key up)?
```

```
        JR      NZ,NOT_CURSOR_KEY       ;Yes So do nothing
                        ;CURSOR KEY DOWN SO CLEAR CURSOR
        LD      D,A
        LD      HL,(VIDEO_PTR)          ;Load VIDEO_PTR
        LD      B,(HL)
        LD      A,0b01111111            ;Clear current Cursor
        AND     B
        LD      (HL),A
        LD      A,D

        CP      75h                     ;Cursor UP ?
        JR      NZ,NOT_C_UP
        LD      DE,FFBFh
        ADD     HL,DE
NOT_C_UP:
        CP      72h                     ;Cursor Down ?
        JR      NZ,NOT_C_DOWN
        LD      DE,40h
        ADD     HL,DE
        JR      UPDATE_CURSOR
NOT_C_DOWN:
        CP      6Bh                     ;Cursor Left ?
        JR      NZ,NOT_C_LEFT
        DEC     HL
        JR      UPDATE_CURSOR
NOT_C_LEFT:
        INC     HL

UPDATE_CURSOR:
        LD      B,(HL)
        LD      A,0b10000000            ;Set Cursor bit
        OR      B
        LD      (HL),A
        LD      (VIDEO_PTR),HL          ;Save screen pointer to RAM

        JR      DONE_KB
NOT_CURSOR_KEY:

                        ;SHIFT KEYS
        CP      12h                     ;Left Shift ?
        JR      Z,SHIFT_KEY
        CP      59h                     ;Right Shift ?
        JR      Z,SHIFT_KEY
        JR      NOT_SHIFT_KEY
SHIFT_KEY:

        BIT     RELEASE_FLAG,B          ;Is the release flag set (Key up)?
        JR      Z,NOT_KEY_RELEASED      ;No So set Shift flag
        LD      A,0b11111001
        AND     B                       ;Yes So Clear Shift and Release flags
        LD      B,A
        JR      SAVE_KB_FLAGS           ;And save flags before exit

NOT_KEY_RELEASED:
        SET     SHIFT_FLAG,B            ;Yes so set shift flag
        JR      SAVE_KB_FLAGS           ;And save flags before exit
```

```
NOT_SHIFT_KEY:
      BIT   RELEASE_FLAG,B      ;Is the release flag set (Key up)?
      JR    Z,NOT_KEY_UP        ;No So Continue

            ;ERROR IF THIS CHAR NOT SAME AS BUFFERED CHAR
      LD    A,0b11111101        ;Yes So Clear Release flag
      AND   B
      LD    B,A
      JR    SAVE_KB_FLAGS       ;And save flags before exit


NOT_KEY_UP:
      LD    L,A                 ;Look up ASCII character
      LD    H,0

      BIT   SHIFT_FLAG,B        ;Is the shift flag set?
      JR    Z,NOT_SHIFT_MODE    ;No So use lower half of table
      LD    DE,ASCII_TABLEH     ;Shift So use upper half of table
      JR    POINTER_READY
NOT_SHIFT_MODE:
      LD    DE,ASCII_TABLEL

POINTER_READY:

      ADD   HL,DE
      LD    A,(HL)              ;Read the char from table into A
      LD    (KEY_BUFFER),A      ;Save current character to Buffer

      SET   CHAR_AV_FLAG,B      ;Set character ready flag

SAVE_KB_FLAGS:
      LD    HL,KEYBOARD_FLAGS   ;Save Flags (they are in B)
      LD    (HL),B


DONE_KB:
      POP   DE
      POP   BC
      POP   HL
      POP   AF
      EI
      RETI



;-------------------- RS232 Transmit INTERRUPT HANDLER -----------------
;RS232_TX_HANDLER
;On entry RX buffer contains received character
;     ORG 0A00h
;TX_INT_HANDLER:
;     EI
;     RETI
```

```
;--------------------- RS232 Receive INTERRUPT HANDLER -----------------
;RS232_RX_HANDLER
;On entry RX buffer contains received character
     ORG ORG_BASE + 0E00h
RX_INT_HANDLER:
     PUSH AF
     PUSH HL

     IN   A,(06h)               ;Read character from RS232 port
     OUT  (06h),A               ;Send character to RS232

     LD   HL,KEYBOARD_FLAGS
     BIT  DOWNLOADING,(HL)      ;Is a file download in progress?
     JR   Z,NOT_DOWNLOADING     ;No so do nothing

     SET  RX_CHAR_AV,(HL)       ;Indicate that a byte has been RX

     LD   HL,(FILE_PTR)         ;Yes so save the received byte
     LD   (HL),A                ;To the current point address
     INC  HL                    ;Increment pointer
     LD   (FILE_PTR),HL
     LD   HL,KEYBOARD_FLAGS
     BIT  FAST_FLAG,(HL)        ;Fast flag set?
     JR   NZ,NOT_DOWNLOADING
     CALL PRINT_CHAR            ;Send character to screen

NOT_DOWNLOADING:

     POP  HL
     POP  AF
     EI
     RETI
```

```
;------------------- ASCII CHARACTER LOOKUP TABLE --------------------
;PS2 scan code to ASCII
     ORG ORG_BASE + 0F00h
;ASCII_TABLE:
     DB    00h,00h,00h,00h,00h,00h,00h,00h
     DB    00h,00h,00h,00h,00h,0Bh,60h,00h
     DB    00h,00h,00h,00h,00h,71h,31h,00h
     DB    00h,00h,7Ah,73h,61h,77h,32h,00h
     DB    00h,63h,78h,64h,65h,34h,33h,00h
     DB    00h,20h,76h,66h,74h,72h,35h,00h
     DB    00h,6Eh,62h,68h,67h,79h,36h,00h
     DB    00h,00h,6Dh,6Ah,75h,37h,38h,00h
     DB    00h,2Ch,6Bh,69h,6Fh,30h,39h,00h
     DB    00h,2Eh,2Fh,6Ch,3Bh,70h,2Dh,00h
     DB    00h,00h,27h,00h,5Bh,3Dh,00h,00h
     DB    00h,00h,0Ah,5Dh,00h,5Ch,00h,00h
     DB    00h,00h,00h,00h,00h,00h,08h,00h
     DB    00h,00h,00h,00h,00h,00h,00h,00h
     DB    00h,00h,00h,00h,00h,00h,1Bh,00h
     DB    00h,00h,00h,00h,00h,00h,00h,00h

     DB    00h,00h,00h,00h,00h,00h,00h,00h
     DB    00h,00h,00h,00h,00h,0Bh,7Eh,00h
     DB    00h,00h,00h,00h,00h,51h,21h,00h
     DB    00h,00h,5Ah,53h,41h,57h,40h,00h
     DB    00h,43h,58h,44h,45h,24h,23h,00h
     DB    00h,20h,56h,46h,54h,52h,25h,00h
     DB    00h,4Eh,42h,48h,47h,59h,5Eh,00h
     DB    00h,00h,4Dh,4Ah,55h,26h,2Ah,00h
     DB    00h,3Ch,4Bh,49h,4Fh,29h,28h,00h
     DB    00h,3Eh,3Fh,4Ch,3Ah,50h,5Fh,00h
     DB    00h,00h,22h,00h,7Bh,2Bh,00h,00h
     DB    00h,00h,0Ah,7Dh,00h,7Ch,00h,00h
     DB    00h,00h,00h,00h,00h,00h,08h,00h
     DB    00h,00h,00h,00h,00h,00h,00h,00h
     DB    00h,00h,00h,00h,00h,00h,1Bh,00h
     DB    00h,00h,00h,00h,00h,00h,00h,00h


     END
```

Appendix F – JMZ Character ROM Listing

```
00 38 44 54 5C 58 40 3C 00 10 28 44 44 7C 44 44
00 78 44 44 78 44 44 78 00 38 44 40 40 40 44 38
00 78 44 44 44 44 44 78 00 7C 40 40 78 40 40 7C
00 7C 40 40 78 40 40 40 00 3C 40 40 40 4C 44 3C
00 44 44 44 7C 44 44 44 00 38 10 10 10 10 10 38
00 04 04 04 04 04 44 38 00 44 48 50 60 50 48 44
00 40 40 40 40 40 40 7C 00 44 6C 54 54 44 44 44
00 44 44 64 54 4C 44 44 00 38 44 44 44 44 44 38
00 78 44 44 78 40 40 40 00 38 44 44 44 54 48 34
00 78 44 44 78 50 48 44 00 38 44 40 38 04 44 38
00 7C 10 10 10 10 10 10 00 44 44 44 44 44 44 38
00 44 44 44 44 44 28 10 00 44 44 44 54 54 6C 44
00 44 44 28 10 28 44 44 00 44 44 28 10 10 10 10
00 7C 04 08 10 20 40 7C 00 7C 60 60 60 60 60 7C
00 00 40 20 10 08 04 00 00 FC 0C 0C 0C 0C 0C FC
00 00 00 10 28 44 00 00 00 00 00 00 00 00 00 FC
00 00 00 00 00 00 00 00 00 10 10 10 10 10 00 10
00 28 28 28 00 00 00 00 00 28 28 7C 28 7C 28 28
00 10 3C 50 38 14 78 10 00 60 64 08 10 20 4C 0C
00 20 50 50 20 54 48 34 00 10 10 10 00 00 00 00
00 10 20 40 40 40 20 10 00 10 08 04 04 04 08 10
00 10 54 38 10 38 54 10 00 00 10 10 7C 10 10 00
00 00 00 00 00 10 10 20 00 00 00 00 FC 00 00 00
00 00 00 00 00 00 00 10 00 00 04 08 10 20 40 00
00 38 44 4C 54 64 44 38 00 10 30 10 10 10 10 38
00 38 44 04 18 20 40 7C 00 7C 04 08 18 04 44 38
00 08 18 28 48 7C 08 08 00 7C 40 78 04 04 44 38
00 1C 20 40 78 44 44 38 00 FC 04 08 10 20 20 20
00 38 44 44 38 44 44 38 00 38 44 44 3C 04 08 70
00 00 00 10 00 10 00 00 00 00 10 00 10 10 20
00 08 10 20 40 20 10 08 00 00 00 FC 00 FC 00 00
00 20 10 08 04 08 10 20 00 38 44 08 10 10 00 10
00 38 44 54 5C 58 40 3C 00 10 28 44 44 7C 44 44
00 78 44 44 78 44 44 78 00 38 44 40 40 40 44 38
00 78 44 44 44 44 44 78 00 7C 40 40 78 40 40 7C
00 7C 40 40 78 40 40 40 00 3C 40 40 40 4C 44 3C
00 44 44 44 7C 44 44 44 00 38 10 10 10 10 10 38
00 04 04 04 04 04 44 38 00 44 48 50 60 50 48 44
00 40 40 40 40 40 40 7C 00 44 6C 54 54 44 44 44
00 44 44 64 54 4C 44 44 00 38 44 44 44 44 44 38
00 78 44 44 78 40 40 40 00 38 44 44 44 54 48 34
00 78 44 44 78 50 48 44 00 38 44 40 38 04 44 38
00 7C 10 10 10 10 10 10 00 44 44 44 44 44 44 38
00 44 44 44 44 44 28 10 00 44 44 44 54 54 6C 44
00 44 44 28 10 28 44 44 00 44 44 28 10 10 10 10
00 7C 04 08 10 20 40 7C 00 7C 60 60 60 60 60 7C
00 00 40 20 10 08 04 00 00 FC 0C 0C 0C 0C 0C FC
00 00 00 10 28 44 00 00 00 00 00 00 00 00 00 FC
00 20 10 08 00 00 00 00 00 00 38 08 38 28 3C 00
00 20 20 38 24 24 78 00 00 00 1C 20 20 20 1C 00
00 08 08 38 48 48 3C 00 00 00 18 24 3C 20 18 00
```

441

```
00 08 14 10 38 10 10 00 00 00 18 24 24 1C 04 18
00 20 20 38 24 24 24 00 00 10 00 10 10 10 38 00
00 08 00 08 08 08 28 10 00 20 24 28 30 28 24 00
00 30 10 10 10 10 38 00 00 00 68 54 54 54 54 00
00 00 38 24 24 24 24 00 00 00 18 24 24 24 18 00
00 00 38 24 24 38 20 20 00 00 38 48 48 38 08 0C
00 00 2C 30 20 20 20 00 00 00 3C 20 18 04 3C 00
00 10 38 10 10 10 08 00 00 00 24 24 24 24 1C 00
00 00 44 44 28 28 10 00 00 00 44 44 54 54 28 00
00 00 44 28 10 28 44 00 00 00 24 24 24 1C 04 18
00 00 7C 08 10 20 7C 00 00 08 10 10 20 10 10 08
00 10 10 10 00 10 10 10 00 20 10 10 08 10 10 20
00 00 00 04 38 40 00 00 00 00 7C 7C 7C 7C 7C 83
FF C7 BB AB A3 A7 BF C3 FF EF D7 BB BB 83 BB BB
FF 87 BB BB 87 BB BB 87 FF C7 BB BF BF BF BB C7
FF 87 BB BB BB BB BB 87 FF 83 BF BF 87 BF BF 83
FF 83 BF BF 87 BF BF BF FF C3 BF BF BF B3 BB C3
FF BB BB BB 83 BB BB BB FF C7 EF EF EF EF EF C7
FF FB FB FB FB FB BB C7 FF BB B7 AF 9F AF B7 BB
FF BF BF BF BF BF BF 83 FF BB 93 AB AB BB BB BB
FF BB BB 9B AB B3 BB BB FF C7 BB BB BB BB BB C7
FF 87 BB BB 87 BF BF BF FF C7 BB BB BB AB B7 CB
FF 87 BB BB 87 AF B7 BB FF C7 BB BF C7 FB BB C7
FF 83 EF EF EF EF EF EF FF BB BB BB BB BB BB C7
FF BB BB BB BB BB D7 EF FF BB BB BB AB AB 93 BB
FF BB BB D7 EF D7 BB BB FF BB BB D7 EF EF EF EF
FF 83 FB F7 EF DF BF 83 FF 83 9F 9F 9F 9F 9F 83
FF FF BF DF EF F7 FB FF FF 03 F3 F3 F3 F3 F3 03
FF FF FF EF D7 BB FF FF FF FF FF FF FF FF FF 03
FF FF FF FF FF FF FF FF FF EF EF EF EF EF EF EF
FF D7 D7 D7 FF FF FF FF FF D7 D7 83 D7 83 D7 D7
FF EF C3 AF C7 EB 87 EF FF 9F 9B F7 EF DF B3 F3
FF DF AF AF DF AB B7 CB FF EF EF EF FF FF FF FF
FF EF DF BF BF BF DF EF FF EF F7 FB FB FB F7 EF
FF EF AB C7 EF C7 AB EF FF FF EF EF 83 EF EF FF
FF FF FF FF FF EF EF DF FF FF FF FF 03 FF FF FF
FF FF FF FF FF FF FF EF FF FF FB F7 EF DF BF FF
FF C7 BB B3 AB 9B BB C7 FF EF CF EF EF EF EF C7
FF C7 BB FB E7 DF BF 83 FF 83 FB F7 E7 FB BB C7
FF F7 E7 D7 B7 83 F7 F7 FF 83 BF 87 FB FB BB C7
FF E3 DF BF 87 BB BB C7 FF 03 FB F7 EF DF DF DF
FF C7 BB BB C7 BB BB C7 FF C7 BB BB C3 FB F7 8F
FF FF FF EF FF EF FF FF FF FF FF EF FF EF EF DF
FF F7 EF DF BF DF EF F7 FF FF FF 03 FF 03 FF FF
FF DF EF F7 FB F7 EF DF FF C7 BB F7 EF EF FF EF
FF C7 BB AB A3 A7 BF C3 FF EF D7 BB BB 83 BB BB
FF 87 BB BB 87 BB BB 87 FF C7 BB BF BF BF BB C7
FF 87 BB BB BB BB BB 87 FF 83 BF BF 87 BF BF 83
FF 83 BF BF 87 BF BF BF FF C3 BF BF BF B3 BB C3
FF BB BB BB 83 BB BB BB FF C7 EF EF EF EF EF C7
FF FB FB FB FB FB BB C7 FF BB B7 AF 9F AF B7 BB
FF BF BF BF BF BF BF 83 FF BB 93 AB AB BB BB BB
FF BB BB 9B AB B3 BB BB FF C7 BB BB BB BB BB C7
FF 87 BB BB 87 BF BF BF FF C7 BB BB BB AB B7 CB
FF 87 BB BB 87 AF B7 BB FF C7 BB BF C7 FB BB C7
FF 83 EF EF EF EF EF EF FF BB BB BB BB BB BB C7
```

```
FF BB BB BB BB BB D7 EF FF BB BB BB AB AB 93 BB
FF BB BB D7 EF D7 BB BB FF BB BB D7 EF EF EF EF
FF 83 FB F7 EF DF BF 83 FF 83 9F 9F 9F 9F 9F 83
FF FF BF DF EF F7 FB FF FF 03 F3 F3 F3 F3 F3 03
FF FF FF EF D7 BB FF FF FF FF FF FF FF FF FF 03
FF DF EF F7 FF FF FF FF FF FF C7 F7 C7 D7 C3 FF
FF DF DF C7 DB DB 87 FF FF FF E3 DF DF DF E3 FF
FF F7 F7 C7 B7 B7 C3 FF FF FF E7 DB C3 DF E7 FF
FF F7 EB EF C7 EF EF FF FF FF E7 DB DB E3 FB E7
FF DF DF C7 DB DB DB FF FF EF FF EF EF EF C7 FF
FF F7 FF F7 F7 F7 D7 EF FF DF DB D7 CF D7 DB FF
FF CF EF EF EF EF C7 FF FF FF 97 AB AB AB AB FF
FF FF C7 DB DB DB DB FF FF FF E7 DB DB DB E7 FF
FF FF C7 DB DB C7 DF DF FF FF C7 B7 B7 C7 F7 F3
FF FF D3 CF DF DF DF FF FF FF C3 DF E7 FB C3 FF
FF EF C7 EF EF EF F7 FF FF FF DB DB DB DB E3 FF
FF FF BB BB D7 D7 EF FF FF FF BB BB AB AB D7 FF
FF FF BB D7 EF D7 BB FF FF FF DB DB DB E3 FB E7
FF FF 83 F7 EF DF 83 FF FF F7 EF EF DF EF EF F7
FF EF EF EF FF EF EF EF FF DF EF EF F7 EF EF DF
FF FF FF FB C7 BF FF FF FF FF FF 83 83 83 83 83
FF C7 BB AB A3 A7 BF C3 FF EF D7 BB BB 83 BB BB
FF 87 BB BB 87 BB BB 87 FF C7 BB BF BF BF BB C7
FF 87 BB BB BB BB BB 87 FF 83 BF BF 87 BF BF 83
FF 83 BF BF 87 BF BF BF FF C3 BF BF BF B3 BB C3
FF BB BB BB 83 BB BB BB FF C7 EF EF EF EF EF C7
FF FB FB FB FB FB BB C7 FF BB B7 AF 9F AF B7 BB
FF BF BF BF BF BF BF 83 FF BB 93 AB AB BB BB BB
FF BB BB 9B AB B3 BB BB FF C7 BB BB BB BB BB C7
FF 87 BB BB 87 BF BF BF FF C7 BB BB BB AB B7 CB
FF 87 BB BB 87 AF B7 BB FF C7 BB BF C7 FB BB C7
FF 83 EF EF EF EF EF EF FF BB BB BB BB BB BB C7
FF BB BB BB BB BB D7 EF FF BB BB BB AB AB 93 BB
FF BB BB D7 EF D7 BB BB FF BB BB D7 EF EF EF EF
FF 83 FB F7 EF DF BF 83 FF 83 9F 9F 9F 9F 9F 83
FF FF BF DF EF F7 FB FF FF 03 F3 F3 F3 F3 F3 03
FF FF FF EF D7 BB FF FF FF FF FF FF FF FF FF 03
FF FF FF FF FF FF FF FF FF EF EF EF EF EF EF EF
FF D7 D7 D7 FF FF FF FF FF D7 D7 83 D7 83 D7 D7
FF EF C3 AF C7 EB 87 EF FF 9F 9B F7 EF DF B3 F3
FF DF AF AF DF AB B7 CB FF EF EF EF FF FF FF FF
FF EF DF BF BF BF DF EF FF EF F7 FB FB FB F7 EF
FF EF AB C7 EF C7 AB EF FF FF EF EF 83 EF EF FF
FF FF FF FF FF EF EF DF FF FF FF FF 03 FF FF FF
FF FF FF FF FF FF FF EF FF FF FB F7 EF DF BF FF
FF C7 BB B3 AB 9B BB C7 FF EF CF EF EF EF EF C7
FF C7 BB FB E7 DF BF 83 FF 83 FB F7 E7 FB BB C7
FF F7 E7 D7 B7 83 F7 F7 FF 83 BF 87 FB FB BB C7
FF E3 DF BF 87 BB BB C7 FF 03 FB F7 EF DF DF DF
FF C7 BB BB C7 BB BB C7 FF C7 BB BB C3 FB F7 8F
FF FF FF EF FF EF FF FF FF FF FF EF FF EF EF DF
FF F7 EF DF BF DF EF F7 FF FF FF 03 FF 03 FF FF
FF DF EF F7 FB F7 EF DF FF C7 BB F7 EF EF FF EF
FF C7 BB AB A3 A7 BF C3 FF EF D7 BB BB 83 BB BB
FF 87 BB BB 87 BB BB 87 FF C7 BB BF BF BF BB C7
FF 87 BB BB BB BB BB 87 FF 83 BF BF 87 BF BF 83
```

443

```
FF  83  BF  BF  87  BF  BF  BF  FF  C3  BF  BF  BF  B3  BB  C3
FF  BB  BB  BB  83  BB  BB  BB  FF  C7  EF  EF  EF  EF  EF  C7
FF  FB  FB  FB  FB  FB  BB  C7  FF  BB  B7  AF  9F  AF  B7  BB
FF  BF  BF  BF  BF  BF  BF  83  FF  BB  93  AB  AB  BB  BB  BB
FF  BB  BB  9B  AB  B3  BB  BB  FF  C7  BB  BB  BB  BB  BB  C7
FF  87  BB  BB  87  BF  BF  BF  C7  BB  BB  BB  AB  B7  CB
FF  87  BB  BB  87  AF  B7  BB  FF  C7  BB  BF  C7  FB  BB  C7
FF  83  EF  EF  EF  EF  EF  EF  FF  BB  BB  BB  BB  BB  BB  C7
FF  BB  BB  BB  BB  BB  D7  EF  FF  BB  BB  BB  AB  AB  93  BB
FF  BB  BB  D7  EF  D7  BB  BB  FF  BB  BB  D7  EF  EF  EF  EF
FF  83  FB  F7  EF  DF  BF  83  FF  83  9F  9F  9F  9F  9F  83
FF  FF  BF  DF  EF  F7  FB  FF  FF  03  F3  F3  F3  F3  F3  03
FF  FF  FF  EF  D7  BB  FF  FF  FF  FF  FF  FF  FF  FF  FF  03
FF  DF  EF  F7  FF  FF  FF  FF  FF  C7  F7  C7  D7  C3  FF
FF  DF  DF  C7  DB  DB  87  FF  FF  FF  E3  DF  DF  DF  E3  FF
FF  F7  F7  C7  B7  B7  C3  FF  FF  FF  E7  DB  C3  DF  E7  FF
FF  F7  EB  EF  C7  EF  EF  FF  FF  FF  E7  DB  DB  E3  FB  E7
FF  DF  DF  C7  DB  DB  DB  FF  FF  EF  FF  EF  EF  EF  C7  FF
FF  F7  FF  F7  F7  F7  D7  EF  FF  DF  DB  D7  CF  D7  DB  FF
FF  CF  EF  EF  EF  EF  C7  FF  FF  FF  97  AB  AB  AB  AB  FF
FF  FF  C7  DB  DB  DB  FF  FF  FF  E7  DB  DB  DB  E7  FF
FF  FF  C7  DB  DB  C7  DF  DF  FF  FF  C7  B7  B7  C7  F7  F3
FF  FF  D3  CF  DF  DF  DF  FF  FF  FF  C3  DF  E7  FB  C3  FF
FF  EF  C7  EF  EF  EF  F7  FF  FF  FF  DB  DB  DB  DB  E3  FF
FF  FF  BB  BB  D7  D7  EF  FF  FF  FF  BB  BB  AB  AB  D7  FF
FF  FF  BB  D7  EF  D7  BB  FF  FF  FF  DB  DB  DB  E3  FB  E7
FF  FF  83  F7  EF  DF  83  FF  FF  F7  EF  EF  DF  EF  EF  F7
FF  EF  EF  EF  FF  EF  EF  EF  FF  DF  EF  EF  F7  EF  EF  DF
FF  FF  FF  FB  C7  BF  FF  FF  FF  FF  FF  83  83  83  83  83
```

List of Figures

About the Author

Jerry has spent many decades running a number of highly successful technology companies which initially specialised in the design and development of cutting edge embedded systems for critical applications.
As his design companies' technologies developed and spread world wide he also became instrumental in the  creation of validation systems and protocols.

His companies became world leading in the development of cold chain management products and applications including global mapping for medical directives and standards.

Following retirement he has returned to working on vintage electronic and mechanical systems of all kinds which is how his career started. He has written several books on these topics including how to build a complex microprocessor from discrete transistors and another on how to design magnetic core memory systems.

He currently undertakes no charge repairs of vintage machines for collectors and enthusiasts while also creating reproduction boards and components aimed at keeping these old devices operational.

This book is another in his series aimed at popularising old school electronics system design.

Milton Keynes UK
Ingram Content Group UK Ltd.
UKHW022238131223
434271UK00006B/149